TF.
OF THE FASCIST YEARS

THE ITALIAN-CANADIAN PRESS: 1920-1942

Essay Series 40

Guernica Editions Inc. acknowledges the support of
the Canada Council for the Arts.

Guernica Editions Inc. acknowledges the financial support of the
Government of Canada through the Book Industry Development
Program (BPIDP).

Guernica Editions Inc. acknowledges the support of the Department
Canadian Heritage (Multiculturalism) for this publication.

Angelo Principe

The Darkest Side of the Fascist Years

The Italian-Canadian Press: 1920-1942

Guernica
Toronto·Buffalo·Lancaster (U.K.)
1999

Copyright © 1999, Angelo Principe and Guernica Editions Inc.
All rights reserved. The use of any part of this publication,
reproduced, transmitted in any form or by any means, electronic,
mechanical, photocopying, recording or otherwise stored in a
retrieval system, without the prior consent of the publisher is an
infringement of the copyright law.

Antonio D'Alfonso, Editor.
Guernica Editions Inc.
P.O. Box 117, Station P, Toronto (ON), Canada M5S 2S6
2250 Military Rd., Tonawanda, N.Y. 14150-6000 U.S.A.
Gazelle, Falcon House, Queen Square, Lancaster LA1 1RN U.K.

Typeset in Times by Selina, York.
Printed in Canada.

Legal Deposit — Second Quarter.
National Library of Canada.
Library of Congress Card Number: 99-71703

Canadian Cataloguing in Publication Data
Principe, Angelo, 1930-
The darkest side of the fascist years :
the Italian-Canadian press, 1920-1942
(Essay series ; 40)
ISBN 1-55071-083-4
1. Italian Canadians — Newspapers.
2. Italian Canadians — Politics and government.
3. Press and politics — Canada.
I. Title. II. Series : Essay series (Toronto, Ont.) ; 40.
PN4907.E84P75 1999   071'.1'0897   C99-900310-0

Contents

Acknowledgements	7
Introduction by Gabriele Scardellato	9
Foreword	19
Chapter One: Failed Attempts: 1923-1929	26
Chapter Two: *L'Italia* (Montreal)	63
Chapter Three: *Il Bollettino italo-canadese* (Toronto)	85
Chapter Four: *L'Eco italo-canadese* (Vancouver)	123
Chapter Five: Anti-Semitism and the Local Fascist Press	146
Epilogue	186
Appendixes	194
Notes	224
Bibliography	253
Index	265

To my daughters, Concetta & Cornelia

ACKNOWLEDGEMENTS

In giving this book to the editor of Guernica, Antonio D'Alfonso, I would like to thank several people for helping me throughout the development of this work. Some of them contributed a great deal with suggestions and critical appraisal; others polished and straightened my convoluted English; and finally, others provided me with assistance and material from several institutions in Italy and Canada. Of cource, it is beyond saying that eventual errors committed and the views expressed are only mine.

I thank therefore my friend Dr. Gabriele Scardellato (Multicultural History Society of Ontario) who encouraged and assisted me and, in addition to graciously introducing this book, used his fine editorial skill for its general improvement. I am grateful to Prof. Roberto Perin (York University) for his much needed assistance. I thank Prof. Luigi Bruti Liberati (Università di Milano), Prof. Rev. Guido Mazzotta (Pontificia Universitas Urbaniana in Rome), Dr. Stephen A. Speisman (Ontario Jewish Archives), Prof. Frank Sturino (York University), Prof. Olga Zorzi Pugliese (University of Toronto). My warmest thanks and gratitude to Brenda Withcombe (York University) and Celestino Dejulis, both of them spent a lot of their time reading and correcting my manuscript. I thank also Profs. Bernard Chandler (University of Toronto), Piera Bertoia Canella, Raymond Culos (Vancouver), Antonietta Principe Giorgi, Mark Giorgi, Teresa Manduca, Aldo Macioce, Giuseppina Gatto Mari, Vito Moretti. Dr. Luigi Pautasso, Luigi Pennacchio, Concetta Principe, Sandra Gourlay Principe, Vilma Ricci, and Francesco Zaffiro (Hamilton).

Special thanks go to my colleagues and friends in the Italian Department of University of Toronto at Mississauga (Erin College), who encouraged me throughout this project. They are Giuliana Sanguinetti Kats, Salvatore Bancheri, John Campana,

Michael Lettieri, Mila O'Brien and, last but not least, Guido Pugliese who, during our weekly squash game, bore with my obsessive repetition of this book's themes which I was able to develop more fully through his keen observations and questions.

Before ending, I feel it is my duty to remember certain people who are no longer with us for spending their time with me, answering my questions and making accessible their personal papers and the documentation in their possession. They are the late Robert F. Harney, Attilio Bortolotti who gave me his collection of *Il Martello* (New York) and other anarchist newspapers, Anselmo Bortolotti (Ottawa), Benny Bottos for *La voce operaia, Il Lavoratore, La voce degli italo-canadesi,* and *La Vittoria,* Mario Lattoni (Montreal), Ruggero Bacci, Frank Frediani and his wife Etelvina, and Donald Di Giulio, Carlo Lamberti (Toronto), Quinto Martino (Hamilton), and Carlo Fera (Sault St. Marie).

Introduction

The publication of Dr. Angelo Principe's study of the pro-fascist press in Canada in the inter-war years is a unique contribution to the field of Italian-Canadian history and one that will be further enhanced by the appearance of a companion volume — now in preparation — on the Italian-Canadian anti-fascist press. Principe is extremely well-qualified for either study. He brings to his work not only sound preparation as a historian of the Italian-Canadian experience but also years of work as a journalist and political activist of the left. In the latter two capacities, he has participated in much of the discussion of the internment of Italian Canadians that has occurred in post-World War II Toronto Italia in particular. Through this engagement Principe has worked hard to understand the social, cultural and political environment which lead to the events of 10 June 1940 and the results of his efforts are wonderfully illustrated in the present volume.

As many readers will know, shortly after Italy's entry into war in June 1940 on the side of Germany, the then Prime Minister of Canada, William Lyon Mackenzie King reassured the Canadian public via a radio broadcast that the Royal Canadian Mounted Police had been instructed "to take steps to intern all residents of Italian origin whose activities have given ground for the belief or reasonable suspicion that they might, in time of war, endanger the safety of the state, or engage in activities prejudicial to the prosecution of the war." Many settlements across the country that included Italian-Canadian enclaves experienced the force of the Defence of Canada Regulations. According to various local newspaper reports, a number of Italian Canadians were taken into custody in Vancouver, one hundred were said to have been arrested in Toronto, and according to the Montreal Gazette, more than 2,200 were detained in Montreal. In many instances, the actions of the RCMP and other police forces were followed by outbursts of violence against Italian Canadians. The storefront windows of Italian-owned enterprises were smashed and Italian-Canadians were threatened in their homes and at their workplaces. According to *The Globe and Mail,* in Glace Bay, Nova Scotia, "Three collieries of the Dominion Coal company were tied up . . . and one was forced to work at half capacity through the refusal of Canadian-born miners to work with Italian-born men after Italy's declaration of war on the Allies." In other areas, municipalities moved quickly to stop the provision of relief for their Italian-Canadian residents and in Toronto, a concert at the Eaton Auditorium was altered to remove "all Italian numbers" that were to have been performed.

No figures have been published to describe the total number of those who were originally detained for interrogation by the RCMP for questioning after 10 June 1940 and there is also some disagreement about the number of Italian Canadians who were actually interned. The most sound investigation of the internment episode that has been produced to date suggests that roughly 600 individuals were detained at Camp Petawawa in northeastern Ontario at the height of the internment at the end of 1940. This total, however, also includes 99 Italian merchant seamen who were seized on Italian ships docked in Canadian ports when war was declared and who were interned for the duration of the war. Of the remaining 500 or so internees, 56 were released by the end of 1940, another 80 were released during 1941 and by the summer of 1942, only 162 remained to be transferred from Petawawa to another internment site near Fredericton, New Brunswick. The latter figure suggests that over 200 had been released in the first six months or so of 1942 before the transfer.

By now many of these facts of the internments, as well as many of the expressions of antipathy toward Italian Canadians exhibited in their wake, are well-known within a relatively large circle of researchers and are even becoming known to a larger public. Predictably, many were highlighted in one of the most recent treatments of the internment episode that has appeared, the National Film Board of Canada's documentary, *Barbed Wire and Mandolins* by Nicola Zavaglia. They are also featured in works like Kenneth Bagnell's *Canadese: A Portrait of the Italian Canadians*; in Antonino Mazza's introduction to his translation of Mario Duliani's *La Ville sans femme* which is a fictionalized account of life in the internment camps by one of the internees; in the brief presented by the National Congress of Italian Canadians in which the Congress demanded financial compensation from the Canadian government on behalf of the internees, and so forth.[1] More scholarly analysts also often report various moments from Italian-Canadian history, whether real or imagined, that occurred as a consequence of the government's implementation of the War Measures Act. The doyen of Italian-Canadian history for example, the late Robert F. Harney, chose to illustrate the impact of the internments and of the imposition of enemy alien status on a very large number of Italian Canadians with images of " . . . [a]cculturated professionals and businessmen of Italian descent, who had as teenagers during the fascist era helped fathers bury a hunting shotgun for fear of the RCMP or walked a nonna downtown once a month so that she could register as an enemy alien . . . " In describing his response to the use of such images, in particular those used in *Barbed Wire and Mandolins* which includes poignant moments of tearful interviews with the children of men who had been interned, Principe has noted that he is able to understand " . . . the feelings of the children . . . I even empathize with their suffering and tragic experience. I understand less the internees themselves . . . "[2] It is the latter phrase which is particularly evocative in the context of the present study as well as Principe's criticism of scholars and others who appear to accept at face value the professions of innocence by self-confessed fascists of any ill-intent toward their adopted country. This criticism in particular, is the foundation on which Principe's research, and thus his observations and conclusions, are based.

In the current volume Principe amasses a wealth of evidence, drawn in particular from the three principal fascist newspapers of the inter-war period, for fascist propagandizing and organizing activity across the country. His concerns therefore, are not necessarily with the consequences of Italian-Canadian fascist activity in Canada — that is, the internments themselves and the hostility toward Italian Canadians that they provoked — but rather with the environment which fascist propagandizing helped to create and with the very vehicles that helped to create it. In these concerns, a reader can detect a desire on Principe's part to address his inability to understand the internees themselves and to challenge those who have allowed themselves to be deceived by them. In short, through his analysis of the history of the black-shirt press and its agents and promoters and proprietors, and in particular of the issues that its various newspapers attacked or defended, Principe silences the often-heard claim of naivety and innocence on the part of many who were interned, and those who have written about them, with numerous detailed examples of the proliferation and attempted dissemination of fascist ideology in Canada amongst Italian Canadians in particular.[3] This is extremely useful for countering the imbalance often found in other works which, as noted, tend to focus on the internments themselves. Many of the latter prefer, if anything, a statement about mixed or changeable attitudes within the Canadian polity itself toward Mussolini and fascism.[4] They rarely consider the fact that there were organized and active fascist groups — either organized fasci or other organizations that had been subverted by fascists — in many of Canada's urban centres and that these conducted aggressive and often effective proselytization amongst Italian Canadians. It remains for the reader, however, to ponder how Canadian fascists would have behaved had the course of the war in Europe and elsewhere around the globe unfolded differently. And, although our present-day perspective cannot help but be different, with the detailed information provided by Principe in this study, we are better equipped to confront the decision taken by Canada's wartime leadership to intern and/or to register some Italian Canadians as enemy aliens.

Principe begins with a wide-ranging first chapter that covers in some detail the rise to power of Mussolini and the fascists in Italy in the 1920s with particular attention to their appreciation for, and exploitation of potential propaganda vehicles like newspapers. Fascist success in Italy is juxtaposed with the relative lack of success in its propagation and spread amongst Italians abroad, and amongst those in Canada in particular. In this discussion Principe includes a survey of the fortunes of a number of early pro-fascist Italian-Canadian newspapers including *L'Araldo del Canada* and *L'Italia* of Montreal and *La Tribuna Canadese* of Toronto. Perhaps the most interesting observation in this portion of Principe's study, however, is his claim that fascism did not appeal to Italian Canadians because of a "nascent inferiority complex." This "complex" was originally proposed to account for fascism's success amongst Italian Americans and has also been adopted as part of the explanation for its success in Canada. For Principe, however, fascism may have succeeded for precisely the opposite reason; that is, because of the high level of self-esteem which Italian Canadians experienced in the period and which was available for manipulation by fascist propagandists.

The three chapters that follow this in Principe's study discuss in considerable detail the three highly-successful Italian-Canadian fascist newspapers that emerged from the mid to late 1920s with a chapter devoted to each masthead. *L'Italia* of Montreal is featured in chapter two, *Il Bollettino italo-canadese* of Toronto in chapter three, and *L'Eco italo-canadese* of Vancouver.

Almost inevitably, the chapters repeat themselves to some extent given that the three newspapers were extremely likely to cover the same events for their respective markets. This is true, for example, of the coverage given by *Il Bollettino* and *L'Italia* to Italy's military aggression in Ethiopia and, more importantly, to the reaction in Canada — both in the mainstream as well as within the Italian-Canadian sidestream — to this "war." Nonetheless, there is much that is different both in coverage and in response to the events in both chapters and it is extremely useful to be able to compare and contrast.

Of course, there were also unique events that occurred within the market-area of each newspaper and which dominated coverage in one newspaper but not necessarily in the other two or three. These types of events are used successfully by Principe not only to reveal various aspects of fascist activity but also to further our understanding of the social and economic environment of the Little Italies in which they occurred. A good case in point is the controversy that arose in the course of the Montreal campaign to erect a monument to Giovanni Caboto or the attempt made in the same city to have a major thoroughfare renamed in honour of Guglielmo Marconi. For Toronto, on the other hand, Principe focuses — amongst other issues — on the campaign led by the Italian Consul General and other prominent local fascists, or fascist supporters to raise funds to purchase what effectively became the Italian consulate as well as a form of Italian-Canadian community centre. The Vancouver newspaper *L'Eco italo-canadese* differs from its two counterparts in this respect, as well as in many others as Principe clearly points out. In part the difference might stem from the relatively late date at which it was created — after the events in Ethiopia, for example — and perhaps because its smaller, more diversified group of Italian Canadians, was not as readily affected by local issues like a proposal to erect a Casa d'Italia.

Principe's chapter five, the last in this study before a useful concluding epilogue, resembles his first in that he returns to an overview of events in the interwar period. It differs from his chapter one because at this point he narrows in on one subject, fascism and anti-Semitism in Italy and, more importantly, in Canada. The promulgation in Italy of racist and draconian anti-Semitic measures caused initial surprise and disbelief in Canada even amongst fascists! They and their newspapers, however, soon fell into line with the dictat from Rome, and some — in particular Tommaso Mari, editor of the Toronto-based *Bollettino* — seized the opportunity to vent their virulent anti-Semitism which they previously had repressed to some extent. Finally, Principe's epilogue to this monograph is a useful summary of his charting of the history not only of the black-shirt press in Canada but also of the political movement which it represented.

Overall, Principe's monograph is an extremely useful one which will advance significantly our understanding of a difficult period in Italian-Canadian history. The study is also to be commended for its systematic and careful use of an otherwise under-exploited resource, the so-called ethnic press. Principe's work clearly shows the value of this type of primary research material for illuminating political and other concerns within a given community. His monograph also raises a number of issues that have considerable resonance within contemporary Canadian Italia and to Canadian life beyond that entity.

Throughout this study, readers will note the important role assumed by local or imported notables, within the various enclaves of Canadian Italia. These usually self-appointed representatives and leaders claimed to be able to speak for others and insisted at the same time that none of the "others" had a right to speak. In this instance, of course, these self-appointed speakers — be they editors of newspapers, minor functionaries, important diplomats and so forth — promoted a message that became anathema to mainstream Canadian society and which brought down havoc on the many genuinely innocent "others" for whom they claimed to speak. This is a lesson whose importance extends far beyond Canadian Italia, for example, either at present or in the inter-war period, and which should be studied in particular by all those who continue to involve themselves with the events of that period and with their aftermath.

Secondly, the experiences of groups like Italian-Canadians in the inter-war period, and their internment after Italy's entry into the war, raises a number of questions in political science and philosophy which touch directly on issues like the responsibilities of citizens in a liberal democracy, to say nothing of the mandate entrusted to that democracy by its members to defend itself against usurpation. This problem is heard in the aftermath of internment, for example, in the claim made by some who argue that in their choice to support fascism they were simply exercising their political rights in a democracy. At the same time, often the same "defenders" of political freedom accuse the government of the day of having failed in its duties. In this accusation the government failed by not preventing the penetration of Canadian Italia by fascist propaganda disseminated, as seen clearly in Principe's study, either via Italian-Canadian newspapers or through other vehicles. It is to be hoped that the present study by Principe will prompt further discussions on these and related topics and we hope that Principe himself will bring his considerable expertise to bear on them.

Gabriele Scardellato

Foreword

At a conference held at the Columbus Centre in Toronto, Ontario, in 1995 to address the subject of the internment of Italian Canadian fascists in 1940, a member of the audience asked rhetorically, "Were those Italian Canadians who supported Mussolini and who joined local fascist clubs (*fasci*) really fascists? After all, they were only expressing their patriotism, their Italianness (*italianità*)." Whether or not individuals were simply expressing their Italianess, the fact remains that shady, unsavoury, and undemocratic political activities had been carried out in Italian-Canadian communities in the name of patriotism. "Were they really fascists?" The question itself implies the current negative view of fascism that is itself a result of World War Two. The war gave to terms like fascism and fascist a meaning which except among leftwing groups was not current in the community and in the country during most of the 1930s.

This post-World War Two view of fascism informs even Kenneth Bagnell's book, *Canadese* (and Nicola Zavaglia's documentary, *Barbed Wire and Mandolins,* aired by the Canadian Broadcasting Corporation). For example, in describing the arrest of Luigi Pancaro, an Italian-Canadian physician based in Sudbury, Ontario, Bagnell in his book writes that, at the rail-road station, when Pancaro was to be transferred to Toronto, " . . . a friend of Pancaro's, a local pharmacist . . . in indignation yelled at the police, 'This man is a gentleman. This is a terrible mistake.' "[1] From the context in which Bagnell recounts this incident it is obvious that he too would like to portray Pancaro as a gentleman, and it is equally obvious that Bagnell also would implicitly conclude that Pancaro could not have been a fascist.

Pancaro undoubtedly was a gentleman but he was also *"un fascista della prima ora"* (a fascist of the very first hour), to paraphrase the Italian saying devised by fascists themselves: that is, he was a fascist even before the momentous events of 1922 through which Benito Mussolini and his supporters seized power in Italy. Moreover, as an appointed fascist "inspector" from 1933 he occupied the highest fascist office possible in Northern Ontario as we learn from the following statement:

> the illustrious Dr. Luigi Pancaro, Executive Secretary of the Sudbury Fascio, has been appointed Inspector of the Fasci for Northern Ontario by the General Secretariat in Rome. This appointment is a reward for his laudable activity in favour of the Fasci abroad, to which the learned Doctor had dedicated all his best time. He also contributed to the [fascist] cause with his continuous medical assistance and innumerable scientific publications which are a dignified ornament of the Italian science. To the inspector Dr. Pancaro our sincere Alalá [a fascist expression of greeting].[2]

Pancaro's new task consisted in regularly inspecting and coordinating the Northern Ontario fasci. The following report, which appeared in *Il Bollettino,* 22 May 1936, is one example of his functions: "Sunday the 17th, we had received a pleasing short visit by the Inspector Cavalier Dr. Pancaro who resides in Sudbury, Ontario. Cavalier Pancaro, because of his high office, was a honoured guest of the Executive Secretary of the local fascio, Italo Gioia. Gioia referred to Pancaro on the activities regarding the fascio [of North Bay]."

Because of his services to fascism both in Italy and in Canada, Pancaro had been knighted by Mussolini in 1936. The Consul General Luigi Petrucci, unable to attend personally the ceremony of knighting Doctor Pancaro, sent the following message with the Vice Consul the Count of Revedin: "In my opinion few decorations have been so deeply felt as this one. In addition to being an illustration of the Italian medical science in America and having enriched Humanity with a great discovery, Doctor Pancaro is a great citizen. He should be taken as an example for his hard work, his honesty and his highly fascist sentiments. Further, he should be taken as an example for having been a fascist of the first hour and, as all those men who belong in this group, he gave all to fascism and asked nothing from fascism because he is inspired by a high and pure idealistic spirit of sacrifice. In closing, I beg you all to shout a fervent Alalà to his Majesty the victorious King, to the Duce Mussolini, to the Royal and Imperial Italy and to the comrade and neo-Cavalier Doctor Pancaro, a very elected son of Italy, illustrious scientist, fascist of the first hour, and a glory of Italy in this marvellous land of Northern Ontario."[3]

Moreover, in the internment camp at Petawawa, Ontario, where he was imprisoned, Pancaro wrote a fascist song which the internees sang regularly. The following are three stanzas of that song as two other prisoners, Franco F. and Ruggero B., remembered it:

> Petawawa prigione di forti,
> di valenti ed onesti pionieri,

dell'Italia, saremo conforti,
e di sue glorie sofferte ed altere.
Coi tedeschi uniti marciamo,
degli onesti noi siamo fratelli,
se ai bimbi assai tutti pensiamo,
la vittoria lontana non è.
Siamo figli d'Italia rinata
ne tradire possiam nostra gente
se la madre adottiva c'è ingrata
Mussolini* (altra madre) giustizia farà.

O Petawawa prison of the strong,
Of valiant and honest pioneers
We praise Italy both in deed and song
Take comfort in her glories and her tears.
We march along with Germany as one;
In brotherhood with honest men and true.
Our children in our thoughts, we will go on,
And victory will surely soon ensue.
We are the sons of Italy reborn,
Her people we can never, e'er betray.
If our adopted land treats us with scorn,
The Duce will defend us in the fray.[4]

[*The commander of the camp objected to the word "Mussolini" and it was substituted with the phrase "altra madre" (other mother).]

Pancaro, then, was one of the many local fascist ducetti — literally, minor leaders — who assumed positions of importance for themselves in various communities of Italian Canadians throughout the 1930s. These gentlemen, even if they were not personally involved in unsavoury activities, closed their eyes to the meanness, the abuse, and the insults perpetrated by the fascist Italian consuls and their cohorts against those Canadians in general and Italian Canadians in particular who refused to acclaim Mussolini and fascism. These ducetti undoubtedly were gentlemen. We don't know, and indeed it seems unlikely that they would be as vicious as some of their counterparts in Italy — men like Italo Balbo, Dino Grandi, Roberto Farinacci and other leaders of the fascist regime. Fortunately, Canadian society and its laws did not allow squadrismo (political hooliganism) of the type practised in Italy by Italian ducetti to flourish.

Moreover, fascism and fascist were respectable words during most of the 1930s. These terms were positive in their connotations, a fact which derived from the convoluted ambiguity in which Italian fascism wrapped itself both at home and abroad. Thus in Canada, where fascism appealed equally to different social classes, institutions, and individuals, as it did elsewhere, Italian fascists were treated well and with respect. For themselves "Fascists were," Angelo Tasca wrote in a very penetrating analysis of fascism, "neither republican nor monarchist, Catholic nor anti-Catholic, socialist nor anti-socialist; they were 'problemists' and realists, and practised in turn, according to the need of the situation, 'class collaboration, class struggle, and class expropriation.' "[5]

Among Italian emigrants, fascism claimed to create a new Italian man (women were only seen as child-bearers and as "guardian angels of domestic virtues") and to regenerate the *fasti* or memorable deeds of ancient Rome for the Italian nation. This ideology demanded that anyone who considered himself to be Italian should also be a fascist and should therefore "believe, obey, and combat." He who did not think of himself as a fascist was not an Italian but rather a traitor. Inspired by this ideology, fascists divided the community into good and bad Italians. The bad ones were spied on, cursed at, blackmailed, and, in some cases, even beaten.

To the Western democracies, fascism presented itself as the knight that had slain the bolshevik dragon. In Canada, as in the rest of these democracies, the upper classes — which had been shaken by the October Revolution in Russia and which feared workers' activities — accepted these fascist claims at face value. They were deaf to the voices which attempted to warn them that fascism as a cure was worse than bolshevism as a disease. In 1937, Giuseppe Antonio Borgese, who cannot be categorized as a sympathizer of bolshevism, pointed out that, "if the Bolshevist peril, as vulgar opinion sees it, consisted of violence, tyranny, and infringement of the rights to individual expression and free use of personal property, it is quite clear that fascism was the particular sort of Bolshevism allotted to Italy."[6]

Even the usually prudent Roman Catholic Church fell into this trap. Seeing in fascism a bulwark against socialism and twentieth-century secular ideology, the Church supported Mussolini's regime even though it had brought forth the rebirth of pagan myths and the cult of war, violence, and domination. The anti-bolshevik alliance between the Church and the fascist state was, however, under continuous strain in Rome and this strain developed into a profound rift with the introduction of Mussolini's anti-Semitic legislation of 1938.

Who is responsible for fascist activities amongst Italian Canadians throughout the 1930s? People joined fasci voluntarily, and they thus assumed responsibility for the misdeeds perpetrated by those same fasci just as they accepted praise for real or presumed accomplishments of their same political movement. Fascists erected five Case d'Italia (or Fascist Centres), one each in Sydney, N. S.,

Montreal, Hamilton, Toronto and Windsor.[7] They assisted needy Italians and they provided Italian-language instruction for Canadian children of Italian origin. The most meritorious students in these classes — generally the sons and daughters of local fascists — were sent on camping trips to Italy. At the root of all of these accomplishments, however, was the indoctrination of youth and the domination of the community.

Fascists demanded and imposed absolute conformity according to their motto — *chi non è con noi è contro di noi* (he who is not with us is against us). Those who did not join were alienated and pilloried. The activities of gentlemen like Luigi Pancaro were extolled and praised by the Italian fascist press in Canada and were rewarded by the regime. It is now time that the ugly, dark side of the Italian-Canadian experience during the fascist period is discussed. This experience is documented in the fascist press which was a mirror for local fascists and the megaphone of the diplomatic representatives of the fascist regime.

CHAPTER ONE

THE ITALIAN FASCIST PRESS IN CANADA: 1920-1940

> *Totalitarianism is not only hell,*
> *but also the dream of paradise.*
> Milan Kundera

After unsuccessful attempts to publish and maintain an Italian fascist press in Canada in the 1920s, similar efforts prospered in the 1930s. In its golden years from 1935 to 1938, three widely-distributed weekly newspapers were available for Italians from coast to coast with a readership that was divided according to the territorial boundaries of the Italian consulates in Canada. Quebec and the Maritime provinces were serviced by *L'Italia* of Montreal. Ontario's and Manitoba's Italians read *Il Bollettino italo-canadese (Il Bollettino)*, which was published in Toronto, and Western Canada was covered by the Vancouver-based *L'Eco italo-canadese (L'Eco)*. In addition to these major journals, three minor publications with strong pro-fascist orientations also appeared in the Montreal area in the 1930s; these were, *Il Cittadino, Il Giornale dei lavoratori,* and *L'Italiano.*

Despite local differences, the three major newspapers played a decisive role in fostering fascism among Italians, in fiercely defending fascist ideology and policy, and in propagating the image of fascist Italy that was elaborated in the offices of the Ministry of Popular Culture in Rome. The Ministry's documents reveal, in fact, that "the main thrust of fascist propaganda in Canada was the press, immediately followed by documentary films which rendered more evident the achievement of the regime."[1]

The fascist leadership recognized that propaganda was an important means of persuasion and the press an indispensable instrument for delivering it. Thus, newspapers were held in high regard under the fascist regime. The leadership believed that if fascism was to have any chance of becoming a world-dominating or, in their own terms, an "imperial" ideology — as they claimed that socialism had become — then fascism had to be accepted abroad. The millions of Italian emigrants were the first targets of a world-wide campaign to achieve this end. According to the official fascist line, emigrants were receptive to fascism because of its patriotic ideals and because of their sentimental links with Italy.

Italian "colonies" would accept fascism if emigrants were made to understand that they lived in symbiosis with their home country. Giuseppe Bastianini, the head of the fasci or fascist clubs abroad, wrote in 1925:

> Explain to the emigrant why when living in a foreign land he lives in symbiosis with his Patria (homeland). Make him understand that his personal behaviour may honour or dishonour his country and in turn his country's fortunes and misfortunes reflect on his own life accordingly. Make sure that he understands this and you'll see the emigrant preserving his national heritage: he solicitously behaves for his country's sake and loves the Patria for his own sake.[2]

Disseminating this principle among Italians in Canada was the essential role of the country's three fascist newspapers: *L'Italia, Il Bollettino,* and *L'Eco*. The extent of their success and as well their failure can be understood first and foremost in the complex social and psychological reality linking Italians to both Canada and Italy. This local and sometimes paradoxical reality was influenced in various degrees by the national and international political events of those years: the rise of fascism in Italy and its reception in the western world in general and particularly in Canada; the Conciliation Pact of 1929; the Ethiopian war of 1935-1936; the Spanish civil war of 1936-39; and Italy's anti-Semitic legislation of 1938.

Fascism seized power in Italy in 1922 where it arose out of the social and economic crisis which followed the end of World War I. In Italy, four years of war had been a harsh period of political tension between pro-war nationalists and anti-war socialists. Economically, the country was in ruins at the end of the war. Spending for the war effort had depleted its already meagre financial resources, causing widespread poverty, high unemployment, and consequently social unrest, fear, and a growing polarization in Italian political life.

Peasants returning from military to civilian life were no longer willing to endure the privations and exploitation they had been subjected to before the war. They demanded the land that had been promised to them in return for fighting the war. The phrase *la terra ai contadini* (the land to peasants) became their rallying cry. They organized themselves into leagues and unions and occupied abandoned lands. The clash between landlords and excited peasant crowds created hotbeds of violence and disorder.

In the industrialized northern provinces rural unrest was matched by strife in urban settings. Workers staged several effective strikes which frightened the well-to-do who were still shaken by the Bolshevik Revolution of 1917. Some landowners reacted to labour unrest by hiring groups of hooligans to intimidate workers and to disrupt strikes. From 1919 to 1922 and beyond, the activities of these bands escalated into what became known as squadrismo, the precursor of fascist revolution.

Led by *ducetti* or minor leaders — like Italo Balbo, Dino Grandi, and Roberto Farinacci — *squadristi* wearing black shirts carried out a systematic anti-socialist, anti-union, and anti-worker campaign. In perpetrating their crimes against protestors, strikers and others, fascists could count on the connivance and support of the police corps, the army, and the courts.[3] Tolerated by these institutions of power, *squadrismo* culminated in the march on Rome. While squadristi were converging on Rome, Benito Mussolini was in Milan, conveniently close to the Swiss border. The show of fascist force intimidated the weak Italian King, Vittorio Emanuele III, who gave Mussolini, the Duce (leader) of the squadristi and the strong man of the hour, the mandate to form a government on 28 October 1922. Black shirt violence, however, did not stop there. It reached its climax with the assassination in June of 1924 of the socialist leader Giacomo Matteotti.[4] That murder created a wave of negative feelings, both at home and abroad, against the newly installed fascist regime and the country was plunged into a deep political crisis. The liberal opposition, led by Giovanni Amendola, refused to attend parliament and instead met on the Aventine Hill in Rome, trusting that the king would rise to the occasion and dismiss Mussolini.[5] The monarch, however, continued to countenance illegal fascist methods in the country and in parliament and left Mussolini free to overcome the most serious crisis of his peace-time political life.

During the following two years, 1925-1926, Mussolini imposed his personal domination on both the Partito Nazionale Fascista (PNF) and the country. Besides holding the position of Prime Minister, he also took personal control of five other ministries: Foreign Affairs, Home Affairs, War, Navy, and Aviation. The historian Renzo De Felice defines such a concentration of power as the transformation of fascism from a "populist-revolutionary movement" to Mussolini's personal "regime."[6] In fact, never before in modern Italy had one man had so much power in his hands. Just before being interned on the island of Lipari, the rebellious fascist Leandro Arpinati, former Under Secretary of Home Affairs, said, "Mussolini doesn't want advice any more, he only wants applause."[7]

Mussolini successfully purged the PNF of radical and independent thinking individuals like Arpinati. He outlawed strikes and announced the creation of corporazioni or corporate boards that represented the different productive forces of the nation and which were presented as the middle way between the major antagonists, socialism and capitalism.[8] And finally, Mussolini eliminated any form of freedom of expression. Opposition newspapers were suppressed; political parties and anti-fascist organizations were declared illegal; a special police corps, the Opera Volontari Repressione Antifacismo (OVRA) and a special political "tribunal for crimes against the state" were created; anti-fascists, or those suspected of being so, were interned in small, isolated mountain towns or on islands in the Mediterranean.

In short, Mussolini put a straitjacket on the Italian people, and a mask resembling order and discipline on the country. Through a well-orchestrated propaganda campaign, all these misdeeds were presented to, and eagerly accepted by the bourgeoisie of the Western world as great achievements of the new regime and of its Duce, Benito Mussolini. Ignoring what Mussolini himself had written in his paper, *Il Popolo d'Italia,* on 2 July 1921 — "to say that a bolshevik danger still exists in Italy is to mistake certain oblique fears for realities: Bolshevism is beaten" — fascists claimed that their "spiritual revolution" had saved Italy and perhaps Europe from the "materialistic bolshevik hordes." The fascist revolution, they affirmed, had brought order and discipline to the land, peace between workers and capital, and it had harmonized the Italian State with the Roman Catholic conscience of the Italian people.

All this won Mussolini the admiration of world leaders like Winston Churchill,[9] the Canadian Prime Minister Mackenzie King, and the leadership of the United States of America who, as David F. Schmitz writes, "in their response to Mussolini and Fascism, developed for the first time the rationale and logic for actively supporting right wing dictatorships in the twentieth century."[10] It is interesting to note that fascism was accepted by the leadership of the Western democracies as it also was imposed as a dictatorship on the Italian people. Mussolini's regime had become "the ideal of capitalism and the conservative classes, however disturbed they may have been as to the principle of his authority."[11] Moreover, the solution of the Questione Romana — that is, the unresolved issue of the position of the Holy See after the Papal State and Rome had been annexed by the new Italian state in 1860 and 1870 respectively — through the Lateran Treaty, gained the backing of Roman Catholics throughout the world and boosted Mussolini's popularity both at home and abroad. Writing in 1926, Kathleen McMillan reported that Mussolini's plan was to entice the Roman Catholic Church to his side, "there has been talk of an ambitious plan of Mussolini . . . to concede certain temporal powers to the Pope in exchange for Vatican support of Italian political propaganda abroad."[12]

Regarding emigrants, fascist policy was not new, only bolder and more aggressive than its previous versions. As part of a new imperialist undertaking, fascist policy was engineered to regain the allegiance of the millions of Italians who had left their homeland to seek work abroad by awakening their *italianità* (sense of being Italian). Presented as the awakening of national pride, it disguised the regime's economic interest and political aims, "our colonies abroad are advertising agencies for exporting our products."[13] The defence of the emigrants' *italianità* and their link with the mother country also had been the objective of the pre-fascist governments' policy, though it had been carried out cautiously, and had sought to avoid conflict with those countries that hosted Italian emigrants.[14]

To this end, the pre-fascist governments had taken several important initiatives. The Commissariato Italiano della Emigrazione (Italian Office for Emigration), which was legislated into being in 1901, already sought to cultivate the emigrants' Italianness and this was also the goal of the schools for emigrants that were established abroad;

the financial support given to Italian language newspapers abroad; and the creation of the Dante Alighieri Society in 1898. To assist the government in these efforts, religious institutions sent Italian priests, monks, and nuns to work among emigrants[15] while private enterprises like banks opened offices in locales where large contingents of Italian emigrants had formed. All of these different but convergent initiatives aimed at assisting the emigrants in maintaining their links with the old country.

Fascists did not essentially change this policy; but they pursued it with a large budget and a considerable amount of noisy rhetoric. First, they proclaimed that emigrants were "Italians abroad" and, as early as August 1921, recognized their right to be represented in the Italian Parliament.[16] It is interesting to note, however, that during some twenty years of dictatorial power, the fascist regime never implemented this principle. Instead, Mussolini ordered that in the new Italian dictionary produced during his regime the word *emigranti* be replaced with the phrase *italiani all'estero*; that is, the definition of the term emigrants was changed to read Italians in foreign lands.

Undoubtedly, fascists had realized the great political and economic resource represented by the multitude of emigrants if only Italy could gain their active support. By the 1920s, over ten million Italian emigrants had spread throughout the world and this population could be seen as a huge potential market for Italian products as well as a powerful political lobby for Italian interests. This was particularly so in North America where many Italians had prospered and where politicians were susceptible to pressure from their voters:

> A foreign policy aiming at asserting vigorously the Nation ... must above all be understood by Italians living abroad.

> Being in daily contact with the opinion of other peoples, they can influence it immensely. The few thousand Americanized Irish men of the United States succeeded in securing North American sympathy for the freedom of Ireland. Equally successful, though they had less right, were the ten thousand Jugoslavs of the United States against our claim in the Adriatic lands.[17]

The question faced by the fascist administration was how to go about regaining the emigrants' loyalty and how to bind them to the interests of fascist Italy. The most natural approach seemed to be that which was provided through the fasci which had sprung up in the large Italian communities of Europe, Africa, and America. Because they were located in foreign countries, these fasci could not engage in *squadrismo,* wrote the ducetto Camillo Pellizzi, and they therefore "lacked . . . the bellicose impulse of the incipient Italian fascist movement."[18] Unable to subjugate emigrants with violence, fascists had to win them over with propaganda. In this endeavour, newspapers were essential.

It was the local newspapers' task to retain the sympathy of emigrants as faithful "children" of Italy. This was the vital element in the process of affirming the principle of a "Grande Italia" (a Greater Italy).[19] Fascist policy was built on the belief that the Italian nation existed wherever there were Italians even if they had become citizens of another country. The preamble to the Fascist Penal Code is quite explicit on this point:

> The loss of citizenship does not free the ex-citizen from the bond of fidelity to his country of origin; still less can it free him from responsibility when he loses citizenship through political misdemeanours. Otherwise, the very loss

would give him immunity and encourage him to commit more and perhaps worse outrages against his county of origin or his former fellow citizens.[20]

Indeed, through the use of patriotic propaganda, newspapers were to work to reverse the process of *snazionalizzazione* — the naturalization of Italian emigrants — by instilling in them and their offspring a sense of belonging to the *madre patria* (motherland).

Through their writing, they had to inculcate in the minds of Italian emigrants the idea that fascist Italy, in bringing the world a new and superior civilization, would be continuing the civilizing mission of Rome. Besides this, the newspapers should support initiatives aimed at rekindling the emigrants' "dormant patriotism." The combination of propaganda and patriotic activities would create the complete citizen, the new Italian abroad who was sure of himself and of his country. It was in this context that in 1925 the Order Sons of Italy in Montreal initiated their campaign to have Giovanni Caboto, rather than Jaques Cartier, officially recognized as the discoverer of Canada.[21]

Newspapers and newspapermen were held in high regard by fascism. Journalists were considered, in Mussolini's own words, "armed militia men guarding the most advanced and most delicate sector of the fascist front, manoeuvring the most powerful and most dangerous weapon of every battle"; and the main task of a newspaper was "to find an essential homogeneity" to serve the cause and "to ignore the rest, treating what is not important to the movement with the most absolute indifference."[22]

In Canada, fascist newspapers essentially followed these guidelines, ignoring everything except fascist activities. Newspapers echoed with obsessive repetition the "great achievements" of the new Italian regime and of its genial leader. Blinded by such chauvinism, fascist newspapers in Canada (and the United States) equated Mussolini with the nation, and the Fascist Party with the Italian people. Thus, anyone who opposed Mussolini's policy or his party was considered not an anti-fascist but rather an anti-Italian and, if he or she happened to be of Italian origin, a traitor as well.[23]

Ignoring everything which did not advance their cause, fascist newspapers in Canada became "monotone," publishing only stories which dealt with events in the fascist sphere and with what the local consul deemed necessary to the cause. This may explain why, in reading local fascist newspapers of the 1930s, one feels that the entire community was solidly behind fascism. They reported nothing but the proceedings of fascist meetings, fascist celebrations, and fascist successes and glories. This distortion perhaps has even misled scholars studying Italian fascism in Canada — the present author, as well as Luigi Bruti Liberati, Martin Robin, John Zucchi, and even Charles Bayley, who was a contemporary of the fascist period — to overrate the extent of fascist success in local communities.[24]

Furthermore, their strict adherence to these guidelines determined the profound difference between community newspapers and fascist newspapers, even though at first glance they seem similar in that they all used a patriotic rhetoric that often bordered on jingoism. Italian weekly newspapers had served the community since 1894 in Montreal and 1898 in Toronto.[25] When the fascists came to power in 1922, there were three weekly community newspapers in the country — *L'Araldo del Canada* and *L'Italia* both in Montreal and the *Tribuna canadese* in Toronto.

In general, these newspapers had a twofold objective. On the one hand, they appealed to the patriotic sentiments of their readers as a means of providing a sense of identity and unity. On the other hand, they facilitated and encouraged the integration of immigrants into the new country. They functioned as a type of revolving door which was open to both the society at large and the ethnic community. They also were very much involved in Canadian politics: *L'Araldo, La Tribuna,* and *L'Italia* supported the country's Conservatives, whereas the newly created newspapers *Il Cittadino* (Montreal), *Il Bollettino,* and *Il Progresso italo-canadese* (Toronto), supported the Liberal Party.[26] Furthermore, in contrast to fascist newspapers, community newspapers in general were open to the many different voices in the community.

Because of their patriotism, these newspapers always supported the Italian government and its leader, regardless of political stripe. They were for Crispi, Giolitti, Salandra, Orlando, Nitti and Mussolini as well. In the mind of the editors, these leaders represented the Italian nation and as such they symbolized the patriotic sentiment which held the immigrant community together. Perhaps the history of the Italian press in Canada or, more generally, of the Italian press abroad cannot be dissociated from this multifaceted and changing but persistent, patriotic core by which the community press has lived, and still lives symbiotically. It may be argued, however, that fascist newspapers, unlike community newspapers, exploited this sentiment effectively and kept emigrants in a continuous state of patriotic excitement.

There are, as mentioned, two very distinct phases in the history of the Italian fascist press in Canada: namely, the failures of the 1920s and the successes of the 1930s. These two phases parallel the two stages in the development of fascism among Italian Canadians. In the 1920s, three fascist newspapers — *Le fiamme d'Italia* in Montreal and *Gente nostra* and *Corriere italiano* in Toronto — failed, just as several attempts to create a functioning fascist organization had failed. During this decade, fascists and their fasci in Canada were few, weak, and existed in a state of constant internal struggle.[27]

The 1920s were a period of active self-assertion and profound transformation for Italian-Canadian communities across Canada and not a period which witnessed the development of a "nascent inferiority complex," as some have argued.[28] The fact is that long "before the Fascists took control . . . Italians abroad were becoming very tired of the eternal organ-grinder" image used to stereotype them in North America.[29] In Canada, the Great War had been a breakthrough for Italians and for their self-esteem. Their active participation in the war effort on the same side as Canada, and the victory that Canada and Italy helped to achieve, boosted their confidence and shifted their sense of subordination within the society at large.

Additionally, after the war second-generation Italians who had grown up and been educated in Canada began to take up positions in the socio-political activities of their communities. Within a decade, a new leadership had emerged.[30] These were individuals who were determined to have a prominent profile in the country. The reaction against an offensive article published by *Saturday Night* (3 May 1919) on Italy's position at the Peace Conference and the enthusiastic receptions given to the Italian General Guglielmotti that same year, suggest both the determination and self-reliance that had come to motivate Italian Canadians.[31]

The 1920s witnessed both profound changes in, and an expansion of Italian-Canadian associations. In Toronto, the Circolo Colombo (Columbus Club), which had been created in 1916 by sixteen young, Italian-Canadian Roman Catholics, grew into a first-rate association. It had its own premises at Mount Carmel Parish which had its headquarters on McCaul St. The Circolo was involved in several cultural and recreational activities and published an English-language monthly bulletin. Two new associations also flourished in this period, l'Italo Canadese and the Fratellanza (Brotherhood).

The Order Sons of Italy was introduced into Canada from the United States in 1915. In the 1920s it branched out, opening several lodges in Ontario and Quebec as well as one, known as the Giovanni Caboto Lodge No. 8, in Alberta.[32] Further, because of a schism between fascists and anti-fascists in the Quebec branch of the Order, the Independent Order of the Sons of Italy was created in 1927.[33] The anti-fascist Circolo Matteotti was created and flourished both in Montreal and Toronto.[34] Two Italian locals of the Amalgamated Clothing Workers of America were organized — Local 274 and Local 235, in Toronto and Montreal respectively. Also in Montreal, then the Canadian city with by far the largest population of Italian Canadians, three cooperatives were formed; the Meucci,

Garibaldi, and Mazzini and the "Cooperative Mazzini was so successful that it built a Mazzini Hall in Ville Émard."[35]

In Western Canada the situation was not different. In Calgary, the Giovanni Caboto Lodge left the Order Sons of Italy and joined the independent "Order of the Flower of Italy," which was based in Fernie, British Columbia.[36] In Vancouver, the Società Veneta, though founded as early as 1911 with eight members, received a charter in 1921 and grew rapidly. Eventually, it was able "to build a large Social Hall on Hastings Street East, in the city of Vancouver." Even the "Società di Mutuo Soccorso Figli d'Italia Inc." developed tremendously in the 1920s.[37]

More importantly in this decade, Italian Canadians switched their federal political loyalty from the Conservative to the Liberal Party.[38] The Conservatives were elected in the 1930 federal election but in Toronto's Spadina riding where the Italian and Jewish vote was heavy, the Liberal candidate Samuel Factor won the election. He was "carried in triumph on the shoulders by his Italian and Jewish supporters."[39] Factor was the first Jew to be elected to the Canadian Parliament. In the 1934 Ontario provincial election the results in Toronto's Bellwoods riding, which then had the largest concentration of Italians in the city,[40] saw the election of the Liberal candidate, Arthur Roebuck.

Seen against this background of political and social renewal and change, the early fascists and their fasci can be understood as another manifestation of the various stimuli that then stirred the hearts of Italian Canadians. Their editorial initiatives — those of *Le fiamme d'Italia* and *Il Corriere italiano* in particular — were an expression of these stimuli and they were intended to harness and direct the changes experienced by Italian Canadians through their use of blistering rhetoric and bragging patriotic statements.

The main reason, amongst several, for the failure of the fascist newspapers of the 1920s, was the attempt by editors, some of whom were newcomers, to introduce into the mostly Canadianized community issues which stirred fascists in Italy but which left Italians in Canada indifferent. By the 1920s, most Italians in Canada were long-time residents who had been in the country for at least sixteen years. For example, the Canadian Census of 1931 reported a total of 42,578 Italian-born, an increase of twenty per cent from the previous Census of 1921 when the number was 35,531. From 1915 to 1920, in particular because of the war, there was practically no Italian immigration to Canada and no sizable repatriation occurred during the decade 1921 to 1931. Therefore, by the late 1920s and early 1930s, about 80 per cent of Italians had been in Canada sixteen years or more and only some twenty per cent had less than ten years of residence in Canada.

Consequently, problems in Italy did not effect this Italian immigrant cohort deeply. In 1925, a visiting Italian, a certain Dr. Muzi, found that Italians had assimilated a "sound democratic disposition for mutual respect for all political and religious opinions"[41] in part because they had been in the country for a considerable period of time. Another visitor, Dr. Costantino Lozima, noted, some two years later in 1927, that "Italy occupied a second place in their [immigrants'] minds."[42] Moreover, in the 1920s, Italian consuls in Canada were not yet involved in promoting fascism and a strong left-wing contingent was in place and able to protest the few and mostly timid fascist activities that were staged.[43] Only a few newcomers, individuals with little or no status in the community together with a few idealists, who were not afraid of being controversial, promoted fascism.

Up to the mid-1920s in fact, most Italian Canadians were indifferent to, some were against, and a very few supported what was taking place in Italy. In this respect, Italian Canadians were in tune with the majority of Canadians who then also held a negative opinion of fascism. Giulio Bolognini, the Italian Consul in Montreal, captured the mood of the country and Canadian attitudes toward fascism in a report that he compiled for Mussolini. In November 1922, he wrote to his superior, then Prime Minister and Minister of Foreign Affairs, that in Canada "Fascism is described as an anti-democratic party serving the wealthy classes, suppressing with violence the freedom of others and, because it is imbued with Imperialistic ideals, a menace to European peace."[44] In this atmosphere the Italian Canadian petit bourgeoisie, which became the backbone of local fascism in the 1930s, would not get involved. These people (doctors, lawyers, clergy, professors, merchants, and others) were seeking approval and recognition rather than the type of confrontation which was essential for the success of the radical position of the first fasci in Italy.

Camillo Vetere, fascist trustee for Canada, stressed the need to confront the indifference surrounding him and his comrades. In 1925 he proclaimed that "having arisen with the goal of renewing the Italians, the fasci must collide with the fossilized and antiquated mentality which is the malignant gangrene of the Italian communities abroad."[45] By the end of the decade, in 1929, Italian Canadians were still suspicious of fascism. According to a report in the fascist *Corriere italiano*, "we had never succeeded in gathering so large a number of our countrymen for a fascist speech, because there still persists in certain Italian centres an unjustified mistrust of our movement."[46]

Dissatisfied with what they considered the lukewarm support that the community newspapers accorded to Mussolini and fascism, individual fascists undertook the publication of their own newspapers; namely, *Le fiamme d'Italia* in Montreal, in the first half of the 1920s; and *Gente nostra* and the *Corriere italiano* in Toronto, in the second half of the same decade. However, because these editorial initiatives found neither enough financial backing nor sufficent readers, the newspapers soon disappeared. Unfortunately, only the first issue of the *Corriere italiano* and only the masthead of an issue of *Le fiamme d'Italia* have survived for study, while only some secondhand information is available concerning *Gente nostra*.

The editor of *Le fiamme d'Italia* was Nanni Leone Castelli, a controversial and turbulent figure and self-described "ultrafascist." Born in 1899 in Sansevero, Foggia, by the age of fifteen he had founded an anarchist club in his home town, *L'alba dei liberi* or The Dawn of Free Men, and he was already under surveillance by the police as a "subversive."[47] On 15 May 1918 from the war zone where he was a soldier, Castelli wrote a letter to the Roman newspaper *L'Unità,* whose editor was Gaetano Salvemini. In this letter he complained that while he was engaged in the defence of the country, police had searched his home and harassed his (common-law?) wife.[48] Salvemini sent the letter to Minister L. Bissolati who initiated a chain of events that resulted in the deletion of Castelli's name from the police records of subversives.[49]

After the war, in February 1921, Castelli emigrated to New York where his father Vincenzo lived. There he worked for the *Corriere d'America,* the big fascist daily directed by the renowned Luigi Barzini, who had made a name for himself as foreign correspondent of the prestigious *Corriere della sera* of Milan. While working at the *Corriere d'America* Castelli met a young woman, Ferdinanda Maria Ingrassia, and the two fell in love. Since Castelli was separated from his wife and children in Italy, the Ingrassia family was against such a relationship. The couple ran away from New York to Montreal where Castelli began to publish *Le fiamme d'Italia* in 1922.[50]

In a letter written to *Il Grido della stirpe* of New York, Castelli recounted that he had been a volunteer in the military expedition to Fiume led by the poet Gabriele D'Annunzio in 1919 and that he was a fascist of "the very first hour."[51] The letter reads:

> I believed that you knew something of me, or that you have read or asked superiors in Italy, or the fascists of the first hour of 1919, about me. I realize now that I was wrong not to inform you directly of what I have done for the fascist cause when there were only two fasci, in Milan and Bologna, and here [Canada and the United States] when no one was a fascist.[52]

The ultra-radical position of the *Fiamme d'Italia* provoked much animosity at the founding convention of the Order Sons of Italy of Ontario, in Hamilton in 1924.[53]

According to *Il Martello,* an anarchist newspaper of New York, in *Le fiamme d'Italia* Castelli "asked the fascists who misgovern Italy that every one of our [anti-fascists in Italy] relatives receive four bullets in the chest."[54]

Further, in a polemic with *L'Italia,* Castelli accused the editor, Camillo Vetere, of being an incompetent journalist, and the owners of the paper of being ignorant. As a futurist, it seems, he preached a new morality, while Vetere defended the old way, labelling Castelli as a moralista da strapazzo (vulgar moralist).[55]

Because of its radicalism, in a period when local Italians mistrusted fascism, *Le fiamme d'Italia* did not live long. It ceased publication after only a few issues had been produced. In a letter dated 7 January 1923 and addressed to Mr. Tempora, editor of the *Don Chisciotte* (Rome), Castelli informed him that "the last issue of my magazine cost me too much and I was forced to end the operation for a while. But now, I will begin publishing again, perhaps under another masthead."[56] There were, however, additional personal reasons for putting an end to Castelli's editorial activities. He was charged by the Ingrassia family, and subsequently prosecuted for causing his pregnant wife's death by "punching and kicking her in the stomach."[57] He was, however, acquitted of the charge. Defending himself in a letter to *Il grido della stirpe,* Castelli reported that "all of the doctors supported my thesis. They absolutely excluded the possibility of a punch [as being the cause of death]."[58] There were cases both before and after the trial in Montreal which suggest that Castelli was prone to violence against women including a request "for a separation" by his wife in Italy because of his violent behaviour.[59] Somewhat later in Mexico City, where he settled in 1926, a certain Ana Maria Alvarado charged him with attempting to strangle her.[60]

After his Canadian court case, Castelli became co-editor with Camillo Vetere of *L'Italia,* for a short period in

1924.[61] This collaboration may have been the turning point at which both Vetere and his newspaper became sympathetic to the fascist cause. Sometime in 1925, Castelli returned to Italy but he failed to secure a position for himself there. Disappointed and disgusted with fascism, Castelli then left Italy for Mexico where he became the most radical anti-fascist as his thick (and re-newed) file in the Casellario Politico attests. He wrote anti-fascist articles for the Mexican press and published two weekly magazines first, *Italia Libre,* followed by *Genio latino,* "an organ of culture, propaganda, and defence of Latin people in America."[62] As a protest against fascism, he voluntarily gave up his Italian citizenship and in a long letter to the King of Italy announcing his decision he wrote:

> Your Majesty ... I am not sending you my war decorations because I am certain that the Italian people will once again rebel to redeem the honour of the country and therefore my decision is only temporary. But, as long as Italy is governed by fascism, I beg of you not to consider me an Italian citizen ...[63]

Further, while he was abroad he was found guilty of desertion by a military tribunal; a charge that Castelli claimed resulted from his decision to abandon his army-corps in order to join D'Annunzio's expedition to Fiume.[64]

In Toronto in 1926, as in Montreal in 1923, it was a veteran of the First World War, Francesco M. Gualtieri, who initiated the publication of the bilingual Italian and English *Gente nostra* (Our People). Gualtieri's publisher was Luigi Ciano and the newspaper was produced to fill a need felt by a growing and changing Italian community in Toronto. The discontinuous and pro-Conservative *Tribuna canadese,* edited by Henry Corti (Enrico Corticelli) did not satisfy the needs of this community. Francesco M. Gualtieri was the brother of the Reverend Domenico Gualtieri, an Italian Protestant Minister and editor of the United Church bulletin, *La favilla.* Francesco Gualtieri was a poet, a nationalist, and a follower of the controversial futurist poet, Giovanni Papini.[65] In 1927, a year after the creation of *Gente nostra,* Gualtieri and Dr. Donato Sansone founded the Toronto branch of the Italian Veterans' Association.[66]

We know very little about *Gente nostra,* although we might infer from Gualtieri's futurist and nationalist convictions that it was a radical-populist magazine which, as he stated in his book, *We Italians,* "was intended to express among Italians abroad 'that sentiment of unity which Mussolini has inspired at home.' "[67] This statement is supported by a news item which appeared in the Toronto *Globe* (5 November 1926) which reported that "in connection with the issue today of the first number of *Gente nostra,* a new Italian-English magazine to be published here, Luigi Ciano . . . and F. M. Gualtieri, promoters of the magazine, laid a wreath on the Cenotaph. Yesterday was the Italian armistice day, and as the first issue of the magazine is to be an armistice number the little ceremony was thought by the publishers to be a most fitting start to their enterprise."

Moreover, Francesco Gualtieri was also the master of ceremonies in 1928 for the Italian-Canadian commemorations that year of both Armistice Day and the March on Rome. He officiated at these events with the Consul General of Italy, Sir Pio Margotti and Mr. Toto Giurato, Head of the Press Office of the Fascist League of North America.[68] The life-span of *Gente nostra* is not known but it seems unlikely that it lasted for any great length of time given that it lacked community support, as had *Le fiamme d'Italia*. The fact that Gualtieri was a Protestant might have been an impediment to his enterprise because he did not have the support of the powerful and Roman Catholic, Circolo Colombo.

The Toronto-based *Corriere italiano* appeared at the end of the decade, on 23 March 1929. This publication consisted of four full-size newspaper pages and it was published with the approval of both the Circolo Colombo and the Italian Consul General in Ottawa, Pio Margotti. In a letter which appeared in the first issue of the newspaper, the Consul General wrote that "it is with intense pleasure that I learned of the imminent publication of the fascist newspaper *Corriere italiano* in that city [Toronto]: today being fascist means being Italian."

The newspaper was intended to serve readers in Ontario, Western Canada, and the northern areas of New York State. It included in fact, a full page of news from "Jamestown [N.Y.] and its Vicinity" and also some advertisements from that area. On the page which carried news from Toronto, there are seven small advertisements — four of them were purchased by well-known local fascists (Marco Missori, Nicola Masi of Hamilton, C. Sansone, J. Grittani). It is unclear whether the other three advertisements — for the Gatto Travel Agency, the lawyer Frank Denton, and a distributor of "excellent quality coal" — were genuine advertisers or political supporters or both.

One of the articles published in *Corriere italiano* attacked the Inter-social Committee, an umbrella organization of Toronto Italian-Canadian associations, and in its attack the article reveals the arrogant manner, typical of Italian *squadrismo,* that was used by local fascists to deal with the people in the community. Local fascists demanded the right of the fascio and the Veterans' Association to lead the community and they objected to an article in the constitution of the Inter-social Committee which gave longer-established Societies precedence over more juniors ones like the local "Fascio Principe Umberto" and the Italian Veterans' Association.

That article in *Corriere italiano* echoed the order to lead the community which was given to fasci in the First Congress of Fascists Abroad which was held in Rome in the fall of 1925. The following paragraph gives the flavour of the article:

> Our friends [a sarcastic way of referring to the leaders of local associations] must understand that the time has come to persuade themselves of some basic facts and to put these facts into their heads: 1. The fascio is not a Society like the others; the fascio represents the Party which forms the Government and as such it is the heart of Italian life; 2. Precisely because it is the heart, from the fascio originate all official activities; 3. For official activities are to be understood even those events organized by other associations which request the participation of the consular authorities. And the consular authorities do not attend any function where fascio and Veterans' Association do not have the leading role.

Furthermore, the tone of the first editorial in the newspaper, titled "Positions," is both peremptory and threatening. Having said that local fascists are ready and willing to speak to anyone who wants to learn about fascism, the editorialist closes with a sinister warning to the community as a whole. It reads:

> Three months from now, after having reviewed the colonial masses, our attitude will change completely: those who still are against fascism and our movement here [in Canada] will find us less conciliatory; some will find us even very hard...With us or against us is the old saying. Of one thing we are certain: those who are against us will get the worse of it.

The warning "with us or against us" was repeated four years later by the Italian Consul General in Canada, Luigi Petrucci, at a banquet held at the Royal York Hotel in Toronto.[69]

The *Corriere italiano* published the speech that Cesare Maccari, editor of the magazine *The Latin World* and member of the fascist Central Committee for Press and Propaganda of the Fascist League of North America,[70] had presented to the Hamilton fascio. This long, bombastic statement ended with a rhetorical appeal that drew on futuristic imagery of machines, speed, motors and a bit of implied misogyny. Maccari declaimed:

> still many men waste the best years of their lives trying uselessly to comprehend their woman or women. Down with sensuality and with sentimentalism! This malignant gangrene that infects the blood of many young men must be cut from our youth. Our entire love, our desire must be for the machine, for the engine. Italian engines! Delicate creatures of iron, bronze and steel, in whose vigorous bodies gasoline and oil flow giving life and impetus, give us your metallic discipline, the instinct of perpetual motion, the virtue of rhythm and intuition!

The *Corriere italiano* can be considered the prototype of fascist newspapers in Canada. It presents a synthesis of the propaganda which engulfed the fascist press in Canada and elsewhere throughout the 1930s. This newspaper also displayed the arrogance that was characteristic of the fascist newspapers that followed and prospered in the 1930s when a new and favourable atmosphere was created for fascism in Canada and, consequently, amongst Italian Canadians.

What had happened to change Canadian attitudes toward fascism so profoundly from those that they had exhibited in the early 1920s? Mussolini's process of normalizzazione had worked effectively. He had taught the Western bourgeoisie how to rid itself of the threat of communism and militant radical unions and his lesson was appreciated by many. The fact that the removal of such threats also entailed the removal of freedom did not worry either industrialists or national leaders like Richard B. Bennett, Mackenzie King, and lesser known large and small "c" conservative politicians. The stability of Italy under an anti-bolshevik regime, which had the blessing of the Vatican, was a sufficient good that could be accepted and even helped.

The following words of admiration for Mussolini are found in Mackenzie King's diary in his entry for 25 September 1928,

> when one hears how he came with his blackshirts to the King, offered his services to clean up the government and House of representatives filled with communists [sic], banished them all to an island, cleaned the streets of beggars, and the houses of harlots one becomes filled with admiration. It is something I have never seen before and one feels it in one's bones.[71]

In reading this passage one cannot help but be dismayed and wonder how much an average Canadian could have known about fascist Italy if the Prime Minister of the country was so naive and grossly ignorant of Italian affairs.

After the Conciliation Pact of 11 February 1929 with the Vatican, Mussolini and his regime received the full support of both the Canadian Roman Catholic clergy and lay leaders across the country. This recognition effectively transformed Italian-Canadian Roman Catholic parishes into centres of fascist propaganda. The Roman Catholic hierarchy was so elated with Mussolini that, according to one fascist newspaper, *Il Bollettino,* during the Parade of the Holy Name in St. Agnes Parish in Toronto, the Archbishop of that city James McGuigan, answered the Italian fascist salute with the words, "Evviva Mussolini! Evviva l'Italia."[72] This, of course, is highly improbable, but as a propaganda gimmick to dupe readers, it was very effective. Bishop McNally of Hamilton, however, was very loquacious both in the church and on the street, supporting Mussolini and his new regime.[73]

In Quebec, the Conciliation Pact triggered a general explosion of enthusiasm for Mussolini which lasted throughout the 1930s. The following are the words of Premier M.L.A. Taschereau: "Mes paroles seraient incomplètes si je ne disais à l'eminent homme d'état qui dirige l'Italie que son dernier geste lui a attiré l'admiration et la reconnaissance de tous les catholiques de l'universe."[74] Even the French-Canadian nationalist newspaper, *Le Devoir* of Montreal, had words of praise for Mussolini in an editorial titled *"La paix romaine"*:

> De la personne et du rôle de Mussolini, de ses principes politiques et sociaux, de son mode d'action, du régime qu'il a donné ou, si l'on veut, imposé à l'Italie, ce n'est pas le temps de nous occuper. Mais ce que personne ne peut contester c'est la puissance de l'homme, l'envergure de son esprit, la grandeur de ses conceptions, c'est, pour tout dire en un mot, son génie. La justification de ce jugement, je ne la cherche ni ne la trouve dans l'etonnant succès de son entreprise, mais dans la source d'inspiration qui l'a conduit à l'acte posé le 11 fevrier [the Conciliation Pact]...[75]

From the private notes of Mackenzie King to the public words of Mr. Taschereau and G. Pelletier, editor of *Le Devoir,* emerge the feelings and views of the leaders of the country and these in turn suggest how profoundly things had changed since 1922.

During the same period, the expansion of the diplomatic network, as already noted, created three new vice-consulates in Canada — those of Toronto, Winnipeg, and Vancouver — and several consular agencies across the country. The men sent to take charge of these new offices arrived in Canada in 1929. Unlike their predecessors, the new diplomats were chosen from fascist ranks and this group of consuls and consular agents were zealous fascists. Their task was to enhance fascism and make it respectable by winning over the "notables" of the community. This was expressed explicitly in a speech given by the Consul General, Luigi Petrucci:

> Today the Italian Consuls abroad . . . are not amorphous, anodyne, limited to the exercise of functions which, however noble, are technical; they represent the strong arm of the Fascist Government, for the full realization abroad of the great new civilization initiated by Benito Mussolini

> and the new regime . . . I, gentlemen, and Chevalier Ambrosi, my colleague, are first of all Fascist Consuls. We will not compromise about our Fascism, we will not descend to compromises with those who still stubbornly remain in the contrary camp.[76]

The new diplomats reorganized the existing fasci and created new ones. Old and new fasci became bureaucratic extensions of the consulates, professional and business people were appointed to leadership positions and the radicals of the squadristi type were expelled from their positions or left out in the cold.[77] To the society at large, the new fasci presented themselves as organizations that were for law and order in support of authority and against bolshevism. To the Italian community they presented themselves as instruments of the "new Italy," reaching out to her sons and daughters abroad. They were to give prestige to the community and to strive for the interest and dignity of the Fatherland.

With praise, promises of knighthood, and sometimes even insinuations of possible reprisal, consuls succeeded in gathering around them numerous groups of subservient individuals. This is reflected in the following servile adulation by Tommaso Mari:

> before the arrival of Consul Ambrosi, we [Italian Ontarians] were nothing. He found a desert in which the Italians rambled as nomadic bands in the Sahara desert. He rebuilt everything . . . Though Ambrosi guided, aided, assisted and gave us pride, we owe also to Consul General Petrucci equal sympathy and love. First of all, Petrucci understood us, then he estimated and presented us in our just merits.[78]

This statement is written in the typical fascist style of the period. One man is placed on a pedestal through the denigration of an entire nation or, in this case, an entire community.

The Italian churches in Montreal, Toronto, Ottawa, Vancouver and elsewhere were open to fascist activities. Most of the Italian priests who were then working in Canada became fascist supporters. Some, like Father Cheli of St. Peter's Parish in Ottawa, Father Truffa and Father Balò in Toronto, Father Maltempi and Father Manfriani in Montreal, Father Belcastro in Sault Ste. Marie, and Father Bortignon of the Sacred Heart Parish in Vancouver became activists. In return, as a mark of appreciation for their great contribution to fascism, Father Zanobi Manfriani and Father Stefano Cheli were knighted by Mussolini. The unity between the Roman Catholic Church and Italian fascist authorities in Canada is best symbolized by the homage that Consul Gian Battista Ambrosi paid to Archbishop Neil McNeil of Toronto in December 1929. Mimicking the visit that the Italian King and his Queen had paid to Pope Pius XI, Consul Ambrosi together with an ensemble of fascists and dignitaries from the Italian-Canadian community called on Archbishop McNeil at his residence in Toronto; in so doing they symbolically bore to him the devotion of their community.[79]

The consuls' work was undoubtedly made easier by the economic depression which devastated North America from the end of 1929. Fascist propaganda, by claiming that the so-called middle way, the way of "Corporatism," had brought social peace, prosperity and plenty of work in Italy, led many politicians to look to fascism as a way out of the social upheaval that was occurring in Canada. Even the socialist Mayor of Toronto, Simpson, deluded by fascist propaganda declared that "in every field of social activity Italy is more advanced than us. And if in Canada political fascism is not necessary, it is necessary to imitate her powerful social and economic activity, for Italy is a vanguard nation."[80] In the early 1930s, Canada was engulfed in misery. Over a period of some three years the export of farm produce and raw materials, the essential economic resources of the country, plunged more than two-thirds from $1,152,416,000 in 1929 to $489,883,000 in exports by 1932.[81]

Canadians were tasting the bitter medicine that had been ingested by Europeans ten years earlier. Unemployment soared and soup kitchens to feed a hungry mass of destitute people, and shanty towns to house the homeless, sprang up everywhere. In the House of Commons in Ottawa, J. S. Woodsworth, future leader of the Cooperative Commonwealth Federation (CCF), in 1931 sketched the drama of the unemployed with these words:

> In the old days we could send people from the cities to the country. If they went out today they would meet another army of unemployed coming back from the country to the city; that outlet is closed. What can these people do? They have been driven from our parks; they have been driven from our streets; they have been driven from our buildings and in this city [Ottawa] they actually took refuge on the garbage heaps.[82]

For the federal government, which was lead by R. B. Bennett, labour activities, "protest groups and mass meetings of the unemployed were, by definition, revolutionary in intent." Delegations of farmers or the unemployed "seeking to speak to the Prime Minister were met with exaggerated show of force." On one occasion, writes Kenneth McNaught, "armoured cars were called out."[83] In Canada, as in Europe ten years before, depression was tearing the social fabric of the country apart.

Politics became increasingly polarized. Smitten by Mussolini's success and Hitler's ideology, scores of anti-Semitic groups sprang up throughout major cities.[84] Bands of men wearing brown shirts, mimicking both Italian squadristi and German nazis, drilled in preparation against the perceived threat of a bolshevik-type revolution. Two new national political parties came into being — the CCF and the Social Credit. In Quebec, the anti-communist Union National led by Maurice Duplessis emerged and was elected to power in 1936. For the federal election of 1935, H. H. Stevens created the Reconstruction Party. Reconstructionists allied themselves with local Italian fascists and boasted that 50,000 Italians were affected by such an alliance.[85] Massimo Jacopo Magi, the leader of the Fascio Principe Umberto of Toronto, was hired as a national organizer for this party. During the campaign, his slogan was "Mussolini in Italy, Stevens in Canada."[86] Because the new constitution of the Fasci abroad did not allow fascists to involve themselves in the politics of their host country, local fascists must have received permission to make this pronouncement from high up in the hierarchy; perhaps from Mussolini himself or from his office.[87]

In this situation fascist consuls and their propaganda succeeded, without much effort, in making fascism acceptable to authoritarian leaders like R. B. Bennett and to provincial and municipal politicians who had become infatuated with Mussolini's strong-arm methods. Populist politicians like Stevens, Duplessis, and the Mayor of

Montreal Camillien Houde and, to a certain extent, Mitchell Hepburn in Ontario, viewed fascism as an effective means for solving the problems that vexed their various constituencies without further damaging the tarnished capitalist system. Duplessis' Padlock Law and his anti-labour legislation and practices bore an extremely close resemblance to Mussolini's totalitarian methods.[88]

Scores of local speakers, wealthy tourists, and Italian visitors presented fascism as the dawn of a new and modern civilization.[89] Returning from her Italian vacation, Lady Eaton spoke highly of Mussolini who, she explained, had "reinvigorated the Italian national spirit."[90] Other speakers affirmed that fascism was as in tune with British traditions as was the maple leaf and fish and chips. Addressing the Empire Club of Toronto on 25 January 1934, Magistrate Alfred S. Jones told his audience that fascism was in harmony with the British Empire. He said, " if there were a line in the fundamental principles of Fascism, opposed in the slightest degree to the best ideals of the British Empire, I would not even be discussing the matter. Should Canada at any time in the future, in its wisdom, adopt Fascism, in whole or in part, it is indeed gratifying to know, Gentlemen, that the system fits so admirably into our Imperial setting."[91] Renzo De Felice was essentially right when he wrote that "in Anglo-Saxon countries particularly, some individuals viewed Italian Fascism benevolently and desired a somewhat similar system for their own country."[92]

In a letter to the weekly *La Vittoria* which was published in its edition of 4 July 1942, Camillo Vetere rightly described the positive feelings toward Mussolini and fascism that had been expressed by a variety of wealthier members of the Canadian population and many other leading individuals. He wrote: "our admiration for Mussolini and fascism was shared by illustrious Canadian personalities: politicians, eminent civil and ecclesiastical authorities, scholars, big business men and even by the large daily papers which reflected the positive feelings of public opinion."[93]

Sympathy for Mussolini and his party extended to Italian fascists in Canada. In contrast to the United States of America, where the New York-based Fascist League of North America was forced to disband in order to avoid the intervention of the Federal Government in 1929, in Bennett's Canada, according to Roberto Perin, "fascists could wear black shirts in public and meet or parade without fear of repression . . . the police were sympathetic to Fascists and Bennett recognized the good work done by the consulates among the Italian communities of Canada."[94] On one occasion, according to *Il Bollettino, The Globe* of Toronto even went so far as to list Consul Ambrosi as one of the "builders" of Canada.[95]

In 1933, the Canadian Attorney General M. Price received Luigi Meconi, leader of a brown shirt Italian club of Windsor, Ontario, who offered his club's help in fighting bolshevism.[96] The Honourable Hugh Cuthrie, Minister of Justice in the same government, however, refused to meet with a delegation of Italians who wanted to ask him to follow the lead taken by the United States and to curtail fascist activities in Canada. The Minister argued that "the Italian government was a friendly government and that the Italians in Canada were justified in wearing black shirts and marching in military formation on public streets."[97]

The Canadian bourgeoisie's change of mood towards Mussolini and his regime, the political and other activities of the consuls, and the involvement of Italian national Roman Catholic parishes were decisive factors that prompted "respectable" Italians, particularly those close to the church, to join local fasci. The country provided a congenial ambience for "prominent" people who sought to enhance their popularity and acceptance to come forward and to join with local fascism which was a respectable mode of being Italian Canadian. The consuls proclaimed that "a good fascist also makes a good Canadian" and, in the community, being a fascist meant being among those who counted.[98] Moreover, in order to silence anti-fascists, the consuls did not hesitate to blackmail them, insinuating that their relatives in Italy might be in danger,[99] or to denounce them to the authorities as dangerous bolsheviks and/or anarchists.[100] The stubborn ones, like Terzo Busca and Antonino Spada of Montreal and others, were sometimes beaten into silence.[101]

Thus, lured by the promise of prestige and by patriotic rhetoric, many petit-bourgeois men and women became promoters or supporters of local fascism. Some of these individuals thought themselves to be "intellectuals because," writes Gaetano Salvemini, "they have been educated above their intelligence."[102] These men cannot be called fascists. To label them as such would imply, notwithstanding its negativity, that they were driven by something beyond their base self-interest and boundless vanity. In this regard, the response many years later of a former prominent fascist of Montreal, Dr. Salvatore Mancuso, to the question "Pourquoi, selon vous, les gens ont-ils adhéré au fascisme?" is symptomatic. "Parce que nous étions stupides" was his lapidary answer.[103]

Reorganized or initiated by the Consuls and their agents, and headed by prominent people (physicians, lawyers, journalists, clergy, and business people in general), the fasci grew in the 1930s. In every Canadian city and town where there was a consul or consular agent or someone aspiring to be knighted by the Italian regime, there appeared a fascio and parallel female and youth organizations. The leaders of the Veterans' Associations and the officers of the mutual aid societies, like the Order Sons of Italy of Ontario or Quebec, sought the prestige and the convenience of joining fascism. A fascist membership card was, according to consul Brigidi, more important than a passport:

> The membership card is a priceless document for everybody who changes his residency, for the Italian who goes back to Italy. From this document is ascertained that, although the bearer has lived far from his country, he has maintained such good faith in himself and such great Italianism as to have earned complete confidence. This is the individual who has well represented our Fascist Italianism in foreign countries.[104]

The wives, sisters, and mothers of these men joined female organizations while their children joined fascist youth clubs.

In this atmosphere, the web of individual interests (ambition, vanity, profit, and pride) and collective resentments (discrimination, both real and imaginary, unemployment, and exploitation) coalesced in the seemingly respectable form of "Italian patriotism." This sentiment was strongly felt by most ordinary Italian Canadians for whom it still held the sense of respectability which it had had during World War I, when Italy and Canada fought on the same side. Moreover, by the end of the 1920s and the beginning of the 1930s, Italian patriotism was also ambiguously tainted with a vein of anti-Semitism and the fervour of the anti-bolshevist crusade in which Canada and Italy were once again on the same side.

In the final analysis, the consuls exploited with some skill and to their own advantage, this ambiguous mix of sentiment and resentment. The community press, which was owned and supported financially and ideologically by the Italian-Canadian élite, became a mouth-piece of the consuls. It was essential as a tool for propagating fascism and the phoney martial image of the new Italy. Community newspapers in general, while they supported fascism in Italy, either rejected or were cool to the idea of importing fascism into Italian-Canadian communities. By contrast, *L'Italia, Il Bollettino,* and *L'Eco* became the magnified echo of the local consuls, dependent on their whim and purse and as such they flourished until 1938. Writing in 1940 — although his research had been completed some time before — on "The European-Canadians and Their Press," Watson Kirkconnell wrote that "the tone of all three papers (*L'Italia nuova,* Montreal; *Il Bollettino,* Toronto; *L'Eco italo-Canadese,* Vancouver) in recent years has been rhapsodically pro-Fascist, and the circulation rate would indicate that this influence is being exerted in more than half of the Italian homes in Canada."[105]

Chapter Two

L'Italia (Montreal)

The weekly newspaper *L'Italia* was founded in Montreal in 1916. It was renamed as *L'Italia nuova* in 1937 and ended publication in June 1940 when fascist Italy entered the war against Great Britain, and thus, technically also went to war against Canada. *L'Italia* was created originally during World War I to inspire and support patriotic fervour among Italians living in Montreal, which was then the largest Italian community in Canada.[1] Because Italy and Canada had been allies in that war, Italian patriotism was accepted as an extension of Canada's war effort. Hence, it was welcomed by the authorities and supported by the Canadian people. After the war, *L'Italia,* like the other community newspapers (*Tribuna* and *Araldo*) in Montreal, continued to provoke the same patriotic fervour which was not easily put to rest, in particular among leading members of the community.

In the 1930s, *L'Italia* added first one, then two pages in French and a monthly supplement, *L'Italia illustrata.* The few issues that have survived reveal that the monthly supplement, full of interesting pictures and short, informative articles, was more in touch with its readers than the weekly *L'Italia* itself. The articles appearing in the weekly often were too long and too abstract for the average reader. In its contents, the paper gives the impression that it was written for the hierarchs in Rome, the Consuls in Montreal and Ottawa, and the few local pseudo-intellectuals who saw their hidden ambitions vented through the bombastic rhetoric in which the editors, first Camillo Vetere and later Giulio Romano, indulged throughout the 1920s and 1930s.

Vetere assumed the direction of *L'Italia* in 1922, taking over from O. T. Mollo who returned to Italy.[2] Except for two short periods, Vetere was the editor until 1937.[3] It was not difficult for *L'Italia* to become a fascist-supporting organ, after Camillo Vetere, fascist trustee for Canada and founder of the Fascio Luparini in 1925, had become its editor. In fact, soon after Vetere took over the newspaper, according to the fascist periodical *Il Carroccio* of New York, *L'Italia* changed for the better. According to *Il Carroccio*, "for some months now, *L'Italia* has appeared in a larger and better format. It is rich with various and interesting articles and a vigorous assertor of the renewal and rebirth of our colonies abroad."[4]

As early as June 1924, and over the period of time that Nanni Leone Castelli was Vetere's co-editor at the paper as already noted, *L'Italia* crossed the line and became a staunch supporter of the fascist regime. At the time, for example, there was a fierce struggle between fascists and anti-fascists within the Quebec branch of the Order Sons of Italy which came to a head in the schism of 1926.[5] *L'Italia* sided squarely with the fascist faction, of which Vetere himself was part. "In our opinion," the paper editorialized, "the Order, because it is a collective and eminently political association, should impose above all the concept and the cult of the Fatherland . . . Is there a reason for the existence of an Order which is deprived of its patriotic virility and made an eunuch by the subtle subterfuge of those few intriguers who, perhaps unknowingly, are victims of ideas that are hatched at night by internationalist Jews?"[6] This long article ended with the declaration that "it is the Order's duty to . . . cry with all its strength 'Viva Mussolini!' " The emphasis on "patriotic virility" and Mussolini and the specific reference to "internationalist Jews" leave no doubt about the ideology which inspired the writer.

Perhaps the owners of the newspaper, Luigi Capuano and Enrico Pasquale, felt that expressing support for fascism would keep away possible competition — that which had been provided previously by the defunct *Fiamme d'Italia* of Nanni Castelli — and rally behind *L'Italia* the support of the Italian Consulate, Italian priests and philofascist leaders including officers of the Order Sons of Italy, members of the Italian Chamber of Commerce, and the fellows of the War Veterans' Association. This was a shrewd move which probably even benefited by the fact that the other Italian newspaper of Montreal, *L'Araldo*, which was then edited by Antonino Spada, was decisively anti-fascist. Later, *L'Araldo* was sold and it too became a supporter of fascism in its political outlook.[7]

Throughout the 1920s, fascist propaganda blurred the difference between fascism and patriotism. For example, on its tenth birthday, *L'Italia* received many congratulatory messages from Italy and local notables in which "the patriotic spirit" of its proprietors and editor was "praised."[8] *Il Carroccio,* a prestigious North American fascist periodical, added its own congratulations to our "confrere which in the land discovered by our Caboto actively promotes the principle of *italianità.*"[9]

It was in the late 1920s and 1930s that the word patriotism gradually gave away to fascism as the following passage from *L'Italia*, commemorating its twentieth birthday, reveals:

> Today, as in that distant 1916 . . . the newspaper *L'Italia* counts on the sincere and affectionate support of its readers near and far. So that together we march on the road to progress in order to accustom ourselves to the rhythm of Italian life which Fascism has renewed in all its most noble manifestations.[10]

The twentieth anniversary of *L'Italia* coincided with the end of the fascist honeymoon in Canada. From 1935 to 1937, *L'Italia* mirrored the exciting fascist achievements and fierce confrontation between fascism and the Canadian people, particularly the anglophone and Protestant population.

This important three-year period was inaugurated by the unveiling of the monument to Giovanni Caboto which finally took place on 25 May 1935, after several delays and ten years of bickering among the various members of the organizational committee and sub-committees.[11] The monument was the source of a bitter polemic between fascists and French-Canadian nationalists.[12] The main problem that divided the two groups, French Canadians and Italian Canadians, was the inscription that should go on the monument. Fascists wanted a plaque stating that Giovanni Caboto was "the discoverer of Canada." French Canadians were decisively opposed to this — they had already erected a monument to Jacques Cartier as the discoverer of Canada. In 1933, the anti-fascist *Messaggero italo-canadese* of Toronto suggested a compromise. The paper argued that in Caboto's time Canada as a national entity did not exist. Therefore, the paper proposed that the inscription on the plaque should refer to Caboto as "the man who first landed on the shores of Labrador."[13] This would accommodate both proud Italian- and French-Canadian nationalists and this was the essence of the wording that was adopted after some two years more of discussion.

The long controversy about the monument, both among Italians across the country and between Italian and French Canadians, inspired the Protestant minister Liborio Lattoni to write the following sonnet which expresses the hard-line fascists' disappointment:

A Giovanni Caboto

Indignatio versum facit!
Juvenalis

Discoverchia la tomba dove tu giaci
Illustre spirito, e vieni in mezzo a noi;
Guarda quest'opera che in tuo nome audaci
Fare volemmo, e ci fustiga poi

Degni noi ci credemmo insiem capaci
Di dire al mondo gli alti merti tuoi;
Giganti ci stimammo ... ma fallaci
Fur nostri vanti, qual veder tu puoi.

Dipicciolette menti al rio volere
Ci siam chinati senza fare motto,
E ancor lasciam che la vergogna duri! ...
Discoverchia tua tomba, e con sicuri
Scudisci ci (sic) fustiga, finché rotto
Ci sentiremo in cor ogni potere.

(To Giovanni Caboto

Indignatio versum facit!
Juvenalis

Escape the tomb wherein you lie
Illustrious spirit, and come be with us:
Behold the monument that in your name
We dared erect . . . then let your lashes fly.

We deemed ourselves both worthy and adept
To tell the world of your exalted worth:
We felt as Titans . . . yet our boasting was
Mendacious ranting as you well may see.

To the savage will of petty minds
We bent our heads and uttered not a word,
And suffer that this shame should still live on.

Escape then your tomb and with firm thongs
Feel free to flail us till deep in our hearts
We know our strength to be completely crushed.)[14]

The inauguration of the monument to Caboto was an occasion for *L'Italia* to exalt the courage and adventurous, warring spirit of the Italian race, "be the names of the Italian navigators close to our heart: they are admirable examples of the physical and moral aristocracy of our nation. They loved risk, the spirits of adventure and conquest, more than the apple of their eye."[15] The community, through the Fronte Unico Morale (FUM), an umbrella organization grouping the philo-fascist Italian Associations of Montreal, was mobilized and the fascists and their youth organizations attended the ceremony in uniform. On that occasion *L'Italia* printed, in large letters that spanned seven columns, the absurd statement: "Half of the World Would Belong to Italy if We Were to Claim All The Lands

Discovered by Italians," implying, perhaps intentionally, that Canada ought to be Italian because it had been discovered by an Italian, Giovanni Caboto.[16]

Consul Brigidi noted to the members of the FUM that "the prestige of Italy has increased very much in this country," signifying that the improved prestige was a consequence of fascism. He cited as an example "the very warm welcome that signor T. Pizzigalli received from the Premier of Quebec, the Honourable L. A. Taschereau, when Pizzigalli recently visited the Legislature building in Quebec City."[17] Moreover, as the following passage reveals, support for fascism and a belief in it as political ideology was developing gradually amongst some leading members of the community. "All compatriots should attend," wrote *L'Italia,* this "rite of love [the inauguration of the monument to Caboto], to show in the spirit of perfect discipline the sentiment of profound attachment that the Italian community feels for this *hospitable* country [emphasis added]."[18] The implication of this type of statement is that Italians in Canada are no longer presented as Canadian citizens of Italian origin but rather as guests in Canada. Charles M. Bayley rightly noted that "*L'Italia . . . ,* rather than serving the local communities in the ways common to an immigration press, has been almost entirely an agent of propaganda."[19]

Until the spring of 1935, Italian fascists and their press had a free hand and were seen by most Canadians as an innocuous and exotic expression of Italianness, even though the fascists' belligerent attitude was often the cause of laughter:

> Oh, Italy, we love your art,
> Your songs have truly touched each heart.

But when a warlike fist you shake,
We sigh, "Please sing, for heaven's sake."[20]

As soon as the Ethiopian crisis arose in the League of Nations and economic sanctions against Italy loomed in the Spring of 1935, the fear of fascist imperialism, which had already been raised by the Corfù incident in 1923, re-emerged in a more palpable and menacing manner. A strong, anti-fascist feeling surged throughout the country. In Quebec, however, where fascist propaganda exploited Roman Catholicism and the anti-British sentiments of French Canadians, Mussolini's position was viewed more favourably. Important newspapers — *La Presse, Le Canada, Le Devoir* — published fascist propaganda articles sent to them by the Italian consulate through its phoney International Press Service, which consul Brigidi himself had created.[21]

L'Italia (as did *Il Bollettino* in Toronto but not *L'Eco,* which was created later) faced the task of explaining to local Italians the reason(s) for Mussolini's activities in Ethiopia. It had to convince them to support generously Italy's war effort by donating their gold rings and/or their money to the Italian Red Cross, and it had to spur young Italians to join their compatriots who were fighting for a new fascist civilization. From Canada some twenty to twenty-five young men, about fifteen of whom were from Montreal, joined the Italian fascist legions fighting in East Africa.[22] A very poor showing compared with the more than 5,000 men who had left Canada to fight with the Italian army during the Great War.[23] The following is how *L'Italia* presented one of the volunteers:

> A few days ago, comrade Gentile Dieni presented the Italian Royal Consul his application as a volunteer in the Militia for East Africa ... Having repeatedly given proof of his fascist boldness, comrade Gentile, a fearless and valorous black-shirt ... enriches the group of volunteers ... The Italian community of Montreal can be proud of its militia men who are about to serve the Fatherland.[24]

In the spring of 1935, *L'Italia* did not yet have a clear view of the Ethiopian question. On 11 May, for example, the newspaper published a piece in which the Ethiopian question was presented as a struggle between European civilization and an African-Asiatic alliance. Because of this alliance, *L'Italia* argued, England and France "are on our side because they themselves feel threatened by the arming of the Abyssinians by the Japanese." This, the paper continued, should be said to Canadians who, being unaware of the colonial situation, "rave about an eventual concession in Abyssinia and of eventually exporting technicians and goods."

By July of the same year, however, *L'Italia*'s view of the Italian-Ethiopian situation had changed drastically; it was now a struggle between good and evil. In this new interpretation, those "groups hostile to Italian policy and in favour of the Abyssinian blacks" were seen to be on the side of evil. This change of view no doubt was prompted by the arrival of propaganda material from Rome which gave the direction and themes that *L'Italia* (and the pro-fascist Italian press abroad) would follow in its presentation of the war. It was in June 1935 that the fascist Under-Secretariat for Press and Propaganda, which was first headed by Mussolini's son-in-law, Galeazzo Cianno, became the Ministry of Popular Culture (Minculpop).

Using the Ethiopian question as an experiment, the new ministry both boosted and tested the effectiveness of its propaganda machine.[25] There were three essential themes to follow:

> 1. the wealthy and well-fed nations like England and France, which were jealous of Italy's prestige, wanted to maintain the status quo, that is, their positions;
> 2. proletarian nations like Italy had the right to expand in order to create a better life for their growing populations; and
> 3. the Italians in East Africa would bring Catholicism and prosperity to an unhappy country which was exploited by its barbarous ruling class, a situation made worse by the mingling of Protestants and Jews.

British Protestant and Jewish interests, wrote *L'Italia,* unleashed a "formidable" propaganda campaign against Italy and in favour of the Negus and they "even excused the existence of slavery." In talking about the Negus, the "Semitic press uses phrases dear to students of the old testament . . . Who pays for this anti-Italian and pro-Abyssinian agitation? From which cells of the international underworld does it originate?" the paper asked rhetorically.[26] The unanswered questions conjured in the possibly naive mind of an Italian-Canadian reader a sinister, Protestant-Jewish conspiracy against Italy and Roman Catholicism.

Moreover, fascist propaganda in Canada played on the feelings of French Canadians who did not want to be dragged into a new European conflict. *L'Italia* maintained not only that Canadians should not follow England in imposing sanctions on Italy, but that "Canada should openly tell Great Britain that she would not send troops to fight in Europe. This would contribute greatly to world peace because it would undoubtedly influence the British Government and English public opinion."[27] This strongly felt theme had been debated throughout the Federal election campaign of 14 October 1935.

The electoral campaign coincided with the Italo-Ethiopian crisis. During the campaign, Liberal Party leaders made critical remarks concerning both fascism and the Italian position in East Africa. Ernest Lapointe said that under fascism "minorities, whether intellectual, economic or religious, are subjected to government brutalities."[28] Mackenzie King, for his part, saw the Italian-Ethiopian question as one in which a big and powerful country was ready to smash a poor and weak one. *L'Italia* reacted promptly, sending Liberal leaders a warning message about the impending election, "the Italians will ... oppose anyone, regardless of his political stripe who would offend their patriotic sensibility with words or deeds."[29] The success of the Liberals in the ridings in Montreal and Toronto where Italians were numerous reveals how vacuous the warnings and claims of the fascists were.

After the Liberal victory, *L'Italia* was less arrogant with Mackenzie King and sometimes even polite with him as in the James Woodsworth case. Reacting to press reports on a speech delivered by Consul Petrucci to the Italian Chamber of Commerce of Montreal, Woodsworth, leader of the CCF, asked the government to inquire whether Consul Petrucci had overstepped his diplomatic bounds. The paper excused the Prime Minister, defended Petrucci, and called Woodsworth "the representative of the human defeating spirit in Canada" and the leader of "a party which is on the border line between Socialism and

Bolshevism, between the Second and Third International."[30] Ironically, Woodsworth was one of the very few who opposed, in the Canadian Parliament, the League of Nations' policy, as did the fascists. He did so, however, from a completely different perspective. For Woodsworth, the League of Nations was "essentially a league of capitalist nations" and, as a socialist, he believed that "capitalism must be done away with ... I cannot be expected to take a very lively interest in policies that are essentially founded on capitalism," he said in the House of Commons.[31]

In defending Petrucci, *L'Italia* presented him as the *capo* (leader) of Italians in Canada who "have proclaimed in this part of the world that the ignominious sanctions would not stop the Italian people from its destined goal" [for the entire text see appendix No.2]. According to *L'Italia*, Petrucci was speaking not only as Consul of Italy, but also as the leader of Canadian citizens of Italian origin. Further, *L'Italia* conducted an intense campaign against the newspapers which did not support this component of the fascist cause. The newspaper accused other organs of being communists or of serving obscure interests. On one occasion, it even asked Italians living in Nova Scotia to boycott the *Sydney Post-Record* because it continuously denigrated their "Fatherland."[32]

The fascists' Ethiopian financial campaign was definitely a great success, a fact recognized even by anti-fascists.[33] Following the example of the Italian King and Queen who, in a church in Rome, gave their wedding rings to the motherland, *L'Italia* asked the Italians of Montreal to imitate their sovereigns and also to offer their gold to the patria. Hundreds of Italians, and women in particular, donated their gold wedding rings. Week after week,

L'Italia published lists of men and women who attended meetings, generally held in the church, and, before the priest and the fascist hierarchs, offered their gold rings. As in a pagan religious ceremony, they reconfirmed their marriage and link to the motherland.[34]

Charles Bayley, a contemporary observer, described one of these church meetings as follows:

> Sixteen Blackshirts marched down the aisle behind flag-bearers and faced the altar. Two girls dressed in Red Cross uniforms and four in Fascist costume of black tam, white waist, and black skirt, were present to assist. The priests blessed the new steel rings. A picture was taken of the group assembled in front of the altar in order that a visual reproduction might be had for the parent church and government. Father Manfraini (sic), in an appeal filled with emotion and pleading, addressed the mothers. The ceremony, he told them, had been performed everywhere in Italy. This sacrifice was to be an expression of faith not only to the Mother Country but also to their husbands. Italy was not fighting in Africa, he pleaded, because she is cruel, but she was attempting to spread civilization and christianity among barbarous natives.[35]

In the whole affair of the Ethiopian war, the paper was satisfied with its "modest contribution" to the great Italian battle "for the triumph of the true civilization."[36]

Once the Ethiopian campaign was over, and in the euphoria of victory, *L'Italia* initiated a petition for naming a main street in Montreal after Guglielmo Marconi, who had just passed away. By this time the paper had changed hands. The new owner was Giulio Romano who took over the position of manager that previously had been held by D. A. Iannuzzi. These changes occurred in September of 1937 and, for the time being, Camillo Vetere remained in place as editor. It is not known when the paper changed hands exactly but it is interesting to point out that the outgoing owners, Capuano and Pasquale, must have been shrewd business men. By the time they sold the paper, perhaps the spring or summer of 1937, a cold wind was blowing against local fascism and divesting themselves of the paper was a clever move on their part.

The new owner reorganized the paper and enlarged it from four to eight full-size pages: six pages were written in Italian and two pages appeared mostly in French with one or two articles in English as well. The following are the headlines of the French section of *L'Italia* of 16 October 1937: "Pour comprendre Mussolini. Les discours et ecrits du Duce depuis 1915 jusqu'à nos jours"; "Après la visite de Mussolini à Hitler. 'La France a recule de cinquante-cinq ans,' écrit M. André Tardieu, Ancien Président du Conseil Francais"; "Au fil de la plume"; "Pour mieux connaître l'Italie"; "Non, ni l'Italie ni l'Alemagne ne 'crevent' pas de faim!"; "Tout de même . . . "; and the English articles were: "On Both Sides of the Water" and a column of brief sports news.

Romano divided *L'Italia* into a number of subsections: namely, "Vita italiana di Montreal"; a page on women's interests which included fashion, cooking and advice on the home; a weekly column titled "Sette giorni — Sette Notti (Seven Days — Seven Nights)"; a social calendar; and a strictly Italian commercial guide. A novel by the writer Mario Duliani, "*il più grande avventuriero del mondo,*" was translated from the French into Italian by Camillo Vetere and published in weekly instalments. Advertising was more abundant. In other words, *L'Italia* underwent a face lift. Emulation of the large Italian newspapers did not change. Articles were still too long and too abstract for the average reader.

Coterminous with the face lift was the already mentioned campaign championed by the newspaper to name a Montreal street in honour of Guglielmo Marconi. This would have placed *L'Italia* at the forefront of the struggle for prestige for Italian Canadians and the affirmation of their Italianness. Guglielmo Marconi died on 7 July 1937 and in September of that year *L'Italia* initiated a petition asking the Montreal City Council to change the name of the prestigious Park Avenue to Marconi Avenue. According to the newspaper the "initiative... to give a main artery of Montreal the glorious name of Marconi received the impassioned support of all Italians and Canadians who signed the petition."[37]

This request found strong opposition among many city councillors and ended in failure less than a month after it began. The day after the petition was begun a delegation of three men, Giulio Romano, *commendatore* A. D. Sebastiani, and Camillo Vetere, presented it to Mayor Adhémar Raynault. The proposal was debated by city council which voted to accept Councillor F. Quinn's motion to name a street in the Italian section of the city after Marconi.

The decision by Montreal City Council was not without precedent. In 1922, council had voted to change the name of Rue Suzanne, a street in the heart of the city's Italian neighbourhood, to rue Dante,[38] and no one felt then that this had diminished the Italian community or the greatness of the poet himself. Further, in 1921, on the sixth centenary of Dante's death, *L'Italia* itself led a campaign for a monument to Dante Alighieri which was successfully erected in Parc La Fontaine.[39] By the late 1930s according to the fascists' over-blown egos and because of their self-delusion, Italy was an imperial super-power and her illustrious sons like Marconi could no longer be confined to a corner of the city as before. An illustrious son of fascist Italy should have as much prestige and exposure in Montreal as she herself had on the international scene. Therefore, the decision of the Council was decisively rejected as soon as it was known.

Promptly, *L'Italia* called a meeting of all the presidents of the FUM and of the notables and fascist hierarchs of the community.

> Prof. Giulio Romano presided over the meeting which was animated by a high patriotic spirit. Not a single voice dissented, but all were united and firm behind the newspaper *L'Italia*. All were determined to win this battle in Marconi's name and to create a stronger coalition which would win other victories in the future.[40]

Notwithstanding the above rhetoric, it was decided to give up the struggle as recorded in the following excerpts from a long letter sent to Mayor Adhémar Raynault on 7 October 1937:

> A Son Honeur Adhémar Raynault
> Maire de Montréal.
> Les présidents et le représentants de plus importantes associations italo-canadiennes de Montréal — réunis autour de leur journal *L'Italia* — tiennent à exprimer à Votre Honneur leur sentiment de vive reconnaissance pour l'accueil très cordial qui a été fait à leur demande de consacrer au nom de Marconi une des rues principales de la Métropole . . . Nous sommes sûrs que Votre Honneur, tout premier, se rendra compte que nous ne pourrions pas

> accepter que le nom de Marconi — d'une portée et d'une résonance mondiales, auquel se trouve rattaché également un souvenir canadien — soit donné à une rue de quartier . . . Et vous nous approuverez certainement si nous vous disons que, dans ces conditions, nous préférons retirer purement et simplement la suggestion faite . . . Veuillez croire, Monsieur le Maire, aux sentiments distingués des sous-dignés: les présidents et représentants des associations italo-canadiennes de Montréal.[41]

The following week, *L'Italia* published a report both on the council's debate over the Marconi issue and the reply from Mayor Raynault to the letter from *L'Italia*. In debating the issue, Councillor David Roche, St. Michael Ward said, "Change Park Avenue into Marconi Avenue? Over my dead body!" While councillor Coyette argued that "now is not the right moment to play with names. In Europe things are getting pretty bad. Who knows how a decision in favour of Marconi would be interpreted in Britain and Ireland... the other aldermen, a bit ashamed and humiliated, listened and kept silent," concluded the paper. The mayor's letter to Giulio Romano, dated 12 October 1937, is a polite condolence for the failure of the initiative. It reads:

> Monsieur le directeur,
> Sur réception de votre lettre du 7 de ce mois, au bas de laquelle les présidents et représentants des diverses associations italo-canadiennes de Montréal ont apposé leur signature, je tiens à vous félicitet de ce geste de civisme si généreux qui laisse en plan pour un temps d'affaire de la rue "Marconi" . . . En dépit de certaine opposition, je ne désespère pas qu'un beau matin il nous soit possible de donner à une rue convenable le nom du génie universel que fut Marconi . . . Avec l'assurance de mes sentiments

distingués, et l'espoir de vous être egréable, je vous prie de me croire.[42]

Understandably, *L'Italia* commented bitterly and with vengeance about this decision, which it characterized as "a slap in the face of the Italian community of Montreal:"

> It is necessary to take this episode as a warning and learn from it. When election time comes, we should remember some aldermen and the enemy press. Italians must pay attention to the people in whom they place their trust. We'll see these councillors . . . come to our doors remorseful and humbled and with a bundle of promises . . . It is then that the next chapter will begin and we will firmly write the final period.[43]

Giulio Romano published three consecutive editorials: *"Fraternità italiana"* (Italian Brotherhood), *"Alla prova dei fatti"* (Factual Evidence) and *"La politica locale"* (Local Politics) all of which reflected on this episode. Unintentionally, these three articles reveal how disorganized Italians were in 1937, despite many years of fascist triumphalist propaganda and notwithstanding their claims of unity and improved prestige in the city of Montreal and across the country. D. A. Iannuzzi's failure in the municipal election of 1933, running against another Italian Canadian, Biagio Farese, editor of *Il cittadino* and member of the Club Ouvrière, was still an open wound in the body politic of Montreal's fascists.

> Everything must be done again. We must start from scratch. We must create a solid foundation on which we can build, piece by piece, the Italian Canadian political organization, and uniting all.[44]

It was enough, Giulio Romano wrote, for a politician to utter words of praise to the Italians "and they like good, naive children, attracted by such emoluments . . . would fall into the trap." To end this exploitation "*L'Italia* called together the forces of the community. The paper wanted to consolidate the unity, reinvigorate its energy and channel its actions in a single direction."[45] To obtain such a goal, it was necessary that the community's leaders, rather than filling their mouths with empty, sonorous phrases, should practice the sentiment of brotherhood, "those who are in a position of privilege or are economically independent have more possibilities than others. They should provide an example and they will be recognized as those who have understood the Duce's commandment: *Andare verso il popolo* (Go toward the people)."[46]

In its 20 November 1937 issue, *L'Italia* again underwent a profound change that was intended as symbolic of the new, imperial Italy. It acquired a new name, *L'Italia nuova* (The New Italy), and it was transformed into a 16-page tabloid. The French section became *Le Canada latin,* which was described as the official organ of the "Ligue latine canadienne." This organization was created, wrote *L'Italia*, "under the auspices of our newspaper." In reality, it had been devised by Consul Giuseppe Brigidi[47] who intended to use it to exploit the "anti-British sentiment" that characterized the provincial electoral campaign of 1936 in which Maurice Duplessis had swept to power.[48] Through this initiative, local fascists attempted to break the isolation to which they were subjected because of the Ethiopian war; Mussolini's help to the rebellious general Francisco Franco in Spain; and the first suggestions of what became Italy's anti-Semitic legislation in 1938. The reaction of anglophone Canadians to all of these events, and the newly changed attitudes of Canadian authorities, isolated local fascists even further. This is reflected in *L'Italia nuova* and in the other fascist newspapers across the country.

In Montreal, *L'Italia* attempted to overcome such situations by devising the Canadian Latin League. The declared intentions of this organziation were to create a bond of solidarity among the Spanish, French, and Italian peoples of the world: "la Ligue latine canadienne est fondée au Canada dans le but de resserrer les liens d'amitié qui existent entre les nations latines du globe." The basic principles of this Association were: "1. La défence et la protection de la patrie; 2. la défence et la protection de la famille; 3. la défence et la protection de la religion; 4. la défence et la protection de la société."

The people targetted in this initiative were not only of the same cultural and linguistic tradition; they were also mostly Roman Catholics. Therefore, the League also was supposed to defend their religious interests. Anyone who believed in the League's basic principles, and who was not a bolshevik, could belong. A bolshevik or communist, however, according to the League itself, was defined as anyone who disagreed with fascism. On this point F. Rose, writing in 1938, noted:

> A glance at the French section of *L'Italia nuova* will remind the reader of things vaguely familiar. Its columns have a halo of religion bordering them. Any statement or person opposing Fascism is characterized with one word — 'communist.' No other comment[49]

The secret, but not too secret, intentions of the League were to rally those targetted for membership in support of Italian government policy. Additionally, the League sought to overcome the isolation surrounding local fascists and fascist authorities operating in Canada by creating a confrontational situation in which "them" (Anglo-Saxon-Protestant) were arrayed against "us" (Latin-Catholics). This strategy is clearly expressed in the following passage, extracted from an English-language article titled "The Immigration Question."

> The fact that a well known magazine [*Canadian Business Magazine,* October 1937], printed in English, should advocate the securing of immigrants, preferably of British Stock, is not in our mind very flattering to our self respect any more than it is to our pride and our ancestors. This sort of discriminating language cannot but be antagonistic to the existing friendly relations between Latins and Anglo-Saxons.[50]

Even the initiative to create the League together with a mouthpiece for it, just like the initiative around the use of Marconi's name, failed. A year later, in fact, *Le Canada Latin* had become *L'Italie nouvelle;* and the Canadian Latin League had disappeared for good. Another initiative undertaken by *L'Italia* to break the isolation was the creation of the Italo-canadian United Political Club. The idea behind the formation of this club was implicit in the editorial titled "Local Politics" already discussed above. This initiative failed as well after only two or three meetings which were held in the spring of 1939.[51] Fascists and their newspapers were not accustomed to working in a hostile environment, with public opinion against them, and the authorities scrutinizing their activities. In reading the 1939 issues of *L'Italia* (and even of *Il Bollettino* and *L'Eco*), one feels that the long-held attitudes of arrogance and ostentatious self-reliance were disappearing: advertising was scanty, the number of pages printed per issue was reduced, and circulation was falling.

The anti-Semitic legislation of September 1938, to be discussed in detail below, had created what local fascists and Consul Petrucci, and therefore *Il Bollettino* in particular, had tried to avoid throughout the 1930s: namely, the open hostility of the sizeable and strong Jewish community.[52] We turn now to *Il Bollettino* itself before discussing, in detail, the last phase of the Italian fascist press in Canada. As will be seen, the three newspapers — *L'Italia* and *Il Bollettino* in particular — became active instruments of the fascist anti-Semitic campaign.

CHAPTER THREE

IL BOLLETTINO ITALO-CANADESE (TORONTO)

In Toronto by the end of the 1920s, there was a need for an articulate and regularly-published Italian-language newspaper. This need was felt so widely that three publications appeared to fill it and they attempted to do so all in the same year, 1929. The three newspapers that made their appearance were *Il Corriere italiano, Il Bollettino italo-canadese (Il Bollettino)*, and *Il Progresso Italo-Canadese*. Their predecessor, the sporadic and pro-Conservative *Tribuna canadese* no longer met the needs of the Italian community which, since the Great War, had evolved into a pluralistic society with multiple political, religious, and cultural orientations, served by a variety of business interests. When, on 20 September 1929, the first issue of *Il Bollettino* appeared, it was welcomed by many people in the community. It presented itself as a true community newspaper, willing to serve Italian Canadians in general and Toronto's Italian Canadians in particular. In its opening editorial it was specific about its intentions to be free from political patronage and independent of the community's squabbles. It read:

> *Il Bollettino italo-canadese* has no links with political parties, associations or groups of people: it is for the Italians or, better, for the emigrants. We seize every opportunity to assert our "Italianness" in this foreign land; but

we intend to cooperate with local authorities in order that our countrymen know the laws governing this country. And that people of other nationalities will firmly understand that Italians have been, are and will always be bearers of civilization, wherever they settle.

Further, the editorial continued, "absolutism is synonymous to despotism and despotism is the beginning of decadence. We are here to stay, to progress and to affirm ourselves." This condemnation of "despotism" does not allude, as it seems at first glance, to fascism in Italy, but to the *Corriere italiano,* which had just been ended, leaving in its wake a train of bitterness.

In its first issue, *Il Bollettino* featured three major items: 1) the coming provincial election (scheduled for 30 October 1929) and relevant information regarding who was allowed to vote; 2) a meeting at the Circolo Colombo to collect funds to send children to fascist summer camps in Italy and; 3) a report of a conference given by the ultra-fascist Domenico Trombetta, editor of *Il Grido della Stirpe* of New York. The conference was not promoted by the local fascio nor by the Veterans' Association, but by the controversial Giuseppe Tomasicchio, so it was boycotted by the officers of Toronto's fascio Principe Umberto. Because of this action, however, Giuseppe Federici, the head of Toronto's fascio, was dismissed in October 1929 by order from Rome and Ettore Fattori was appointed to the position of fascist commissary for Ontario.

Initially, *Il Bollettino* was a modest, four-page newspaper and a one-man operation: Attilio Perilli was both editor and publisher. It grew to six pages per issue by 1930. Tommaso Mari, who called himself a "militant [Roman] Catholic" and posed as an expert in the history and policy of the Roman Catholic Church, was an early contributor to *Il Bollettino* whose contribution began with a number of long letters. Additionally, he wrote three articles on the need for a school to teach the Italian language to children of Italian parents. Mari argued that the school should be "Italian and Christian," a combination that was loaded with political and religious implications for discrimination.[1] In fact, late in 1929, when a committee of community associations in which Mari had a leading role, voted for the constitution that would regulate the Italian school, the committee made certain that "anti-Catholic and/or anti-Italian [read Protestant and/or anti-fascist] associations" were not allowed to participate.[2] The seemingly innocuous combination revealed its true meaning, Roman Catholic and fascist.

Soon after those first three articles had appeared, Mari became editor of the paper in January 1930. From that moment his religious and political ideas and biases informed *Il Bollettino* and they continued to do so for its entire existence. When, in June 1930, the Vice-Consul Gian Battista Ambrosi made the first public move to control the community press, Mari's *Il Bollettino* was already in line with the rules that Ambrosi laid down for Italian newspapers. In a public meeting, directing his words to the three Toronto newspapers of the time (*La Tribuna canadese, Il Progresso italo-canadese,* and *Il Bollettino*), vice-consul Ambrosi said:

> In taking over my office, on 29 April 1929, I declared that, having no knowledge of the past, the Italian associations begin to exist today for me . . . Now that my second year in office is about to begin, I'll say to the Italian press: bury the past; all Italian newspapers of this jurisdiction are born

on 2 June 1930. Anyone who wishes to have the trust of the Vice Consul has to prove the seriousness and dignity of his paper. 1. Avoid articles which create discord, suspicion and mistrust among our countrymen. 2. Do not incite resentment or ill feelings. 3. Do not publish news before checking its authenticity. If they are official documents or government provisions, check by asking at the Consulate.[3]

These rules had two basic objectives: 1. presenting a polished view of the community; and 2. submitting the paper to fascist propaganda. Further, not only was *Il Bollettino* in line but, from 1932 on, when Tommaso Mari was hired as secretary to Vice-Consul Ambrosi, it became the Italian Consulate's mouth piece.

In Italy, Tommaso Mari had been a member of the Roman Catholic Partito Popolare which was founded in 1919 by Don Luigi Sturzo, a Sicilian priest. Don Sturzo went into exile soon after fascism gained power because, against the Vatican's advice, he refused in 1924 to support Mussolini's coalition government. In his book, *Italy and Fascism,* he explains why he, a democrat, could not support fascism: "Every approach made to Mussolini to obtain the cessation of local violence came to nothing . . . In spite of Popular [Popular Party] collaboration in the Cabinet, there were continual assaults on individual members of the Party and on Catholic clubs where the Popular element was strong."[4] Mari did not follow Don Sturzo; instead he became a staunch supporter of Mussolini and a fanatic believer in fascism.

Catholicism was a determinant element of Mari's fascism. For example, because of its pagan and anti-Christian trend, he considered nazism "antithetical" to fascism: ". . . no one dares to affirm that national-socialism and fascism are equivalent; and that Mussolini's conception of life and Hitler's revolt, in the name of the God 'Thor', against Western civilization are similar. Who does not know that fascism has been a revolution which changed the course of history in Italy and has transformed the nation while nazism is, above all, the polemic position of a defeated people?"[5]

Later, Mari returned to the same argument with an article on the religious struggle in Germany. Hitler, he wrote, following an insane dream, "would like to erase Christianity from the German people and create a great nation by substituting its century old Christian basis with the vaporous fancy of a near to madness pseudo scientific theory." Like Luther, Mari argued, Hitler "aimed at avoiding the authority emanating from Rome with a sophistic expedient which . . . does not bring peace to the strong conscience of a people that consider God the Supreme Master of men and things."[6]

He interpreted fascism as a religion — a religion that celebrated the cult of the motherland which Don Sturzo denounced as the cult of a "pantheistic State or deified nation."[7] Unfortunately, Mari was not alone in this approach to fascism. He and many other petit bourgeois accepted fascist propaganda coming from Rome a-critically, as if it were holy scripture and Mussolini a modern oracle endowed with unknown and unknowable superior powers. Often he was referred to as one having attributes usually reserved only for the Roman Catholic God. For example, the Duce was said to have created many great things for the people, which "he loves with an infinite love."[8]

For Mari, Christ himself had been a precursor of fascism — fascism, as Mari himself conceived it, was a blend of patriotism and catholicism:

> For patriots Church and country are two aspects, two different moments of the same problem; for Catholics it is the practical application of Christ's example: on the road to the supreme sacrifice of his earthly life, from the hills surrounding his beautiful city of Jerusalem, he shed the bitter tears that all patriots, who foresee the ruin of their country, shed.[9]

Inspired by quasi-mystic interpretations of fascism of this type, *Il Bollettino* under Mari celebrated, in the yearly cycle of Italian national holidays, the solemnity of patriotic events: 21 April, the myth of ancient Rome; 24 May, the cult of the fallen soldiers; 28 October, the glory of the fascist revolution; 4 November, the apotheosis of the heroes; and all year long, Mussolini's almost divine powers.[10]

In these holidays and other occasional meetings, the director of *Il Bollettino* was one of the major actors. He delivered high sounding speeches which became, through the 1930s, bold and even rhetorically aggressive. The main themes *Il Bollettino* treated throughout the 1930s were dictated by fascist propaganda and some were aimed directly at Italian Canadians, while others were addressed to a larger Canadian audience. The themes presented were: 1. the struggle against the many faces of communism; 2. the *Corporazioni* and their function; 3. reinvigorating the Italian national consciousness among the emigrants and; 4. supporting a-critically the consul's efforts in coercing the community.

The first task of *Il Bollettino,* once it had aligned itself with the consul, was to take sides in the struggle within the local fascio, by promoting the new course that the consul had in mind for the "colonies." This new course was initiated with the appointment of Ettore Fattori, as noted, to the position of fascist commissary for Ontario. Fattori "was not a [card carrying] fascist but he accepted this difficult task," wrote *Il Bollettino,* "because he feels himself profoundly to be Italian and fascist." Disappointingly, lamented the paper, he was not receiving help from his comrades and they "do not follow in his footsteps."

In fact, some fascists even charged that Fattori's approach to the community's problems lacked the energetic and forceful manner proper to fascist activities. In a press release to *Il Bollettino,* Fattori defended himself: "It is not with violence, impetuosity and fanaticism that one serves the cause of fascism, but with calm, deliberation and composure." He also reminded his critics that his work "is in harmony with orders received from above."[11] This was an astute way to remind them of fascist discipline.

The commissary's main objective was to bring the fascio under the control of the vice-consul by liquidating the squadristi type radicals who had dominated the Toronto fascio of the 1920s. *Il Bollettino* had harsh words for those rebellious fascists:

> After the consolidation of the new regime in Italy, Italians abroad felt the need to affirm the prestige of their country of origin. Some Italians understood fascism only as an instrument to defend those common interests which preceded fascism. Others considered it as an ignoble means of revenge and these caused much grief. We don't shy away from labelling them with the harshest words but, exercising restraint instead, we say that they are as ignoble

and defamatory as the anti-fascists. Others thought that fascism was an easer way to ascend to social position and these are deluded.

There are, continued *Il Bollettino,* few people who think of fascism as an association of Italians willing to keep alive the flame of patriotism, to propagate its ideals, generate interest for its culture, and stimulate commerce with the host nation. Among those few, concludes the article, "we modestly place ourselves."[12]

This rapid change — or betrayal, as some called it — of *Il Bollettino*'s initial program brought much criticism to its director not only from the warring fascist factions, but also from the community in general. In defending itself, *Il Bollettino* revealed unintentionally the sentiments that stirred Italian Canadians at the beginning of the 1930s. "Unfortunately, there is malaise in the community; diffidence is spreading among the people. We are accused of submission [to the consul] . . . in defence of some who-knows-what hidden 'business'; which we assure our readers does not exist."[13]

In harmony with the Roman Catholic side of the pairing mentioned above, *Il Bollettino* undertook a campaign to persuade Italian Canadians in Toronto to pay their school tax to the Separate School Board. On 19 February 1930, the Toronto Board of Controllers announced that the tax was $14.60 per thousand dollars of property value for the Separate Schools but only $10.25 for the Public Schools. Archbishop Neil McNeil appealed to all Roman Catholics in his diocese to enroll their children in the Roman Catholic school system. This would reduce the high tax that Roman Catholics who supported Separate Schools were forced to pay in relation to the rest of population. It was thought that many Italian-Canadian Roman Catholics sent their children to the public school to avoid paying higher property taxes.

Il Bollettino informed its readers that it would publish the names of those Italians who, Ward by Ward, paid tax to the Separate Schools and reveal the names of those who did not. "With our publication," wrote the paper, "we intend to achieve two goals: 1. one is what we mentioned above to induce Catholics to pay their school tax in their proper board in order to effect a reduction in the tax burden; 2. to prove that our people are not inferior to any other race in supporting its own faith, as was wrongly accused."[14] The newspaper sought to pressure and intimidate those who, for whatever reasons, did not support the Separate Schools. This campaign was another of the many knots which bound together local fascists, the consulate, and the Roman Catholic hierarchy.

The financial situation of the Separate School also was an issue in the provincial election of 1934. *Il Bollettino* urged its readers to vote for Mitchell Hepburn and his Liberal team because the Conservatives had not kept their promise: "The Hon. Henry had many times promised to find a just solution to the [Separate School] question, but he has always deceived the Catholics' expectations. He does not, then, deserve our support, nor does his party deserve our support. The conservatives, in their long period in power, were unwilling to recognize Catholics' indisputable rights."[15]

After 1932, when the newspaper had created a fair circulation and when it was receiving financial support from advertising as well as grants from agents of fascism, *Il Bollettino* openly put forward fascist viewpoints in its responses to community and national issues. The struggle for the ideological control of the community and the Separate Schools campaign were questions which had involved the community long before the advent of fascist political ideology. The exposition of fascist doctrinal issues as elaborated in Rome was the real task of a newspaper like *Il Bollettino*.

The topic to which Rome wanted to give wide exposure was the Corporazioni or the fascist theory of the "corporative state." This theory was held to be the miraculous third way between socialism and capitalism, the fascist panacea that would cure every social evil and so it was thought to be of universal interest by fascist ideologues. Fascist corporatism was proposed as the way which rejected both capitalism and socialism and it had the support of the Roman Catholic hierarchy.[16] Hand in hand with the theory of corporatism went the related problems of the "totalitarian state" and consequently freedom of the press, freedom of speech, and a free electoral system. For Italians abroad the themes to be prosletyzed were those that would reflect the profound economic, social, and moral rejuvenation of Italy that fascism had acheived.

Il Bollettino articulated these themes as opportunities arose through the reporting of events in Italy and Canada which affected the community and, thus, stirred passions among Italian Canadians. In this task, the newspaper continuously defended fascism by debating with local daily newspapers and arguing with politicians who equated fascism with bolshevism and nazism. Mari was particularly furious with those clerics, mostly Protestants, who thought fascism was anti-Christian.

In almost every issue *Il Bollettino* mentioned, referred, or alluded to the corporatives and it published several lengthy articles which addressed this subject directly. Among these, the most important were "The Corporative State in Canada" by Charles Crate, Toronto organizer of the Canadian Union of Fascists (CUF); and *"Fini e metodi della Corporazione"* (Aims and Means of the Corporative). This was a page-long review of a book by S. E. Biagi, *Scritti di economia corporativa.* The review proclaimed that:

> In contraposition to the principle of the French Revolution, Mussolini conceived the Corporatives; which surpass, theoretically and practically, both the chaos of the Liberal economy and the Marxist class struggle. Corporatives promoted class collaboration in the production and distribution of goods and a 'fair' distribution of national wealth. The principle of Corporatives is universal and every country by learning from the Italian experience might solve its 'grievous social problems, which demand everywhere a decisive solution.'[17]

Like much else written about corporativism, this review-article did nothing to explain it as an economic or any other type of theory. In his article Charles Crate, however, did present the finest political version of the Corporative State ever published by *Il Bollettino*. He argued that in its third and last phase, capitalist-democracy had:

> delivered people over to the slavery of finance-capital . . . A dying Capitalism shall not drag Western civilization into the bogs of economic chaos and cultural decay, the people of the world, their corporate consciousness aroused, are rising to establish in their nations the Corporative State of Fascism, begun in Italy almost thirteen years ago.[18]

In conclusion Crate claimed that the future of Canada would lie in the "Corporative and Totalitarian State."

What is most interesting is the casual way *Il Bollettino* presented the corporatives to its reader. The following is an antipasto or a taste of a dinner which was never served: "In the present state of affairs, only fascism has penetrated to the core of the social problem; only Mussolini's 'corporativism' has succeeded by giving it the majestically just solution worthy of Rome, Mistress of Rights."[19] Of course, the fascist or totalitarian state was directly connected with this view of the Corporative State. The corporatives were discussed with great interest and viewed very favourably in Canada because they were economic experiments which fascists claimed produced extremely good results. Nevertheless, the totalitarian state was perceived negatively even by staunch supporters of fascism like Dr. Cody who felt that "fascism is not a political system for nations with a long parliamentary tradition as British countries are."[20]

Because of its totalitarianism, liberal-minded political, religious and civilian leaders equated fascism with communism and it was this equation that most enraged Mari. He accused those who held this point of view of being grossly ignorant or bolsheviks in disguise. In promoting the totalitarian system, *Il Bollettino* was even able to claim that freedom of the press and free speech, as practised in the democratic countries, were detrimental to the genuine interests of the people. Instead the newspaper argued that the authoritarian state was a new and more advanced form of democracy which found full development in the social harmony made possible by the corporative state which was the economic side of the fascist state. The Toronto municipal election of 1 January 1934 and the provincial election of 19 June of that same year, offered *Il Bollettino* the occasion to expose what Mari called the decadence of democracy or, better, the perversion of freedom and the uselessness of elections. Quite expressively, he titled his articles *"Ludi cartacei"* (Paper Games)), a phrase which Mussolini also used to express his contempt for elections.

In these pieces Mari claimed that elections were "a mirage" for the masses. In reality, he affirmed, elections protect the interests of powerful *cricche* (gangs). "We are in the middle of an election campaign . . . [and] in keeping with our [fascist] ideas, we once again express the conviction that elections are a big fraud committed by politicians and demagogues against the people."[21] *Il Bollettino* held this view about elections throughout the decade. In 1938, for example, the newspaper claimed that "every candidate presents his usual tirade regarding cutting taxes, better traffic control, reducing expenditures . . . It is the usual decrepit old programme of the democratic countries."[22] According to Mari, politicians made shady deals behind voters' backs and against the most needy people. Speaking of the municipal election of 1934, the paper wrote:

> We have seen the masters of the C.C.F. consort with conservatives; conservative leaders share out their spoils; communists (even if they call themselves differently) litigate with socialists. The press without character, dignity and decor, serve. Who? Public interest? Ohibo? It is pretending too much. It serves the more or less confessable interests of more or less obscure gangs or clients. This is call freedom of the press.[23]

Against such corruption and degeneration there was need for a new political system which goes "toward the people," another of Mussolini's slogans. The new system could not be the "dictatorship of the proletariat," which Mari and his newspaper interpreted as being the same yoke as democracy with a different name; rather the new system had to be the totalitarian state.

In the new fascist political system, leaders are chosen by their individual merits not by the numerical support they can muster among the ignorant and the drunkards of the disinterested masses. "If my vote or consent," argued Mari, "is so great and strong that it allows me to endure any sacrifice, then it is not right that my vote is worth as much as the vote of a drunkard who doesn't even know to read the names of the candidates but goes to vote anyway because someone put a piece of paper in his hands."[24] Every sound individual, according to Mari, ought to accept this principle of the authoritarian state.

Hand in hand with the uselessness of *"Ludi cartacei"* went the other aspect of fascist authoritarianism: namely, freedom of the press and freedom of speech. The problem of freedom in general haunted local fascists throughout the decade and *Il Bollettino* returned over and over again to this argument; it was one that was strongly felt inside and outside of the community. According to *Il Bollettino* these aspects of democracy were outdated; the new and more advanced form of democracy which had been developed in Italy could do without such clumsy forms of freedom. In Italy, the Press was "controlled by the Duce in the interest of the nation," whereas, in the democratic countries, the Press is "controlled by Jews, in the interest of their banks."[25]

During Italian Week in 1934, a week-long programme of events that were held in Toronto, at the Convocation Hall of the University of Toronto, *Il Bollettino*'s main concern was, in fact, to neutralize the anti-fascists' effective criticism of the lack of personal and collective freedom in Italy. Thus, Mari interviewed Luigi Villari, one of the fascist speakers imported for Italian Week activities and, of course, Villari replied appropriately. "Freedom of the press? The Italians do not think of it at all . . . they do not feel there is a problem." This argument, Villari continued, "is a blunt sword which only a few clumsy groups of Italians abroad make use of." After all, he concluded, "you have here [in Canada] a much more strict law regulating the press."[26]

But the problem did not disappear with such simplistic statements and *Il Bollettino,* to cool the continuing criticism, returned often through a name-calling campaign that it carried out against the three Toronto daily newspapers — *Globe, Star,* and *Telegram* — which persisted with the charge that democratic freedom did not exist in Italy. The following attack against the *Telegram* is an example of *Il Bollettino*'s typical response in this debate:

> Signori of the Tely and not of the Tely, gentlemen, you need sunglasses to look at the splendour emanating from fascist Italy's life, otherwise you will be blinded. We have enough courage to tell you that freedom of the press, and in part even freedom of thought and association, are trifles of bygone times. You, gentlemen, are old men in your dotage, unable to comprehend the problems of the new generations.[27]

More calmly, in a long English-language article, *Il Bollettino* responded to a criticism by L. Morgan, then Professor of Economics at the University of Toronto, on the same subject. It seems that in a lecture Professor Morgan had observed that a newspaper like *Il Bollettino* "could not be published in Italy by a British community." The editor of *Il Bollettino* agreed but, he went on to explain that the Italian system was superior to the Canadian one because in Italy newspapers published only the truth. The argument put forward by Mari was not unusual: in Canada, the privately controlled press "accumulates lie after lie, conceals and invents news, falsifies and contorts the truth so that it cannot be recognized." This is not freedom of the press, but shameless license; in Italy "readers are guaranteed truth and exactness of news, because the press is inspired by national interests."[28] We do not know how convinced Mari was of what he wrote.

By the end of 1934, *Il Bollettino* had reached its maximum expansion in terms both of distribution and advertising. In fact, in February 1935, the administration felt sufficiently secure financially to offer that *Il Bollettino* would be sent gratis to the unemployed who were willing to pay the mailing cost.[29] Editorially, the paper had become bold, self righteous, and even aggressive. It had a corespondent in every major Ontario city, as well as in Winnipeg, Manitoba, and Montreal. Through this period, *Il Bollettino* normally appeared in an eight-page format, but some special issues could run to ten or even twelve pages. Every issue included a fairly consistent number of advertisements which varied in size and in number from a minimum of twenty-two ads to a maximum of thirty-two.[30] It ran this number of advertisements until the summer of 1938, when its advertising began to decline and so did its readership.

The year 1934 began with Italian Week — 12 January — and closed with an announcement by the new consul, Giorgio Tiberi, a fascist, announcing that Toronto would have its Casa d'Italia or Fascist Centre.[31] Between these two community milestones, other important events occurred that year. These included a visit to Toronto by Piero Parini, the highest-placed fascist hierarch ever to visit the city; the death of Maestro Domenico Angelo Carboni, leader of the local Fascio Principe Umberto; and the Franciscan Brothers takeover of the Italian National Parish churches of Toronto after they had been vacated by the Salesian Brothers.[32] Coverage of these events made *Il Bollettino* the centre of the community, helping it to expand its influence and enlarge its readership.

Fascist propaganda reached its widest dimension and highest point during Italian Week at the University of Toronto. The Canadian National Education Council had asked countries to send delegations to Canada to illustrate what was taking place in the socio-political lives of other nations. Italy was the first country, after England, to accept the Council's invitation. A fascist delegation of four speakers arrived in Toronto on 6 January 1934. They were Duke Mario Colonna, a graduate of Cambridge; Professor Luigi Villari, a publicist; Amy Bernardi, author and journalist; and Eugenio Crozat, art critic. A fifth speaker was Professor Cody, then president of the University of Toronto. Lectures on different aspects of life in fascist Italy were given in the University's Convocation Hall and in other locales in front of a variety of associations, including the Empire Club, the Canadian Club, the Eaton Centre, and the Circolo Colombo.

The presentations by these speakers generated so much interest that they were asked to stay in Toronto a second week before proceeding with the rest of their itinerary of speaking engagements but they were unable to alter their plans. From Toronto they travelled to Ottawa, Winnipeg, Vancouver, Calgary, Edmonton, Montreal, and the Maritime Provinces and their speaking tour ended in Quebec City. The principal mover behind Italian Week was Major F. J. Nay, Chairman of the National Council of Education. "We owe to Major Nay," wrote *Il Bollettino,* "the Italian activities that are going on in Toronto these days."

> Major Nay is a true friend of Italy, a warm admirer of Mussolini and fascism, and a personal friend of our Vice Consul, Cav. G. B. Ambrosi. Together they worked untiringly for the extraordinary success obtained by Italian Week.[33]

For the occasion the Toronto daily papers discovered the Italian community and its prominent members as indicated by a passage from *The Star:* "With the advent of 'Italian Week' which featured a series of lectures by famous Italians brought over from their native land by the National Council of Education, an opportunity has arisen to point out the number of Italians residing in Toronto who have made names for themselves in the arts, in science, and in commercial life."[34] *The Star* mentioned scores of distinguished Italians living in Toronto;[35] most of whom were active in the local fascio or its satellite organizations: Order Sons of Italy, Veterans' Association, Comitato Scolastico (School Committee), Comitato Economico (Economics Committee), and the Gioventù Italiana del Littorio

Estero (Italian Lictorian Youth Abroad). Recognition, acceptance, and respect were what most of the petit-bourgeois Italian Canadians — businessmen, artists, professionals, clerks, merchants — were seeking.

Interpreting their sentiments, *Il Bollettino* exulted over the success of Italian Week and the hearty reception accorded to the speakers: "The Toronto press never spoke so much of Italy, fascism, and Mussolini. Even those newspapers which ordinarily are Italo-phobic [the *Toronto Star* and *Telegram*], have been correct, better, we may say, kind."[35] The paper attributed all this to fascism and Mussolini who had brought to Italy and to Italians, wherever they might live, prestige, admiration, and recognition.

The Italian delegation had just left Toronto when the highly praised fascist dignitary Piero Parini, leader of the fasci abroad, arrived in Toronto for a thirty-six-hour visit. He arrived Thursday morning, 1 February, and left Friday evening, 2 February. During his short stay, he was wined and dined in the luxurious villa of the successful contractor, James Franceschini, and he dined at the Royal York Hotel and Angelo's Restaurant. The Veterans' Association and the fascio offered him what they, in the fascist rhetoric of the time, called *il rancio* (a military ration), rather then a dinner. The Circolo Colombo made Parini honourary member for life and Franceschini presented him with the gift of a white horse from his renowned stable.[37]

Il Bollettino welcomed Parini with a special twelve-page issue, which opened with the headline, "La Nostra Colonia accoglie con entusiasmo il ministro Parini" (Our Colony Welcomes Enthusiastically Minister Parini). After the parties and the private conversations with the consul and fascist leaders, Parini met the community in a public meeting at the Canadian Foresters Association. Apart from the usual fascist rhetoric about inept liberal governments, bolshevik chaos, and the healthy fascist reaction and revolution, the main thrust of his speech was an appeal to the community to remain Italian or to regain its Italianness:

> It is necessary that . . . the characteristic and distinctive qualities of our race be maintained in order to secure its continuity. It is therefore necessary that the Italian people wherever they live remain always and, above all, in their fundamental aspect, Italians.

He even proposed the idea that fascist Italy was no longer the impoverished country that the emigrants remembered but "she is wealthy enough to feed its 45 millions of children." In a Depression-plagued Canada, such words induced awe and admiration.

Following fascist guidelines to publish only what was useful to the movement, *Il Bollettino* ignored a protest organized by the Italian antifascists during the public meeting at the Foresters Hall.[38] There is, however, what might be an allusion to the protest in the words Parini addressed to his fellow fascists before he left the city. In exhorting them, he said "do more and better without paying much attention to the donkey's brays which never reach heaven." The phrase "donkey's brays" is surely an allusion to the anti-fascists' protest and a more specific reference to that incident was printed in *Il Bollettino* a few months later. In a party given for fascist youth to celebrate their return from their camping trip in Italy a mother, hearing her daughter speaking highly of Parini, commented "a gentleman like him [Parini] . . . was mistreated by those scoundrels and no one broke their heads."[39]

Another example which unintentionally documents the presence of anti-fascists in the community occurred when Maestro Angelo Carbone, Secretary of Fascio Principe Umberto, lay ill in the hospital only days before his death. On that occasion, *Il Bollettino* informed its readers of the many messages that had been received that wished Carboni well — "even from adversaries." But otherwise *Il Bollettino* remained mute about who those adversaries were and what they thought and did. By rule, in fact, any opposition by Italian Canadians to the regime in Italy was ignored throughout the decade: "Let us bury anti-fascism by ignoring it completely. For pity, let it fall into oblivion and let its ashes be dispersed by the winds of memory."[40]

What Parini and local fascists had discussed in private during his visit no one knew but the likely topic of conversation was learned later. During his visit Parini had promised $5,000.00 for a Fascist Centre in Toronto. In October of the same year, the new Vice Consul Tiberi announced that Parini had kept his "fascist promise" and that consequently:

> a Casa d'Italia would be built: the fascist government proves with facts and generosity its interest and love for the Italian abroad and for the Italians of Toronto in particular. The Fascist Centre of Toronto will stand as a splendid monument and a symbol of the patriotic passion of our *stirpe* (people).[41]

He also announced that he personally, rather then a committee, would collect funds for the centre. Later, however, he changed his mind and a committee was formed for this task.

In a series of articles, *Il Bollettino* illustrated the fabulous practical advantage, the national pride, and the great spiritual achievements that would result for Italian Canadians in Toronto, once the Fascist Centre was completed. All of the Italian associations would be housed under the same roof and social, recreational and cultural activities for young and old would be programmed at the proposed centre. There, a swimming-pool, a gymnasium, and a library would enrich the lives of Italian Torontians for generations to come. In describing all these grandiose, patriotic wonders, *Il Bollettino* did not forget to appeal to the narcissistic ego of the people then fawning over the Consul. These individuals were enticed by the promise of "a golden book and marble plaques for the founders of Casa d'Italia."[42]

The consul's announcement generated enthusiasm among fascists and their supporters and surprise and scepticism in the community in general. When it was learned, however, that the Casa d'Italia would be owned by the Italian government, scepticism and surprise turned into open criticism.[42] Critics had realized that the Consul's rhetoric about Parini's particular interest for Toronto's Italians was a ploy used by the fascist government to buy and own, with a mere $5,000.00 (which, as will be discussed, probably never arrived in Canada) a valuable property to house the consul, his family, and the Consulate offices, and have the largest part of this property paid for by local Italians.

Moreover, having the associations concentrated in an Italian government property would make them much easier to control and impose on them the totalitarian view of the PNF.[44] Further, critics realized that Tiberi's initial decision to monopolize the project was a subtle form of intimidation; he knew very well that his move would make it difficult for well-to-do Italians to refuse their contribution to the Fascist Centre, if it was the Consul himself who asked for their financial assistance. All Italians who read the newspapers knew about what had happened to Professor Antonio Sabetta of the University of Montreal who, during a vacation in Italy, had been arrested in his home town of Ururi, Campobasso, because he had declined to be part of the fascio of Montreal.[45]

The timing of the Fascist Centre even caused friction between the fascio and the Franciscan Brothers who were then in the process of renovating St. Mary of the Angels Church on Dufferin Street in Toronto. They feared that, because unemployment was very high among Italian Canadians in their parish, the community would not be able to support financially two very expensive initiatives, their church renovation and the Fascist Centre appeal, at the same time.[46]

Il Bollettino did all it could to dispel any mistrust in people's minds and to generate enthusiasm and expectation in the community.[47] It dismissed the general criticism about the ownership of the proposed Centre with the claim that "Casa d'Italia belongs to all Italians, but no one should have the right to remove his individual brick because he has contributed a dollar" to purchase it.[48] And justifying the Consul's exclusive control of the Casa d'Italia project, *Il Bollettino* argued that the decision was not yet well understood but: "When the community has absorbed better the importance of Consul Tiberi's appeal even those who have doubts will realize that their social position and their patriotism demand from them no less than from the others the largest financial contribution possible."[49]

In its 23 November 1934 issue, a manifesto from the consul to the community, and a list of 101 pledges was published (see appendix No. 6 for details). The pledges totalled $26,307.00 in funds plus 174 days of general labour, $380.00 in painting and decorating work, one painting by Professor Pietro Carollo, as well as an artistic work in plaster by Primo Danesi.[50] The list was shrewdly prepared. It showed that people of every walk of life had answered the consul's appeal and that it had been supported generously. In fact, next to the fabulous pledge of $15,000.00 by the wealthiest Italian of Toronto, identified only as V. F. (no doubt the initials of Vincenzo Franchesini), there was the pledge of a $1.00 donation by Camasta Francesco, a sickly individual who was then living on a small pension.

On 21 December 1934, a second list of pledges, made of prominent fascists and their friends, was published, bringing the total amount of pledges to $28,126.25 (for details, see appendix No. 6a). Early in the new year (1935), news of a $500.00 donation by the Eaton Company was the last report published by *Il Bollettino* (1 March 1935) on the fund-raising campaign for Casa d'Italia. Apparently, its strategy of publishing, one after the other, two impressive lists of campaign contributions was not enough to encourage many donations by average Italian Canadians.

In fact, two years later, when the fascists with great fanfare and much jubilation bought the prestigious Chudleigh mansion at 136 Beverley Street, only a fraction of the fabulous pledges announced in 1934 had been honoured. The mansion was bought in September 1936 for $25,000.00 with a down payment of $5,000.00.[51] The sum pledged by the Italian government had not yet been received as Mari's statement in *Il Bollettino* (25 September 1936) confirms: "The Consul [Tiberi], and with him, our Consul General [Petrucci] ... have spoken so well of us to the Italian government which, through the affectionate interest of Piero Parini, has promised to give us $5,000. This promise was repeated to us recently [the summer of 1936] in Rome." It seems likely that the money promised by the Italian government never arrived in Canada. The $5,000.00 for the down payment was money that had been collected in the community in the course of the 1934-1935 fundraising campaign.[52]

Once the Beverley Street property was bought by Casa d'Italia Limited, the consul initiated a new campaign for collecting funds. He nominated a committee to help him and sent the following letter to most Italian Canadians in Toronto:

> Dear Sir,
> A committee of compatriots will soon initiate a voluntary money collection for the Casa d'Italia of Toronto ... The Casa d'Italia Ltd. has bought the property at 136 Beverley Street where the most important activities of the Italian Colony of Toronto will be concentrated. All Italians by birth or by origin who have contributed to the initiative in proportion to their means could participate in these activities and enjoy their numerous advantages ... I am sure that when the delegates from the Committee call on you, you will once again prove your generosity and patriotism which will constitute a noble act among compatriots residing in Toronto.
>
> With much esteem.
> Il Regio V. Console, G. Tiberi

In the 4 December 1936 issue of Il Bollettino an article, titled *"La seconda ondata per la casa d'Italia"* (The Second wave for the Casa d'Italia), gives a preliminary list of funds collected which totalled $550.[53] to be added to a previous balance of $7,299.52 On the eve of the official inauguration of Casa d'Italia, which occurred on Sunday 14 February 1937, it was reported that $9,501.11 had been collected.[54] It is impossible to know, however, how much money was actually collected and how the funds were spent. By the summer of 1939, the mortgage for the Beverley Street property had been reduced by half.[55]

In the spring of 1935, the Italian-Ethiopian crisis put an end to the frenzy of activity around the Casa d'Italia. The attention of *Il Bollettino* and of fascists in Toronto was directed mainly to the development of that crisis: diplomatic initiatives, sanctions, and then war. Attention also was given to international and Canadian events which proved, according to *Il Bollettino,* the irresistible march of fascism throughout the world. For example, the long editorial of 12 April 1935, titled "Peaceful Fascist Revolution in Canada," maintained that Canadian leaders were moving toward fascism, but that they lacked the courage to admit as much.

That editorial took its cue from a declaration by the then new Governor General, Sir John Buchan, who claimed that Canada was going through a "peaceful constitutional revolution." According to *Il Bollettino,* the Canadian middle class had been awakened by the recent investigation by H. H. Stevens of big business in Canada and the middle class strongly felt the need for a third party — a party which was not the socialist CCF — to look after true Canadian national interests. Conservatives and Liberals were restrained from looking after these interests by their "plutocratic" supporters who were British and American respectively. Inspired by national interest, the emerging "third party would stand between the two contending parties" and the plutocracies. This, concluded the editorial, "is the fascist principle" which imposes itself inexorably on modern nations and their governments. This analysis explains the alliance that fascists sought with H. H. Stevens and his Reconstruction Party in the October 1935 election already discussed above.

The paper produced a similar commentary on the occasion of a speech by W. D. Herridge, Canadian Minister in Washington. According to *Il Bollettino* (5 June 1936), Herridge had said: "In a world of economic nationalism, Canada should practice economic nationalism." This prompted the paper to ask:

> Is the Honourable Herridge converted to fascist doctrine? Is he, by chance, one of those men who are afraid of the word fascism, but they sense all the economic and political goodness implicit in that word? Are there courageous men in Canada who, aware of the grave problems facing the country, dare to face their solution?

Il Bollettino returned to the subject of fascism in Canada with two long articles: "Canadian Fascism Towards Unity" and "Canadian Fascists," which it published on 24 March and 7 July 1938, respectively. The former is a report on the progress toward unity of the various Canadian fascist groups. The paper noted that anti-Semitism animated all these groups, except the Toronto based Canadian Union of Fascists (CUF) which, inspired by Mussolini, was more "temperate" regarding the Jewish problem. In keeping with this theme *Il Bollettino* published (14 February 1938) an article, "Fascism and the Christian Ideal" by W. F. Elsey, the secretary of the Woodstock branch of CUF. The writer argued that fascism "is the most perfect form of working Christianity yet devised for Fascists believe in the most practical manner of rendering unto God the things that are God's."

More interesting is the editorial "Canadian Fascists: 2,500 fascists met at the Massey Hall" which was the report of a meeting addressed by speakers from Quebec, Ontario, New Brunswick, and British Columbia. As good fascists, they stood for the Corporative State: "Everything is in the State, nothing is outside the State or against the State." Fascists were against the "inept, incapable, egotistic, stingy Minister of Justice [the Honourable Ernest Lapointe] and his corrupted democracy." And, the paper added: "They are against Masonry and even here they have a point. They are certainly right in their stand against communists." *Il Bollettino* approved the Party's new and truly Canadian symbol which replaced the swastika but it rejected the Party's program because "it is as long and detailed as that of a democratic party." Good fascists should think only in slogans. *Il Bollettino* did not forecast the Party's future but it noted that "Canadian fascism has almost all of the elements necessary for success, particularly a negative view of its political adversaries."

Besides these long articles, the occasional comment on fascist success in Canada and in the Italian community were often expressed in a messianic language. For example, speaking of Hamilton Casa d'Italia, *Il Bollettino* wrote:

> Its facade is exquisitely fascist. Four huge Lictorian Fasces
> rise from the ground to the sky and over them flies the flag
> ... They stand as a categorical affirmation, not only of a
> political ideal but of a way of life which our people affirm
> in the awareness that they are the initiators of a system.
> This system with its higher social justice will even be here
> [in Canada] in a different form some day. It is fascism that
> affirms itself.[56]

From the spring of 1935 to the summer of 1936 and even beyond, *Il Bollettino*'s main interest was the Ethiopian question. It is now known that in Ethiopia Mussolini sought a military victory to increase Italy's prestige, re-assert his position internationally, and consolidate his grip on Italy.[57] After Hitler was elected in 1933, the major European powers — England, France, and even Russia — cast Mussolini in a minor role and Italy, once again, among the second-rate nations. Mussolini could not tolerate the fact that his own disciple Hitler, the last arrival on the political scene, would upstage him.[58] Hence, the Ethiopian campaign was intended to return both himself and fascism to a leading role and to place Italy among the ranks of the great powers.

To launch the campaign which he had prepared in secret for many months,[59] Mussolini waited for the right opportunity. It came after the signing of the Paris-Rome bilateral accord which occurred in January 1935, and the Stresa accord among Britain, France, and Italy, which was signed in April of the same year. It was, however, Germany's decision to re-arm, in violation of the peace treaty, that created the opportunity for which Mussolini was waiting. Majors powers like Britain and France were too preoccupied with nazi Germany to alienate an ally like Mussolini in defence of a poor African nation like Ethiopia.

Mussolini knew well that in such circumstances England or France would do nothing but talk in order to appease a public outcry. In fact, when Dr. Riddell of the Canadian delegation at Geneva proposed to extend sanctions on petroleum products against Italy, England and France became deaf. Ironically, as Mussolini confided to Hitler, such a measure would have compelled him to get out of Ethiopia within a couple of weeks.[60] The sanctions imposed by the League of the Nations against Italy were ineffective because two of the strongest economic powers, Germany and the United States, were not members of the League. The sanctions helped, more than harmed, Mussolini. Italians saw them as an external menace and, whether at home or abroad, they were spurred to rally behind the Duce and, later, their support gave him the chance to boast that Italy won the war against the entire world.

In *Il Bollettino,* the Ethiopian question first appeared as a news item about the frontier incident at Ual Ual where, in December 1934, some Italian soldiers had been killed. In its issue for 22 February 1935, *Il Bollettino* introduced the Ethiopian question with an opinionated article, titled "Roma Civilizatrice," written in English by Frank Molinaro, a very active young man who often was called on to speak about fascism by various associations in the city of Toronto.

Molinaro took his cue from the Ual Ual incident in order to present his ideas on the subject. He argued that only fascist Rome "is peculiarly well suited" to bring civilization to Ethiopia. He painted the East African country in the sombre hues which fascists used to portray their enemies. The country was plagued with social and economic chaos, incompetence and corruption in government, and slavery. In Molinaro's words: "Under the guiding hand of Mussolini, the incarnation of Nietzsche's Superman and Creator of Fascism which shall entirely dominate and decide the life of the twentieth century, she [Italy] resumes her ancient role as Roma Civilizatrice." Molinaro did not speak openly of either war or conquest. But for the conditions he attributed to Ethiopia, only military intervention could introduce "civilization."

Two weeks later, in its 8 March 1935 issue, *Il Bollettino* published an article, *"L'Etiopia ed i suoi vicini"* (Ethiopia and her neighbours), which took a different position. The incidents on the borders of Abyssinia and Italian Somalia were raids carried out by unruly bands. Obviously the article opined, the Ethiopian "government does not have the authority or the means to keep under control the situations in the periphery." In fact, the article cleared the Ethiopian government of any direct involvement in the incidents. The two pieces reveal that *Il Bollettino* (like *L'Italia*) lacked a definite editorial position on the situation in East Africa. By that summer, however, the paper had defined a clear policy regarding the Ethiopian question which by that point had become the focus of fascist propaganda and a hot issue at the League of Nations in Geneva. *Il Bollettino*'s position had three main features: 1. check the overwhelming public opinion against fascism by rebuking opinions and news items appearing in the Toronto daily newspapers; 2. present the fascist alternative with material sent from the Minculpop in Rome; and 3. incite and rally support for Mussolini's policy.

Fascist propaganda contained essentially two richly-articulated reasons for the invasion of Ethiopia. The first of these was a self-proclaimed need to find new lands for the growing population of Italy as a redress for the iniquity imposed by the wealthy nations, England and France. Secondly, Italy was undertaking a "noble mission" in Abyssinia to reaffirm the position of the white race and of Christian values in East Africa.

Canadian public opinion against fascist aggression in Ethiopia, as expressed by the daily papers (*The Globe, The Star,* and *The Telegram*), was *Il Bollettino*'s main target. Given, as already noted, that for the Italian-Canadian paper a free press necessarily meant a corrupted press, it accused all three newspapers of being anti-Italian, of publishing false news and even fabricating news, in order to put down Italy and to portray Mussolini as an aggressor. In reality, the paper argued, Italians had suffered the continued aggression from Ethiopian troops for years. It gave dates and figures to support this claim, as prepared by the Minculpop in Rome.

Such attacks against the Toronto press escalated throughout the conflict in Ethiopia and they reached their maximum pitch at the end of the war, in May 1936. The excitement created by the Italian victory in Abyssinia prompted *Il Bollettino* and its editors to daring arrogance never equalled by *L'Italia*. In what seems to have been a symbolic squadrista reprisal for the newspapers' support of Ethiopia, *Il Bollettino* sent

> the Editor of the *Star* and its foreign correspondent Signor Van Paassen and the Editor of the *Telegram* and its correspondent Signor Robinson MacLean, a small present. A very nice bottle of castor oil and a business card on which was written, "This pure Italian castor oil may help you digest the Victory of the Italian army."[61]

The *Star* returned this courtesy with a cool editorial titled, "It Looks Very Nice," in which the editorialist calmly explained what the "innocent" castor oil really meant.

> His [Mussolini's] Black Shirt supporters drowned all opposition in castor oil. Who, however brave, can take in by forced feeding half a pint of castor oil and remain in opposition? We do not recall that any Caesar in ancient Rome ever hit upon an expedient so demoralizing to his adversaries . . . Still we must point out to our esteemed confrère who edits *Il Bollettino* that . . . we don't have to take it. Fortunately for us, the fiat of Il Duce does not run outside the Kingdom of Italy.[62]

The *Vancouver Daily Province* wrote a strong editorial about this act of fascist bravado in which it noted that "it certainly remains to remind the editor of *Il Bollettino* that he abuses hospitality with his blackguard insult."[63]

Il Bollettino reacted as usual with spurious arguments, phrased in tones of self-righteousness. In a piece written in English, it dismissed the charge of having issued an insult which it maintained "existed only in the head" of the Vancouver editorialist. Then the article continued with an accusation against the Vancouver newspaper of superficially judging fascism and giving unsolicited advice. In turn, *Il Bollettino* offered to send material to Vancouver so the editor could learn about fascism which it described as a phenomenon that was so "great" and "complex" that it is "impossible to judge it as did the Vancouver daily."[64]

If the gift of castor oil was an implicit insult, the printed words were insultingly explicit and openly vulgar as well. For example, for *Il Bollettino* Robinson MacLean was "a buffoon," the editor of the *Telegram* "a gross ignorant . . . a *facchino* (base individual); and the paper itself stinks like a skunk."[65] Referring to the editorial board of *The Star*, *Il Bollettino* wrote, you deserve "a sound cudgelling that would redress your thinking."[66] In reading these obscenities one could be excused the impression that it was in fact *Il Bollettino* and its editor that had been affected by the castor oil.

Such bravado and name-calling did not earn Tommaso Mari rebukes but rather admiration from the Consul General, Luigi Petrucci, and Dr. Vittorio Sabetta, then Grand Venerable of the Order Sons of Italy in Ontario. In a speech Sabetta praised the "bellicose . . . Toronto newspaper *Bollettino italo-canadese* which through polemical articles has been in this Province the knight of the new Italian ideas, defender of Italy's rights and supporter of our faith."[67] Consul General Petrucci expressed his appreciation in a letter:

> In this era of fascistic greatness of Royal and Imperial Italy, *Il Bollettino italo-canadese* must be noted as an example. It distinguishes itself in battles against innumerable enemies which it led on a most difficult ground throughout the year that is about to end . . . To you, dear Mari, who has an easy, daring, and sharp pen, I send a word of special recognition and my best wishes.[68]

The campaign to rally Italians in support of Mussolini's invasion of Ethiopia was a success in every respect. Italians, except for staunch anti-fascists, supported Italy at war. Some young men, as already mentioned, volunteered to fight in the East Africa campaign (see appendix No. 7). In this, *Il Bollettino* and fascists in general were unintentionally helped by the major daily newspapers which continuously ridiculed Italian soldiers. This was a very sensitive issue that was strongly felt even by left-wing Italian

Canadians.[69] *Il Bollettino* explained that conquering Abyssinia was beneficial to both Italians and Ethiopians. The sanctions against Italy were spurred by the envy of wealthy countries. England, in particular, feared that she would be out-classed by Mussolini's Italy. All of these elements of a defence for Italy's aggression were presented well in a piece which *Il Bollettino* presented as a fable for children.[70]

To affirm the religious nature of the Ethiopian campaign, *Il Bollettino* rebuked the Anglican Bishop of Montreal, Mons Farthing, who had stated that "fascism was anti-Christian." With indignation Mari replied that the Anglican Bishop was ignorant because "fascism stands perfectly on the same ground as Christianity." Mari concluded that Monsignor Farthing would learn much about fascism by asking his Roman Catholic colleague McNally, bishop of Hamilton, who knew "what [fascism] . . . has done for religion, and . . . has had the courage of a real Shepherd to affirm the truth" publicly.[71]

With regard to the political-religious dimension of the Ethiopian question, *Il Bollettino* published a circular letter from Damiano Neri, Supreme General of the Franciscan Order, to the Franciscans in Toronto. In that letter, Father Neri said to his brothers:

> Let us work in conformity with the Government's wise instruction for the triumph of the common cause. But above all let us pray that the day in which our Mother Country may exultantly sing thanks to God is near. Thanking God for having insured wealth to her own sons, broken the chains of slavery and opened the road to Christian civilization to Abyssinia, the land towards which once so many of our brothers desiring martyrdom directed their steps.[72]

The Franciscan position toward the Ethiopian war followed the general orientation of the Roman Catholic intelligentsia both in Italy and abroad. Most Roman Catholics supported Mussolini's policy, hoping to keep him from joining Hitler's side. For example, in 1935-36, the influential Jesuit periodical, *La Civiltà cattolica,* published a series of articles by Father Antonio Messineo in which colonial wars were justified. According to Danilo Veneruso, Messineo argued that when "a country is overpopulated, pressed within its boundaries and without the release of emigration, it is forced to expand in lands beyond the sea."[73] This statement could easily have been taken directly from a fascist propaganda sheet.

It is not surprising then that Italian Canadians, most of whom were Roman Catholic, supported in mass Mussolini's African war. The magnitude of their support is clearly seen in the huge sum of money they collected for the Italian Red Cross and in the quantity of wedding rings and gold objects they offered in support of the motherland. In the consular district of Ottawa — which consisted of Ontario and Manitoba — together with that of Western Canada — comprising the provinces of Alberta and British Columbia — $20,825.24 was raised but this was only a portion of the final total.[74] This was a large sum of money to be raised from a community made up mostly of manual workers, many of whom were then out of work.

The collection of gold rings and jewels was undertaken mostly by women who, more than men, were influenced by the sermonizing of priests in their parishes. We cannot know how much gold was collected during the entire fund-raising campaign which ran from the fall of

1935 to spring of the following year. In 1936 the *Montreal Star* wrote:

> Italians in Canada are selling gold to the mint and getting money to send to Italy, according to Dr. V. V. Restaldi delegate-general of the Italian Red Cross and Vice-consul of Italy. The Italians have collected 430 ounces of gold in Quebec and 421 ounces in Ontario. This gold has been sent to the mint in Ottawa and there it was exchanged for money which was to be sent to the Red Cross in Italy."[75]

One of the fundraising efforts was undertaken in Sault Ste. Marie, Ontario and some of its details provide a glimpse into the success of the *Oro pro patria* or Gold for the Fatherland campaign. Mrs. Isabella Pilo of the Lodge Princess Maria José of the Order Sons of Italy of Ontario, presented a list of twenty-seven people (twenty-two women and five men) who had contributed thirty-four gold pieces which included wedding rings, ear rings, necklaces, and other items as well as seven silver pieces. Mrs. Renzoni, former Venerable or president of the same lodge, had canvased seventy women and collected 157 gold pieces, mostly wedding rings, together with some silver objects, and even a brass tray.[76]

At the end of the Ethiopian war, a wave of enthusiasm and excitement surged through Italian Canadians across the country from Nova Scotia to Vancouver. The title with which *Il Bollettino* announced the Ethiopian conquest was childishly arrogant: *"L'Etiopia è Italiana. Ci siamo e ci restiamo — Guai a chi ci tocca"* (Ethiopia is Italian. We are there and there we will stay. Beware those who would tamper [with our conquest]) (see appendix No. 9). The victory gave fascists swelled heads and dreams of new and greater victories and mythical conquests.

> We have just lived a year of struggle, of battle, of glory. Those who like us think of life as a struggle would like to live again the eventful year which is about to end . . . Imperial year, year of the Italian redemption. We are not, however, at apogee yet. Our toil is not over. Our ascending is not completed. We are too far from our goal. But today we can see it clearly up there in the blue sky near glory and justice.[77]

Unable or unwilling to see the Ethiopian war in its true military proportions, as the action of a modern war machine pitted unfairly against an unarmed people, *Il Bollettino* presented the African campaign as one of history's famous military events.

Undoubtedly the wave of patriotic excitement of surprise and joy that swept through Italian-Canadian communities across the country boosted their self image. In turn, fascists were spurred by this outpouring of patriotism to do more and to assert themselves more effectively. In less then one year after the Ethiopian war they were able to establish five Case d'Italia or Fascist Centres — one each in Sydney (N. S.), Montreal, Hamilton, Toronto, and Windsor — which had been neglected because of events in Ethiopia. In Vancouver, Italians fulfilled their long-held aspiration; namely, the publication of a local newspaper. *L'Eco italo-canadese* (*L'Eco*) made its appearance in Vancouver at the end of the Ethiopian war. It was the first Italian-language newspaper to be published west of Toronto,[78] and the most junior of the Italian-language fascist newspapers in Canada.

Chapter Four

L'Eco italo-canadese: 1936-1940 (Vancouver)

The first issue of *L'Eco italo-canadese (L'Eco)* appeared on 24 October 1936. Bruno Girardi was the owner and editor until 11 June 1938 when "as a consequence of painful circumstances," he handed the paper over to his assistant, Alberto Boccini. Free from the presumption of emulating the great Italian national newspapers *L'Eco,* a twelve-page tabloid, served the community better than did the more pretentious eastern newspapers, *L'Italia* and *Il Bollettino.* The articles were short and easy to read, and thus they were in tune with the paper's readership — mostly manual workers who had had three to five years of schooling.

L'Eco was created on the wave of patriotic euphoria which swept over Italian Canadians following Italy's success in the Ethiopian war. Pietro Colbertaldo, the Italian Vice-Consul, seized the opportunity offered by this patriotic fervour, and with the help of newly-arrived Italian priests in Vancouver and the Italian associations of that city, succeeded in creating the necessary support for the publication of an Italian-language weekly.

Even the renowned Vancouver lawyer Angelo Branca contributed to the success of this editorial initiative by lending it his support. W. Ruocco, president of the *Società Figli d'Italia,* not to be confused with the Order

Sons of Italy, recognized Branca's decisive contribution in *L'Eco*'s first issue. He wrote:

> Several times before we wanted to initiate this project, but we always encountered insurmountable difficulties, and we gave up before beginning. This time, however, thanks to the Vice-Consul, signor Pietro Colbertaldo, to the various presidents, male and female, of the Italian Associations of Vancouver, to our newly arrived priests and in particular to A. Branca, renowned and well-liked lawyer of this city, we found our way not only cleared, but even replete with advice and help.

Angelo Branca's mild anti-fascism,[1] a smaller and more integrated Italian community coupled with a strong socialist tradition among the Italian-Canadian miners of British Columbia,[2] hindered the boldness of local fascists in Vancouver and British Columbia in general when compared with their comrades in central Canada. Moreover, it is clear that *L'Eco* was inspired by the nationalistic side of the twofold soul of the Partito Nazionale Fascista (PNF). The *movimento fascista*, created in 1919, and the *movimento nazionalista*, which had been formed in 1910, came together in the founding of the PNF in 1923. *L'Eco*, however, followed fascist guidelines and firmly opposed the process of naturalization of Italian emigrants. On this point *L'Eco* editorialized:

> We must overcome this or that temptation that weakens our love for la Patria. To overcome such temptations, to ensure that our patriotic sentiment remains strong, the emigrant must nourish his Italian roots. We must develop in him his will to remain Italian.[3]

On the other hand, never a word was written to explain or even mention the possible advantages of becoming a Canadian citizen.

The classic propaganda themes of fascism were closely linked to the need to develop "the will to remain Italian," namely, the revival of Rome's military and Imperial glories and Italy's eternal mission to bring "civilization" to the world. Furthermore, in line with its eastern counterparts, *L'Eco* ignored the Italian anti-fascist activities which occurred both in Vancouver as well as in various mining towns of the British Columbia interior. *L'Eco* also ignored union activities and any reference to conditions experienced by Italian Canadians and other miners or workers. All of this news was reported by two anti-fascist newspapers published in Toronto, *La Voce degli italo-canadesi* and, before it, *Il Lavoratore*. Instead, *L'Eco* devoted its coverage to the Veterans' Association, the local fascio organization, Club Giulio Giordani, and related associations. But even in this coverage, and even though the Vancouver paper followed fascist guidelines, generally the tone of its leading articles and editorials was less rhetorical and arrogant than those published in eastern newspapers.

In contrast to its eastern counterparts, *L'Eco* did not say much about local fascist activities. For example, throughout 1938 the local fascio was mentioned only once and this was in the context of a report about a social event. The paper reported that the event was attended by, among others, the Consul, Dr. G. Brancucci, and Ennio Fabbri, a lawyer and *secretary of the fascio*. For the remainder of the year, *L'Eco* did not mention the local fascio again.

Allusions to local fascists were made indirectly. For example, when describing social activities, the paper would report that the meeting began by playing the Italian national anthems; namely, the Royal March and *Giovinezza* (Youth), a song that was very popular during the fascist regime. Similarly, in mentioning certain individuals, the paper used the appellative "comrade," implying that the individual mentioned belonged to the fascio or to the Veterans' Association. Not even during the commemoration of the fascist March on Rome which was organized by the Club Giulio Giordani, which was in fact the Fascio Giulio Giordani, was the word fascio used. This "Club" was named after the fascist Giulio Giordani, a decorated war amputee who had been killed during the tragic events in Italy known as *i fatti di Palazzo D'Accursio,* which had occurred on 21 November 1921, in Bologna.[4]

Though not as brazenly fascist as its counterparts in the East, *L'Eco* was extremely nationalist and often crossed over into jingoism. The paper defended the local Italian-Canadian community and Italy against the big Vancouver daily newspapers which openly or implicitly, in *L'Eco*'s view, denigrated Italy and Italians. For example, in its 30 July 1938 issue, *L'Eco* published an editorial titled "The Italian People," in which it attacked the *Vancouver Sun*. The anti-Italian *Vancouver Sun,* wrote *L'Eco,* "tells us that during the Great War our army did not have a notable strength; and conquering Abyssinia was a childish affair." After a long diatribe about Italy winning the war for the allies, the editorial concluded that "[the *Vancouver Sun*] knows that, without Versailles which taught the Italian people to rely only on themselves, Italy would not have had fascism so soon; without the betrayal of her allies, she would not have her colonial Empire; without the sanctions, she would not have had her *autarchia*,[5] and without the bolshevik agression in Spain, she would not be on her way to a spiritual Empire."

The condescension shown by some Canadians toward Italians as fighting soldiers, as already noted, was a sore spot for all Italian Canadians, regardless of their political stripe. Reacting to such denigration, fascist newspapers like *L'Eco* printed absurd, jingoistic statements and highlighted trivial successes which, in the editor's mind, confirmed the superiority of the Italian people. To make this point, *L'Eco* (3 September 1938) claimed that even the communist experiment in Russia had an Italian origin: "Moscow, which was only a mere village when Rome dominated the world, pretends to lead the world because she tried to put into practice the utopian dream of Tommaso Campanella's *Città del Sole* which originated on Mediterranean shores five hundred years ago."

Moreover, in keeping with the eastern fascist press and the directives emanating from Rome, *L'Eco* reminded its readers, over and over, that Italy had given a great deal to the world and had received very little in return. "We must remember," wrote *L'Eco,* "that most of those who have contributed to the well-being of the human race were Italians or of Italian origin."[6] To prove his point, the editor did not refrain from spewing nonsense so long as in some vague way it pointed to the presumed superiority of Italians. The following are two examples: 1. "every time that a poor beggar became a hero, it turned out that he was an Italian" and; 2. in the "Folk Festival [in Vancouver] . . . the Italian cake was chosen as the best national cake."[7] In almost every issue *L'Eco* announced some type of Italian "supremacy" and, in some obscure way, these silly statements played a role in the psychology of Italian Canadians who felt that they were being, and sometimes were, treated "contemptuously" or, at best, with "condescension" by some Anglo-Saxons.[8]

As a paper that served a number of small communities, *L'Eco*'s yearly calendar was marked by the activities of local Italian Associations; picnics in the summer, dances in the winter, and elections for association officers in the fall. In addition, the Italian national holy days were solemnly commemorated both in the community and by the paper. These memorable dates were celebrated with religious ceremonies during the day and dinner-dances and rhetorical speeches in the evening. Local talent was on hand to entertain the participants by playing music, dancing, singing, and acting.

The associations, according to their main interests — patriotic, political, religious — organized the respective national events to be commemorated. Twenty-four May, Italy entering the Great War, and 4 November, Victory Day, were the domain of the Veterans' Association. The fascio Giulio Giordani looked after the celebration of the birth of Rome, commemorated on 21 April and the March on Rome, 28 October. The recurrence of Cristoforo Colombo's famous voyage was a Roman Catholic affair and so the celebration was organized by the female section of the Figli d'Italia Society. Although one or two associations were responsible for organizing each of these special ceremonies, the other societies and the community in general collaborated and supported such initiatives, participating in large numbers.

L'Eco paid a great amount of attention to these activities by reporting on and advertising the events, highlighting the interesting moments, and praising those responsible for the event's success. The paper's dominant interest was the teaching of the Italian language in Vancouver and surrounding cities. Throughout the province, committees responsible for organizing Italian-language teaching were created. To attract and interest students various activities were undertaken including writing contests, athletic games, and theatrical performances. Prizes were given to worthy students for their intellectual, artistic, and athletic achievements. All of these activities were covered extensively by the Italian Vancouver paper.

Often, conflicts arose between people who wanted to have more direct fascist indoctrination in Italian-language classes and those who simply wished to teach Italian. The echo of such disputes sometimes reverberated even in the paper. The following letter sent to *L'Eco* by one of the organizers of such classes in North Vancouver is an example:

> Let me please point out that in the preceding issue of your paper, I read with much disappointment a report by your correspondent from North Vancouver, Mr. Colombo Vagnini, regarding the Italian School. His conclusion is completely wrong... I firmly disagree with the following paragraph: the Italian schools are in no way linked to Mussolini and their scope is not to develop Italian soldiers.[9]

In this paragraph and in the entire letter, it is not clear if the writer of the letter was for or against Italian schools being "linked to Mussolini." Speculation on this question is irrelevant here; the issue is raised simply to illustrate the divergence of views which existed in the Italian communities of western Canada.

Although *L'Eco* did not speak much about local fascism, it did have much to say about Italian and international fascism. Throughout the five years of its existence, its first page usually was devoted to Italian and related international news; that is to say, fascist propaganda in which fascism and Mussolini were central protagonists. This front-page material was propaganda prepared by the Minculpop in Rome and distributed by the Italian consulates. For example, on the first page of the 8 October 1938 issue the following articles appeared, "Laissez-faire" (editorial)," *"L'Inaguarazione dell'ARA PACIS dell'Impero"* (The Inaguration of the Peace Altar of the Empire), and *"Il Sacrario delle Bandiere alla Casa dei Mutilati"* (The Shrine of Flags at the Home of the War Disabled). The front page also included two short pieces of about sixty words each, on milk production in Canada and a rise in the import tax on wheat by some European countries. The most important front-page piece in this issue was titled "29 Settembre," and it was an article devoted to the Munich accord of 29 September 1938.

This piece is a celebration of Mussolini's dominating role in the Munich conference which included Neville Chamberlain, Edouard Daladier, Adolf Hitler and, of course, Mussolini, which resulted in the partitioning of Czechoslovakia. "In Munich [Mussolini] designed the plan. He dictated the boundaries of the new Czechoslovakia. Master of the situation, he alone could treat the argument without the help of an interpreter. He spoke in English, German and French . . . pages and pages of the Universal history will be devoted to Him."

Canadian politics rarely appeared and, when it did, it was linked in some way to fascism. Once a year in December, during the municipal election, candidates and civic issues made the first page of the paper, as did the federal Canadian election of 26 March 1940. During the civic election, any Italian candidates who participated received a great amount of exposure in the newspaper.

In the 1939 municipal elections in the province, two Italian Canadians were successfully elected: Angelo Branca was elected to the office of Park Commissioner in Vancouver and Carmine Catalano, an emigrant from Cosenza, was chosen as School Trustee in Trail, in the province's interior. *L'Eco* printed Branca's picture on the first page in a prominent position together with that of the newly elected CCF Mayor of Vancouver, Dr. J. Lyle Telford.[10] *L'Eco* was jubilant over Branca's success:

> Our warmest congratulation to Angelo Branca, son of Italians, who gave the Italian community the great satisfaction of being represented at city hall, for the first time in Vancouver.[11]

Branca confirmed that his election had been a "memorable date not only for himself but for all Vancouver Italians."

In Canadian national politics *L'Eco,* like its eastern counterparts, was pro-Liberal but, unlike *L'Italia* and *Il Bollettino,* it maintained a balanced position in relation to the other two parties. In the 26 March 1940 election the newspaper spoke in favour of Mackenzie King but, though its position was obviously pro-Liberal, *L'Eco* presented a fair summary of the political platforms of both the National Conservative Party and of the CCF.

In its coverage of that election, *L'Eco* published four leading articles, one each for the three major parties who were contesting it, and an epilogue. In the first article (2 March 1940 issue), *L'Eco* presented the Liberal party. The main thrust of this piece was to point out that, in 1935, Mackenzie King had opposed the inclusion of petroleum products in the sanctions against Italy.

> Examining the past, we must conclude that the Liberal Government had pursued a policy of Canadian interest; we particularly remember how Mackenzie King acted in 1935 when people, total strangers to this Dominion, suggested extending Sanctions against Italy to include petroleum products. The Canadian representative at the League, gave his support without waiting for the Canadian Parliament approval . . . the Hon. Mackenzie King . . . immediately called back the zealous representative and informed the League of his opposition to such coercion.

Because of this action, the paper suggested that Mackenzie King and his Party deserved the Italian-Canadian vote.

The following week, on 9 March, the leading article presented the programme of the National Conservative Party in a ten point synthesis of the party platform, which stressed Canadian ties with England. The conclusion was, according to *L'Eco,* that this programme was not sufficiently nationalistic: "from a Canadian point of view," the programme was "more Conservative than Nationalist." However, in order not to alienate voters from the Liberal Party who might consider the Canada-England relation essential, *L'Eco* hastily added that both parties, Liberal and Conservative, profess "undivided loyalty to the Mother Country, England."

Even the programme of the CCF was presented with fairness. *L'Eco* did not try to smear the party nor did it resort to scare tactics by charging the CCF of bolshevist and communist connivance as *L'Italia* had done in the 1935 federal election, or, as the more doctrinaire Ontario paper, *Il Bollettino,* did in the Ontario provincial elections of 1934 and 1937.[12] The negative aspect of the CCF, according to *L'Eco*, was that its "programme mentions neither the Homeland nor Race, leaving a lacuna which leads to different interpretations — interpretations which we," continued *L'Eco,* "gladly leave to our readers who are the most intelligent people in the world, as Mussolini recently said."[13]

On 23 March, three days before the election, *L'Eco* openly but tactfully sided with the Liberals. The position taken may have resulted from the criticism of some prominent Liberals (Angelo Branca?) who had criticised the editor for not taking a clear pro-Liberal stand. *L'Eco* defended itself with the claim that "our support for the Liberal Party was clearly expressed in our first article on the election. We thought that the specific reference to the sanctions was a precise and convincing indication of how Italians should vote." On the other hand, concluded the Editor, "to overcome the adversity [the Second World War] which fell on the Dominion, unity, decision, and experience are necessary. Today, Mackenzie King's government has all these. Why then shouldn't we vote for it?" Even in this pro-Liberal epilogue, *L'Eco* was not as forceful and doctrinaire as its eastern colleagues, suggesting that it had respect for its readers' ability to make their own decisions.

Besides these exceptional occurrences, the first page was, as noted, normally devoted primarily to Italian affairs. The remaining pages were mostly filled with news of local Italian-Canadian communities in Vancouver and nearby New Westminster and the smaller cities of the British Columbia interior, namely Fernie, Trail, Michel and Natal, Kelowna, and Revelstoke. From these settlements, local agents sent information about everyday affairs: who was arriving from, or going to, Italy or other Northern American centres; who had been released from, or was about to be admitted to, hospital and, births, deaths, marriages, and serious accidents on the job, mostly in mines. Musical news and sports events were extensively covered when Italian, particularly local-Italian artists or athletes were involved.

Over the years, *L'Eco* published brief historical sketches of some local societies or associations. Particularly interesting for its wealth of information are the reports on the Società Colombo in Trail, the Female League of the Italian Canadian Mutual Assistance Society, and the Società Figli d'Italia, which appeared in the issues of 12 August 1939, and 24 February and 23 March 1940, respectively.

News and reports of this type not only created a network of social relations and connections between Italian Canadians in Vancouver and other British Columbia locales; it was also a means for exalting local Italian-Canadian talent, activities, and achievements. Thus, *L'Eco* confirmed locally and assiduously the official fascist propaganda which appeared on its first page and which credulously asserted that Italians were superior to any other race in every sector of human endeavour. Local news and reports of Italian events reinforced each other and served to assert naively the superiority and supremacy of Italy and the Italian people. This encouraged Italian immigrants to retain their identity as Italians and this, of course, was the main goal of fascist propaganda. In contrast to other, more open, more community-oriented newspapers, *L'Eco* presented to its readers a narcissistic image of their community; it promoted the existence of a community that looked inward on itself and away from the reality by which it was surrounded.

When Mr. Boccini became the owner and editor in June 1938, *L'Eco* became more openly fascist. An extensive number of short, editorial-style articles of about 350 words each on different aspects of fascism and its socioeconomic system appeared after this date. And, although all of these articles were signed "Littorio," the signature and sharp style suggest that they had been taken from propaganda material that the Minculpop prepared for dissemination abroad.[14]

The entire series of articles, fourteen in all, gives a comprehensive view of the Corporative State and fascism, expounding its theoretical principles and illustrating the presumed progress that fascism had brought to Italy and even to the new Germany.

The first piece, *"Corpus juris civilis"* (Body of Civil Law), attempted to demonstrate that, because Italians are descended from Rome, "no other nation of people sums up like Italians do the essential spiritual tradition of Western civilization." Consequently because of this framework, the Italian nation cannot fail to "regenerate the world." Fascism is able to do this by creating the Corporative State which is essentially articulated "on three bases: control, discipline, harmony in economic activities." The system is "as clear as the sun and its practice incarnated in modern economy."

The articles, "Laissez-faire," "Production and Trade," and "Labour Civilization," sought to explain that the liberal formula "laissez-faire" is inadequate in today's world: "Its star has set forever." In the capitalist countries, economic activities are left to "individual egoism," and this is "anti-social." In the ethical fascist state, the socio-economic experiment as demonstrated in Italy, has shown socialists "that Capital and Labour can live side by side with equal rights," and, it has shown the "so called democracies . . . that only a new civilization, a society of working people, can resolve the social question."

The articles, "Two Worlds," "Rome-Carthage, Rome-Munich," and "Fascism and Democracy," deal with the present struggle for the solution of the social problem of Labour versus Capital. According to these pieces, there were two worlds in existence: "one clinging to the past and one already in the future." The democratic states cling to the past; totalitarian states are in the future. Analogous to ancient Rome, which had defeated Carthage and brought the world a new civilization, fascist Rome had crushed the "old world" and seeded a new civilization in Europe. Under fascism, Hitler's Germany has its soul, as did Charlemagne's Holy Roman Empire, in the eternal spirit of Rome and "Munich was only the first leg of a long voyage" for Germany and Europe.[14] In conclusion, wrote *L'Eco,* while "fascism has led Italy to greatness and power . . . and other fascist nations are on their way to solving their social problems," in all capitalist democracies, where

LE CANADA LATIN

SECTION RESERVEE A LA
ORGANE OFFICIEL DE LA **LIGUE LATINE CANADIENNE**
LIGA LATINA CANADIENSE - LIGA LATINA CANADENSE - LEGA LATINA CANADESE - LATIN CANADIAN LEAGUE

TEL. LAncaster 2260   MONTREAL, CANADA   Samedi 9 Avril 1938 — 5c

LAVAL CONTRE LES DESTRUCTEURS

Pierre Laval, ancien Chef du Gouvernement Français s'est insurgé contre les destructeurs de l'amitié franco italienne

Au cours d'une des dernières séances de la Commission des Affaires Etrangères du Senat Français, M. Pierre Laval — ancien Président du Conseil des Ministres de France, et membre de la Commission elle même — établit d'une manière péremptoire devant vingt-cinq de ses collègues, les effroyables responsabilités du Front Populaire dans l'isolement politique dans lequel se trouve son pays, et dans le desaccord franco-italien.

M. Pierre Laval établit un parallèle saisissant entre la situation de la France présente et celle d'il y a trois ans.

— En 1935, du fait de nos accords avec l'Italie et avec l'Angleterre, dit-il, l'Allemagne se trouvait dans l'impossibilité matérielle de réoccuper la Rhénanie, de réaliser un Anschluss et de menacer la Tchécoslovaquie.

M. Pierre Laval entra dans le détail des engagements réciproques pris à Rome et à Paris, engagements qui, par leur portée et leur précision, domaient à la France une sécurité quasi absolue et garantissaient la paix en Europe centrale.

M. Pierre Laval montra comment, en ruinant l'accord franco-italien, le Front populaire avait sacrifié la sécurité des communications françaises avec son empire colonial, avait découvert deux frontières françaises et donné les mains libres à l'Allemagne.

— Il faut de toutes urgence, dit-il, en finir avec cette politique criminelle, il faut reprendre avec l'Italie les rapports de collaboration et d'amitié.

— Trop tard ! s'écria un sénateur d'extrême gauche.

— Il n'est jamais trop tard pour sauver la paix ! répliqua M. Pierre Laval. Une guerre, à l'heure actuelle, serait pour la France un "suicide".

Vingt-deux sénateurs de la commission approuvèrent chaleureusement la courageuse intervention de M. Pierre Laval, à laquelle M. Paul Boncour, l'actuel Ministre des Affaires Etrangères de France, qui assistait à la réunion, ne trouva rien à répondre....

Ceux qui au Canada — sans rien savoir de ce qui se passe dans les coulisses politiques européennes — parlent souvent des "menaces de l'Italie contre la France" et de "convoitises italiennes sur la France" devraient savoir au moins deux choses:

1ère — que c'est le Front Populaire qui a détruit l'amitié entre la France et l'Italie, solidement établie en 1935;

2ème — que c'est le Front Populaire en la personne de son chef M. Léon Blum, qui au mois de juin 1936, repoussa pour des raisons de haine

L'OEUVRE DU PRÉSIDENT DE SAINT-DOMINGO exposée par le Docteur E. Ginebra

Avant hier, dans une des salles de l'Hôtel Windsor, le Consul Général de la République de Saint-Domingo l'eminent Docteur Emilio Ginebra — fit en tant que simple particulier une belle et très érudite conférence sur l'oeuvre accomplie en son pays par le Président Rafael Trujillo y Molina, qui prend de plus en plus figure d'un des plus grands chefs d'état de l'Amérique du Sud.

LE PRETENDU INCIDENT AVEC HAITI

Le Dr. Emilio Ginebra commença par refuter avec des preuves indiscutibles à l'appui, la campagne calomnieuse faite il y a quelques mois contre son pays, lorsque des journaux affirmèrent que "douze mille haitiens avaient été noyés par les milices dominicaines à la frontière saint-dominicaine, à la suite de deux pays..."

Et ceci, entre autres, pour une simple raison d'impossibilité matérielle, car la rivière où au-delà de laquelle on ferait passer les "noyés", les douze mille haitiens, n'a à peu près grande volume... une salle d'hôtel...

Bon!

Mais il vient de se dérouler à Paris un procès de presse, dont le compte-rendu a été publié, comme par hasard, sensiblement par tous les organes canadiens en question...

Le procès est pourtant instructif à plus d'un point de vue, il nous sommes très heureux de le placer sous les yeux de nos lecteurs....

Voici d'abord les faits.

Le ler juin, tous les journaux français portaient leur prix de vente de 30 à 40 centimes.

Seul "L'HUMANITE" organe communiste restait à six sous.

"LA LIBERTE", acquise depuis peu par Jacques Doriot, publait un dessin montrant le "camarade" Thorez debout devant le Grand Livre du Doit et du Avoir, avec cette légende:

"L'Humanité" ne reflète à six sous, sous gagnons des roubles."

"L'HUMANITE", qui est susceptible à ses heures, réclamait cent mille francs de dommages-intérêts, à LA LIBERTE. Une sorte. Les débats qui se sont déroulés devant la douzième chambre correctionnelle de Paris la semaine dernière ont ré-

PROGRES DE L'INSTRUCTION

"Il ne faut pas oublier" dit encore le docteur Ginebra, "que chaque petit village de la République Dominicaine possède une école pour l'instruction y est obligatoire. La Trujillo est par sa mère, la descendant d'une très vieille famille de la noblesse française, et le nom de Trujillo est très connu dans plusieurs régions de la vieille noblesse espagnole: mon pays ne tient à être qu'une simple terre d'Amérique du Sud."

AMOUR DU PEUPLE

En terminant le Dr. Emilio Ginebra fit valoir que le Prési-

LE GOUVERNEMENT DE MOSCOU achète et paye la presse etrangère

Une tourbe de petits journaux, de feuilles de choux n'ayant pas de tirage, pas de publicité pas de vente, et se prétendent "purs", affirment "ne dépendre de personne" et, sous couvert de "libéralisme", font plus ou moins sournoisement une propagande habile en faveur du communisme....

A entendre les excellents confrères qui rédigent ces journaux, tous ceux qui dans la presse canadienne ont le malheur de n'être pas "hégémonistes", tous ceux qui ont admirent pas les massacres des Ouy d'Espagne, ou les massacres qui ne sont pas disposés à offrir la patrie canadienne en holocauste aux destructeurs de la Famille et de la Religion, nous canadiens... sont "payés par Mussolini"!!

Bon!

Mais il vient de se dérouler à Paris un procès de presse, dont le compte-rendu a été publié, comme par hasard, sensiblement par tous les organes canadiens en question....

Le procès est pourtant instructif à plus d'un point de vue, il nous sommes très heureux de le placer sous les yeux de nos lecteurs....

vélé au grand public les sources inavouables des "revenues" de "L'HUMANITE".

Tous les témoignages apportés à l'audience ont été écrasantes.

M. Henri Barbé a été, durant quatre ans, le representant du Parti Communiste Français au Comité Exécutif de l'Internationale de Moscou. Il connait la question. Il a parlé d'une voix claire avec des précisions accablantes:

— Que ce soit en marks, en dollars ou en livres... declarat-il — "L'HUMANITE" de 1928, à 1931, recevait son argent... ainsi que six ou huit millions de Moscou. En 1929, une subvention extraordinaire de plusieurs milliers fut adressée à Moscou à "L'HUMANITE" pour renflouer la banque ouvrière et paysanne.

Chaque témoin apporte une précision nouvelle.

M. Drot, Trelude, charpentier ancien agent de liaison entre Paris et la commission exécutive du parti communiste de Moscou, qui raconte comment la Banque du Nord payait à qui des chèques pour l'échéance de L'HUMANITE.

C'est M. Camille Fery, ancien rédacteur de "L'HUMANITE" et ancien secrétaire des Jeunesses communistes, qui vient expliquer comment les reçus sont établis pour la comptabilité.

— Reçu tant mille brochures, cela signifie "reçu tant mille francs"!

Moscou en a pour son argent Ce n'est aucun des Directeur ni Cachin, ni Thorez, ni Duclos, qui veillent à la confection du journal, c'est un de légue de Moscou. Thorez secrétaire, l'ancien secrétaire général de "L'HUMANITE". M. Lebrun declarait.

— Très souvent il m'assistait à la mutation et au changement total, quant aux idées ou politiques qu'ils exprimaient. les articles rédigés par les collaborateurs de "L'HUMANITE" et notamment ceux de MM. Cachin et Gabriel Perri. Les clichés étaient diminués d'un émissaire etranger, c'est l'Emissaire étranger avec du parti communiste.

La preuve est faite, c'est "L'HUMANITE", la mutilation et le changement total, quant aux idées les politiques qu'ils exprimaient. les articles rédigés par les collaborateurs de "L'HUMANITE"...

IL NOSTRO GIORNALE È VOSTRO
Esso è di Tutti, ma non è di Nessuno
è per Tutti, ma non è per Nessuno.

Published by
The ITALIAN PUBLISHING CO.
111 Elm St. — Toronto — Canada

A. PERILLI, Edit.   T. MARI, Dir.

Entered at Toronto Ottawa P. O. as
Second Class Mail Matter.

il BOLLETTINO

ITALO-CANADESE
'THE ITALIAN-CANADIAN BULLETIN'

Anno II. No. 42.   Venerdì, 17 Ottobre 1930   TORONTO, Canada

L'Arcivescovo di Toronto concede il Circolo Colombo per $10,000

Martedì' scorso in un'assemblea straordinaria del Circolo Colombo, il presidente Sig. Angelo Teolis ha reso noto che, tra egli, quale fiduciario Autorizzato dal consiglio d'Amministrazione, e l'Arcivescovo di Toronto, Mons. Neil McNeil, è stato firmato un compromesso con il quale questi cede al Circolo il terreno, il fabbricato con tutti gli annessi e connessi, per la somma di $10,000; riservandosi che i principii morali, ai quali il Circolo é, nostro, non debbano essere cambiati.

Le trattative di questo affare, sono durate 9 mesi, il vecchio consiglio d'Amministrazione ha studiato, invano e a varie legalità, la questione per altri tre mesi. Il nuovo consiglio amministrativo ha approvato il progetto, che venne di studiare sul presentato all'assemblea e che martedì 21, v. p. dovrà essere approvato, o respinto.

L'affare come tale, costituisce una donazione da parte di S. E. l'Arcivescovo a gl'italiani che gliene saranno grattissimi. Tutta la proprietà, esclusi i mobili, è stata valutata oltre $25,000; sicché la donazione sarebbe per $15,000.

Merito precipuo di questo affare va dato al presidente del Circolo Sig. Angelo Teolis, che ha condotto e preparato con perizia che attesta delle sue ottime qualità d'uomo d'affari. L'idea originaria spetta al Segretario del Circolo Sig. Vincenzo Piccinnini con felice intuito ha potuto divinare quale erano le disposizioni d'animo di S. E. l'Arcivescovo nei nostri confronti.

La passata amministrazione ha avuto il merito di entrare subito nella cosa e di studiare il progetto, con l'organizzazione e di finanziamento per l'acquisto.

Quando al piano di ammortamento, giacché è risaputo che il Circolo non ha disponibilità di cassa per pagare i contanti, l'amministrazione, più che un progetto ha presentato dei dati contabili, su i quali ha chiesto venisse intavolata la discussione. Qualcuno ha affacciato dubbi a riguardo; specie quando il presidente ha chiesto l'assidua ed efficace collaborazione di tutti i membri per alzare gl'introiti.

Senza entrare nei minuti particolari, ci sembra che anche questo lato dell'affare, sia, la più benevola considerazione. L'amministrazione non s'è presentata con la mente bianca a riguardo, ma ha segnato una strada che, se seguita da tutti i soci, darà, i risultati sperati sia per la natura di Circolo che risiede ad Hamilton, é sia, che deporrà in Inghilterra e senza, che della cosa fosse stato nemmeno informato il marito. Il fatto che la donna fosse rimasta nel Canadà per di cinque anni non ha avuto valore per quelle autorità giacché esse affermano che il male che le affligu.

Circolo Colombo Honors Patron

The 438th anniversary of the audience would permit him to

COMMEMORAZIONE VIRGILIANA

Come accenniamo la settimana scorsa, la celebrazione Virgiliana, a cura del Comitato Interessociale, avrà luogo martedì, 28 ottobre, nella Sala Biblioteca, Trinity College, dell'Università di Toronto, alle ore 4,45 precise. E' Chairman il Prof. N. W. De Witt e parleranno il Prof. E. Goggio di Toronto e il Prof. R. S. Conway dell'Università di Birmingham.

OTTAWA DISTRETTO FEDERALE

Nelle prossime elezioni municipali di quella città gli elettori saranno chiamati a votare sulla proposta di considerare la città di Ottawa un Distretto Federale indipendente da tutto il resto dello Stato, come Washington è considerato negli Stati Uniti.

E' INFAMIA!

Si tratta di un caso veramente doloroso. Le autorità d'immigrazione sono state chiamate a dare informazioni riguardo a un caso che potrebbe definirsi una enormità. Una donna che da 18 anni risiede ad Hamilton, è stata deportata in Inghilterra senza, che della cosa fosse stato nemmeno informato il marito. Il fatto che la donna fosse rimasta nel Canadà per di cinque anni non ha avuto valore per quelle autorità giacché esse affermano che il male che le afflig-

IL CONSOLE GENERALE DI PASSAGGIO A TORONTO

Ieri mattina, giovedì, giunse alla sazione alle 7,30, il Regio Console Generale d'Italia ad A-

Virgilio e Manzoni

Non un articolo per un settimanale, ma un libro, e forse voluminoso, si potrebbe scrivere tra questi due sommi artisti.

Il parallelo tra il primo romantico latino e il più grande degli italiani, è pieno di tante analogie e di infiniti contrasti, dai quali le loro figure s'adergono maestose, come due cime dei monti sopra il mare grigio della nebbia, che avvolge la pianura e le valli sottostanti, in un manto che non stanca l'occhio, è non tedia lo spirito.

Si dice che siamo stati maestri a Manzoni gl'inglese Walter Scott, il francese Chateaubriand e forse il tedesco Heine. Ma questi, a nostro avviso, furono alimenti di mente e non maestri del divino Virgilio. Noi pensiamo che a lui non poco abbia attinto il grande poeta italiano. Parini non è quello ironico a Manzoni, Questi gli avrà forse ispirato "a'ngresto" per ciò nel silenzio dei campi più fluente scorreva la vena poetica e più sincera si svolgeva, la vi del alfiere nella vena d'animo. Manzoni ama la stessa sincerità d'animo, con l'equilibrio mentale di chi sa sottoporre i sentimenti alla ragione. Ma del due, primo l'amò e la cantò Virgilio insuperabilmente.

In entrambi è la serenità au-

CORRIERE ITALIANO

26 Queen St. East TORONTO, SABATO 23 Marzo 1929

Discorso del Duce all'Assemblea Quinquennale del Regime

il BOLLETTINO

ITALO-CANADESE — the BULLETIN

IL NOSTRO GIORNALE è VOSTRO
Esce il di Tutti, ma non è di Nessuno
è per Tutti, ma non è per Nessuno
Published by
The ITALIAN PUBLISHING CO.
12 Elm St. — Toronto—Canada

Ignored at Ottawa, Post Office as
Second Class Mail Matter.

Anno VI. No. 23.

Venerdì 8 Giugno 1934

Telefono: WA. 7306

Noi edifichiamo i nostri monumenti più belli sono: La Scuola Italiana di Toronto - Il Comitato Economico Italo-Canadese
A. PERILLI, Edit. T. MARI, Dir.

TORONTO, Canada.

Nota Elettorale Dominante

La nota dominante di questa campagna elettorale settimanale è accesa in lotta ad affermare che tra i conservatori appoggianti l'Inghilterra, i liberali appoggianti gli Stati Uniti, la C. C. F. sono pronti a scendere in lizza e altri 25 lo saranno tra poco.

L'Ontario sarebbe stato accolto giocosamente nelle file del partito conservatore con divisione in quelli liberali.

La campagna elettorale liberale è basata sulla necessità di un cambio di amministrazione provinciale, per riordinare un andazzo di cose deplorevole. Se un terzo partito entra in campo a dividere le forze di coloro che intendono effettuare un tale cambiamento, diminuiscono le possibilità di successo, a vantaggio di quelli che difendono le posizioni, dei conservatori in questo caso.

Forse l'Ontario ha avuto una lotta elettorale così accanita come quella che si concluderà il 19 corr.

Tale è la situazione e sta così incerta.

La C. C. F., partito socialistoide, indefinito, inconcreto, gioca nelle mani dei capi conservatori che attraverso di esso intravvedono la possibilità di un'altra vittoria, dividendo le forze degli avversari. Esiste un accordo tra conservatori e C. C. F.? Non sorprenderebbe nessuno. Ormai l'arrembaggio al po-

appoggiante la Russia e magari il Giappone, può esistere un patto appoggiante il Canada.

Strana, questa benefetta politica!

A forza di favorire l'uno o l'altro ci si è dimenticati il Canada.

LA "CASA LITTORIO"

Per la erigenda "Casa Littoria", che sorgerà a Roma sulla Via dell'Impero, giungono continuamente al Governo Italiano contributi da molti italiani all'estero. Il "Foglio d'Ordini" annuncia che verranno pubblicati i nomi dei contribuenti. Chi volesse dare qualche cosa, può esso

rivolgersi al locale Consolato o al Segretario del Fascio.

LIBRO D'ORO DEL FASCIO

La Segreteria Generale dei Fasci Italiani all'Estero ha creato il Libro d'Oro del Fascio, nel quale verranno scritti gli eventuali nomi dei contribuenti più importanti della vita illustrativa.

ITALIANI!

Siate attivi nelle prossime elezioni e fate conoscere agli altri popoli i vostri interessamento nella politica locale. Tutti i comandamenti, e specialmente quelli interessati nella sezione politica St. George, sono invitati all'adunanza che si avrà nella sala del Circolo Colombo, 202 St. Patrick St.

Martedì, 12 Giugno, alle ore 8 p.m.

per sentire la' parola del candidato Liberale Ian T. Strachan. Parleranno anche il Maggiore John Inwood, Presidente della St. George Riding, il Dott. W. C. Wickett e altri nostri connazionali.

Siate Presenti Coi Vostri Amici

TIME FOR A CHANGE

Are you satisfied with present economical conditions, fellow Italians? Many of our people who have In days gone by this question always been noted for their would be labelled as foolish saving qualities, have fought a question 1,000,000,000. Of course, you are not satisfied! How sorting to accepting charity. can you be, when you see so They have seen their little samuch misery, and destitution vings gradually dwindle away around you? The Italian race year by year, waiting for the as a whole is proud, honest and promised prosperity of the so-hard working. These great attributes of our race are gradually being smothered by the lings mouths of their children

finally broke down their resistance and they have had to accept relief.

In the history of the building of Canada, the Italian immigrant has always been given favorable mention for the manner in which he labored to build this great land of our adoption. A great majority of these pioneers bought homes on the time plan. It took them years, what with small wages and the raising of large families, to pay off the mortgages on these homes. Now owing to their inability to secure work, (Continued on last page)

Ambrosi promosso

GIORGIO TIBERI NUOVO CONSOLE A TORONTO

PER LA LINGUA ITALIANA

E' stato detto che il Parlamento non ha nulla a fare con l'insegnamento della lingua italiana nelle Scuole Secondarie, ma che questa questione è di competenza del Board of Education.

A questi sapientoni diciamo: Chi ha fatto e fa le leggi in Ontario? Il Board of Education e i Direttori delle Scuole, oppure il Parlamento?

presa a Toronto, ove si rinnovera cosi sino a la prossima. Quarta giostra Italiana a la C. N. E. e gli sarebbe rimasto quel la bella notizia lo ha raggiunto mentre egli è in viaggio per l'Italia, sul "Vulcania".

Chi ha seguito, come noi, da vicino il fattivo lavoro del Console Ambrosi, sa bene quanto gli meriti la promozione che gli giunge oggi, perquanto possa dispiacere la sua partenza, gioisce al pensiero che tanto nobile cuore s'abbia il meritato premio del proprio lavoro.

L'ITALIE NOUVELLE

TÉL. LAncaster 2269 — MONTRÉAL, CANADA — Samedi 10 Septembre 1938 — 5c

D'où viennent les volontaires rouges

Une documentation accablante

C'est presque un lieu commun, pour la grande presse internationale asservie plus ou moins ouvertement à la propagande de Moscou, d'affirmer ou d'insinuer que le Généralissime Franco, qui depuis deux ans mène en Espagne le bon combat en défense de la Religion, de la Patrie et de l'Ordre, contre les partisans de la révolution et de l'anarchie, qu'il n'y a qu'une "intervention étrangère en Espagne": celle de l'Italie et de l'Allemagne en faveur des nationalistes.

Quant à celle en faveur des rouges, on n'en parle jamais. On l'oublie toujours !...

Et pourtant les grands journaux français indépendants, se chargent de dévoiler chaque jour la vérité. Ces journaux publient des listes interminables de cargaisons complètes d'armes et de convois nombreux de volontaires rouges qui franchissent la frontière franco-espagnole, et vont aider les communistes de Barcelone.

Les volontaires

D'après ce que publie LE JOURNAL de Paris, par exemple, le passage des hommes — et malgré la "fermeture" officielle de la frontière de la part de la France — s'effectue actuellement sur une large échelle.

On calcule qu'environ 200 hommes par jour passent les Pyrénées et s'en vont grossir les hordes des massacreurs de prêtres et de religieuses... qui règnent en maître dans l'Espagne Rouge.

Le port de ravitaillement

D'après GRINGOIRE, le grand port de ravitaillement des rouges est Oran, en Algérie, qui, comme on sait est une colonie française. Ces marchands de canons y ont leur quartier général. Et ceci parce qu'importe quelle petite embarcation peut accomplir la traversée et se rendre jusqu'à un des deux ports rouges, Alicant ou Carthagène...

C'est à Oran qu'arrivent les grands cargos chargés à Odessa de tanks, de mitrailleuses et de bombes. Là, ils dispersent leurs cargaisons sur quatre ou cinq petits navires qui entreprennent la traversée en une nuit, aux moindres risques.

Il y a une autre raison au choix d'Oran.

Les polices d'assurances contractées au bénéfice des transporteurs, font à ceux-ci obligation — en cas de danger — de chercher réfuge à Oran.

On voit l'intérêt des Soviets à multiplier les envois dans ces conditions. La poursuite d'un navire ravitailleur, par l'escadre ou l'aviation nationale de Franco, peut provoquer un incident international dans un port français....

Le Matériel

Le Quartier Général nationaliste espagnol a publié un état du matériel capturé au cours des dernières opérations.

Ce matériel provient de Tchécoslovaquie, des Etats-Unis, du Mexique. Mais en plus grande proportion de Russie et de France.

En voici le détail:

Russie 84 tanks, 809 avions, 577 fusils-mitrailleurs, 35,912 fusils; 23 millions de projectiles divers et 25 millions de cartouches.

France: 24 tanks; 139 avions; 112 mitrailleuses; 463 fusils-mitrailleurs; 35,912 fusils; 23 millions de projectiles divers et 25 millions de cartouches.

Après quoi — n'est ce pas? — on peut toujours parler de la "neutralité" française !.......

Les Fabricants de Fausses Nouvelles

Il ne passe pas de semaine; Voici donc ce qu'écrivait sans que l'on découvre une fausse L'HOMME LIBRE:

Le IVème Congrès International d'Archéologie Chrétienne à Rome

VISITE DE NOUVELLES FOUILLES

Nombreuses adhésions d'étrangers

Du 2 au 9 octobre prochain aura lieu à Rome, comme nous l'avons déjà annoncé, le Quatrième Congrès international d'Archéologie Chrétienne, organisé par le Comité permanent existant à cet effet près l'Institut pontifical d'Archéologie chrétienne. Les travaux porteront spécialement sur les origines et le développement de la basilique chrétienne antique, et sur les décorations. Les spécialistes les plus éminents en la matière et en premier lieu Mgr. Kirsch, président de l'Institut pontifical d'Archéologie chrétienne, et M. Giovannoni, de l'Académie italienne, présenteront des rapports sur les monuments les plus importants de l'antiquité chrétienne de ce genre étudiées par les savants, et qui se trouvent en Italie, en Tunisie, en Algérie, dans l'Afrique italienne, en Syrie, en Asie Mineure, en Grèce, dans les Balkans, etc.

A l'occasion de ce Congrès, on pourra pour la première fois aux Congressistes les fouilles exécutées sous la face centrale de la Basilique de Saint-Jean-de-Latran, les nouvelles collections du Musée chrétien de la Bibliothèque vaticane, le Cimetière de Saint-Alexandre sur la Via Nomentana, entièrement restauré, et d'autres monuments intéressants. De très nombreuses adhésions sont parvenues déjà de la Belgique, du Danemark, de la France, de l'Algérie, de la Grèce, de l'Angleterre, de l'Espagne, de la Suisse, de Hollande, de Pologne, de Syrie, de Tchécoslovaquie, de la République Argentine, etc. Pour l'Italie, on a déjà reçu les adhésions de l'Université de Rome, et d'autres Universités royales.

L'amélioration de la race italienne

D'après les chiffres communiqués par l'Institut Central de Statistique de Rome, sur dix années d'observations, la taille moyenne de la race italienne est en voie d'amélioration progressive.

C'est pour cela qu'à partir de l'année scolaire 1929-40, la limite minima de la taille des jeunes aspirants à l'Académie Militaire, comme officiers d'infanterie, de cavalerie, d'artillerie, ou du Génie, sera portée à 1 mètre et 65, et la limite minima pour l'admission ...

LES ASPECTS DE L'ACTION RACISTE EN ITALIE

Au sujet du racisme italien qui occupe actuellement l'attention de la presse internationale, l'"Agit" fait remarquer qu'il s'agit la simplement de l'action tout à fait normale d'un Etat responsable qui veut défendre un élément primordial pour la vie d'un peuple: la pureté de son sang. Si Dieu, dans sa sagesse infinie, a cru bon de peupler la terre de groupes d'hommes différant entre eux par des caractères biologiques très nets, on ne voit pas pourquoi les pouvoirs responsables ne devraient pas garder aussi intactes que possible ces différences de groupes.

D'ailleurs le Fascisme n'a pas attendu le moment actuel pour envisager cette question. Mussolini aut toujours au moment voulu. Il a commencé par mettre en pratique le racisme pour une grande échelle il y a déjà 16 ans, et présentement il les italiens. Et simplement, en 1928, il voit que le peuple a conscience de lui-même et M. Giovannoni, de l'Académie italienne, présente... tous les maux et les habitudes de vie susceptibles de la diminuer physiquement, doit avoir pour autre plus profonde.

Autrefois, la vie des italiens s'accomplissait dans le domaine fermé de leur péninsule, et il ne pouvait être question d'un problème racial, dérivant d'un abâtardissement de leur sang. Mais le peuple a conquis un empire et se trouve en contact avec d'autres races, surtout en danger que la race italo-romaine puisse avec le temps se fondre avec d'autres pour donner un type hybride qui ne posséderait plus ses vertus. Cela peut évidemment faire sourire quelques sceptiques, qui pensent qu'il ne se produira pas. Mais il lorsque nous ne serons plus que poussière.

Evidemment, des italiens ou italiennes vont s'établir dans les territoires de l'empire, et il ne se produit pas encore de croisement de races, ni de bâtards, mais cela peut arriver d'ici 10 ou 20 ans, peut-être seulement dans un ou deux siècles. Mais Mussolini sait bien que des lois ne suffisent pas à assurer l'intégrité d'une race, si elles ne s'appuient pas sur une solide conscience raciste.

On voit par là que le racisme est tout fondamental du moment voulu caractère de la vie impériale de l'Italie. En ce qui concerne les Juifs, ... le racisme ... couple question numéro ..... Italie en .... nombre de Juifs qui normale ... se multiplient pas .... ter qu'il n'ait pas ... gration. Il y a .... hommes .... pays ... mesures ... et ce mouvement .... netraliser, le Juifs .... tent s'affirmer .... Italie trop hospitalière. Mais Italie est un pays d'émigration, non d'immigration, et elle ne peut ouvrir ses territoires déjà trop restreints à des groupes étrangers, juifs ou non, lorsque le Gouvernement a le devoir de considérer la question. En ... admettant qu'il y ait de la place en Italie, elle devrait être réservée à ses nombreux enfants qui vivent à l'étranger. Et tranger, parfois sans point de sans travail, parce qu'ils n'ont pas voulu renier leur patrie.

Le sort des Juifs est donc, évidemment. Mais nombres plus triste est celui de ... milles Italiens qui demandent leur rapatriement, faute de pouvoir vivre à l'étranger. Et en matière de drames humains, l'Italie ne peut se payer le luxe des sentiments ..... celui de l'envoyer ... ennemie est aussi pré ... son nombril.

Un autre principe ... se proportionner la politique des Juifs à la ... étranger. On n'a ... attention aux Juifs italiens qui ... par quelques per ... gloise. Ils savent ... ta sera perdu ..... livrer en proie ... et à leur mœurs ... jadis. "Discriminer ...... persécuter" Ye ..... inception de ... istes.

LES BIENFAITS DU FRONT POPULAIRE

Comment les communistes ont détruit une fraîche industrie française plus que centenaire

On a tout dit sur les méfaits constitués de ... A la cause bien un grand pays commis, en effet, de ... nations me la France par le Front Po... engagées sur le M. Vin... Février...

L'Eco Italo-Canadese

Redazione e Amministrazione
1204 Dominion Bank Bldg.

Direttore:
ALBERTO BOCCINI

THE ONLY ITALIAN WEEKLY NEWSPAPER PUBLISHED IN WESTERN CANADA.

L'UNICO GIORNALE SETTIMANALE ITALIANO PUBBLICATO NEL CANADA OCCIDENTALE

Non dimenticarti
sei
ITALIANO

VANCOUVER, B.C., 1 OTTOBRE, 1938.   ANNO II, No. 50.

LA MODERAZIONE E' VENUTA DA ROMA

IL DISCORSO DI MUSSOLINI ALLE CAMICE NERE DI VERONA FATTO IL 26 SETTEMBRE

Ciò che Hitler ha ottenuto

1) Evacuazione da parte delle truppe e polizia cecoslovacche entro il 10 ottobre, senza arrecare alcun danno, incluse le fortificazioni.

2) Occupazione da parte delle truppe tedesche di quattro distretti dei Sudeti entro i primi sette giorni, cominciando dal primo ottobre, e l'occupazione rimanente degli altri distretti dei Sudeti, entro il 10 ottobre.-

HITLER

3) Congedamento entro quattro settimane di tutti coloro che vogliono volontariamente lasciare il servizio militare e di polizia cecoslovaco.

4) La liberazione dei prigio-

Ciò che Hitler chiedeva

1) L'evacuazione delle forze armate e di polizia della Cecoslovacchia dalla regione dei Sudeti, senza apportare alcun danno, ed entro il primo ottobre.

2) Occupazione da parte delle truppe tedesche, per il primo ottobre del territorio dei Sudeti.

3) Licenziamento immediato di tutti i sudetici che fanno parte dell'armata e polizia cecoslovaca.

4) rilascia immediato di tutti i prigionieri politici di origine tedesca.

5) Un plebiscito da aver luogo non più tardi del 25 novembre in quelle regioni ove i sudetici sono in minoranza. La votazione deve essere fatta sotto il controllo di una Commissione internazionale.

L'ITALIA

ORGANO DELLE COLLETTIVITÀ ITALIANE DEL CANADA

Anno XX, No. 21 — Membro del F.U.I.M. (Fronte Unico Italiano Montreal) — Sabato, 15 giugno 1935 - XIII E. F.

Il discorso del signor Baldwin

RIVISTA MILITARE A ROMA NELL'ANNIVERSARIO DEL XXIV MAGGIO

S. M. il Re d'Italia passa in rassegna le truppe schierate a Piazza Venezia, in Roma, nel giorno anniversario dell'entrata dell'Italia in guerra (XXIV Maggio).

(Foto CANADA)

L'ITALIA BASTA A SE STESSA

Le giornate del Duce in Sardegna

BOLLETTINO ITALO-CANADESE
111 ELM ST.
TORONTO, ONT.

DEO ET PATRIAE

L'ARALDO DEL CANADA

DEO ET PATRIAE

Organo Ufficiale del Fascio di Montreal

FONDATO NEL 1906

C. VETERE, Direttore — Telefono: Lancaster 2011 — (Corda Corrente con la Posta) — 31 Notre Dame East — Cav. Avv. GIACINTO LECCESI, Proprietario

ANNO XXV No. 46 — MONTREAL, SABATO 15 NOVEMBRE 1930-ANNO IX

TESSERAMENTO | TARIFFE DOGANALI | IL GENETLIACO DEL RE | Complotto antibolscevico?

Il tesseramento fascista sarà quest'anno accompagnato da una attenta revisione degli iscritti al Partito.

Gli elementi infidi che sotto per spirito di opportunismo o per un interesse personale o per altri scopi inconfessabili, cercherebbero di infiltrarsi nella tessera criminosa, saranno inesorabilmente esclusi dalle file del Partito.

Le istruzioni dell'on. Giurati in proposito non ammettono equivoci.

Tutti coloro che ottennero l'onore della tessera non hanno compreso che il Fascismo è operante milizia, ma hanno lungamente conteggiato appieno o si sono limitati a dare prove di fedeltà poco sentite e che in certi tempi, e che si limita a formulare istituzioni dentro a commuoversi nelle feste comandate, distanziandosi anche nei giorni in cui si è richiesta la loro parte di fatica, di responsabilità e di perfetto non di mostrino di essersi ravveduti.

In fine agli iscritti che hanno carpito il distintivo ai servizio con inganno per ingrandirsi o per impieghi di comodità etichetta il loro affare o a quelli che con qualsiasi atteggiamento abbiano dato motivo di dubitare del loro fede. Le tessere non dovranno essere rinnovate.

Gli stessi criteri varranno per i Fasci all'estero. Le iscrizioni quest'anno saranno definitivamente chiuse e dei Fasci in piena si apriti solamente ai giovani.

L'on. Giurati nella sua parte di onore giovarsi ed ordinare logica e naturale delle cose.

Chi non ha sentito fino ad oggi il bisogno di passare, come i soldati della buona causa, la sua parte di trincea; chi si è tenuto in disparte attento il crescere dell'avvenire, e se spesso accompagnato da una buona dose di presunzione, e un fenomeno estraneo al carattere fascista, che ha per virtù fondamentale la schiettezza, il settarismo, il sacrificio e la dedizione completa.

Dopo nove anni di prova si possono con sufficiente sicurezza distinguere i fedeli-istinti della vigilia e le contemplare dalla rivoluzione dalla schiera dei maffiosi e dubbiosi.

Il questo processo evolutivo e purificatore del Fascismo, si attende degli 'epochs dei fascisti non altre manifestazioni di fede che la buona volontà di partecipare all'umile, ma buona fede e di lavoro per la causa Nazionale e per...

Richiamamo l'attenzione dei commercianti e di tutti quelli che si occupano di affari sulle disposizioni della nuova tariffa doganale sulla Ottawa l'altra settimana presso il Ministro delle Finanze.

A nostra e di quelli del nostro commercio tipografico di cui parliamo specialmente sono stati colpiti con alte tasse certi generi di merci non rinvenientesi in Canada e le nuove imposte di classe da parte di cotone limitato al Paese.

PER LA SERIETÀ DEL COMMERCIO

Il Ministero del Commercio ha emanato una disposizione dopo l'altra in ragione alla creazione dalla Ruggedità, delle tariffe e alla più esatta osservanza sulla gerarchia. Confusionata e permanente della Sicilia.

Roma — S.M. il Re Vittorio Emanuele III

Roma 13. — In data 11 corrente, S.M. il Re ha compiuto 61 anni di età, e l'Italia ha salutato la ricorrenza con un entusiasmo pari al suo amore alla dinastia di Savoia. Il Principe del Piemonte recandosi insieme alle cariche di governo a porgere gli auguri a S.M. nel Quirinale, ha dato luogo a manifestazioni di devozione per la Corona, che riecheggia il suo riflesso di un mondo.

SOSTENETE LA STAMPA DELL'ESERCITO

Con tutti i quali ormai ha dovuto abbracciare la grande solidarietà della nostra istituzione al nostro dovere, sostenere la stampa del Fascio e dell'Esercito e della Patria, è indicare il lavoro che è l'orgoglio e la missione della generazione nascente, alla quale è riservato di costituire il grande luogo l'atteso un giorno in cui il mondo sarà.

Ogni uomo iscritto al Fascio possiede la sua carta di iscrizione nel Partito e nelle future generazioni, cui compete il dovere, in cui si persuaderà di tutta la luminosa gloria della rivoluzione e una parte cieca del fascismo grazie alla sua confessione di se stesso.

La fede del Partito del Fascio non si è spenta negli uomini della nuova generazione e si alimenta in particolare nei giovani Italiani di tutto il mondo, nelle Terre d'oltremare.

LO "ZEPPELIN" AL POLO

Si ha da Mosca che l'Ammeraglio Lida, nella campagna per l'esplorazione aerea delle regioni polari, sta organizzando una spedizione polare del polo scientifico dal comando del dirigibile tedesco "Zeppelin" in collaborazione e di comune accordo con gli scienziati tedeschi.

La base di partenza verrà organizzata sul punto d'Aarè e l'accesso più favorevole al Polo Nord avverrà attraverso la zona d'altezza e servirà la base di decollo regolare lungo la rotta dall'Europa al Polo Nord passando per la Terra di Franz Giuseppe, l'Alaska, la Terra di Grant fino all'Alaska.

Al ritorno il dirigibile tornerà attraverso la Groenlandia alla Terra di Grant fino all'Alaska.

Scopo del volo è di studiare le condizioni di Artico, in Norvegia sarà organizzato un osservatorio magnetico.

La missione avrebbe la possibilità anche della effettuerà a stabilire la più diretta comunicazione aerea fra l'Europa e l'America attraverso le regioni artiche.

UNA FUCILATA CONTRO UN SACERDOTE

Napoli, 14 — Il sacerdote Antonio Carafolino di anni 45, abitante nel casale di Pozzoreale, mentre si recava in 8 mattina per officiare...

government by intrigue reigns, "the same lamentable spectacle exists: unemployment and misery."

In line with fascist propaganda and its eastern confreres, *L'Eco* painted an idyllic picture of the relation between the Vatican and the fascist state that surrounded it. Occasionally, however, news of conflict between the two authorities appeared. The role of Catholic Action, a Roman Catholic youth organization, was one cause for discord that arose between the two institutions. Both institutions claimed the right to the education of the young, but fascist ducetti like the extreme right-wing Roberto Farinacci saw in Catholic Action an intrusion of the Roman Catholic Church in the affairs of the State. Though Church and State had found some form of compromise on this issue in 1931, the question was never fully resolved. Additionally, as we shall see, even the anti-Jewish legislation created profound strife between Pope Pius XI and Mussolini in 1938.

Notwithstanding disagreements of this type, *L'Eco* and its readers continued naively to conceive of the two institutions as partners in an harmonious marriage. A leading article signed F.R. gives an idea of this credulous view. The writer argued that (contrary to other great leaders of the past, including Napoleon), Mussolini's triumph was due to the fact that he and the Italian people, inspired by a profound faith and guided by a mysterious divine power, had "accepted the supreme law" of God and of Christ's vicar on earth, the Pope. Thus, "in the entire world, Italy is the most peaceful and happy nation. She has the purest population," the writer concluded with satisfaction (see appendix No. 10). Further, when Pius XII on 28 December 1939 returned a visit paid him the week before by the

Italian monarchs, King Vittorio Emanuele III and Queen Elena, *L'Eco* labelled this act of Papal courtesy as "the Greatest Historical Event of Our Epoch,"[16] and implied that the spiritual leader of fascist Italy was the Vatican.

Even the Italian intervention in the Spanish Civil War was interpreted within this mind set. Fascists and a large portion of the Roman Catholic intelligentsia portrayed it as a conflict that had a religious dimension: spiritualism versus materialism. By reading *L'Eco*, readers learned that fascism could not let the godless "reds" take over Roman Catholic Spain. In the paper's view, Spain and Italy had shared a common culture and the same religious roots — commonalities which bound them closely together. From ancient times, Italy had always been ready to intervene to save Spain and how could fascism now remain indifferent while Spain was being plundered by the "reds"? Pontificated *L'Eco*, "a Latin blood nation calls another Latin blood nation."

Italy's alliance with nazi Germany was seen as similar to the intervention in Spain: another link in the forging of the Christian-fascist chain. Throughout 1938, *L'Eco* paid a great deal of attention to Hitler's visit to Italy: an event which the paper considered to be the most exciting of the year. According to *L'Eco*, a documentary on this visit, which was screened in Vancouver and other British Columbia locales, fired the imagination of the multitude of Italians who rushed to see it: "The spectacle . . . was continuously interrupted by cheers and acclamations (17 September 1938) which reached a peak at the end of the film." It was, noted *L'Eco*,

> a perfect and realistic vision of the welcome that Hitler received in Italy, last May . . . The long and spectacular

film stirred enthusiasm and very intense emotions in each member of the audience. He who reflects upon what he has seen will reach a conclusion for himself about conditions today in Italy." (10 September 1938)

The paper, however, failed to report a very important event which marked Hitler's visit to Italy, the refusal by Pius XI to meet with the German dictator. During the Fuhrer's visit the Pope left Rome for his residence in the Alban hills at Castle Gandolfo.

Another event which was given ample space in *L'Eco* was Consul Brancucci's visit to the cities of Trail, Revelstoke, Kelowna, Michel and Natal, Fernie and other smaller centres, in the fall of 1938 and the spring of 1939. It was the first time that an Italian Consul had visited some of those communities, many of which were dependent on the province's mining industry. Thus, according to *L'Eco*, Italians in those regions were delighted to see him. The presidents and officers of the patriotic societies and mutual benefit associations were particularly excited. In Natal, for example, the leading people of the city — including George Fisher, the President of the local Board of Trade and Mr. R. Winstandley, Manager of the Crows Nest Pass Coal Company — attended the banquet given in honour of Consul Brancucci.

As a fascist paper *L'Eco* followed a policy of ignoring the anti-fascists and their activities but, even so, their voices became louder and on this occasion they reverberated in Brancucci's speech as it was reported in *L'Eco*. In answer to what might have been charges made by anti-fascists, the Consul said that "his visit was not political propaganda, but a pure and sentimental link between [the local] colony and *la Patria lontana* (distant Fatherland)."[17]

Nevertheless, *L'Eco* returned to this argument a few months later with an attack against "pseudo-Italian squealers" who "informed some communist elements that who knows what subversive fascist design against Canada existed."[18] This charge probably was intended to calm the growing anxiety created in the community by the reports of an imminent war in Europe.

The fear of war and the apprehension that Italy might side with Germany cooled much of the ardent patriotism that had been displayed in British Columbia from 1936 to 1938. The emerging crisis of loyalty revealed the contradictions on which the ambiguous "patriotism" was built and the community split neatly into two parts. One was formed by a few who were ideologically-convinced fascists while the other side was made up by a the large majority of Italian Canadians who merely felt a sentimental attachment to their country of origin. *L'Eco* mirrored these two souls of the community. It continued to publish the bravura of the few fascists and it also gave ample space to leading Italians who in Vancouver and British Columbia more generally attempted to prevent the growing anti-Italian sentiment from sweeping everything before it.

The change of mood toward fascism in the community is well illustrated by the 1939 activities for the commemoration of the March on Rome. Unlike previous years, in 1939 it was a very modest affair that was attended by only about seventy staunch supporters. This small number included the captains, Penne and Zullino, and several crewmen of the Italian ship Cellina, which happened to be anchored in Vancouver harbour at the time. Some of the prominent people attending the ceremony were Consul Brancucci and his wife, Mr. Gregorio Fuoco, leader of the fascio Giulio Giordani, Mrs. Rosa Puccetti, secretary of Club Roma, Mr. Italo Rader, manager of the Catelli factory in Vancouver, Father Gioacchino Bortignon and Mr. Fred Tenisci. As if unaware of the grave situation looming over the community, the defiant speakers carried on as usual. They exalted Mussolini as the leader of the "revolution which had brought the world a new civilization — a civilization which is both Christian and Catholic, ancient and modern, Roman and Italian," said Father Bortignon, who added that under Mussolini, Italy "astonishes the world." He concluded his speech by reading from a letter "praising Mussolini for his far-sighted policy," which the Pope had sent to the Roman Catholic clergy in North America.

Continuing on Father Bortignon's theme, linking politics and religion and fascism and Catholicism, Fred Tenisci, the main speaker of the evening, said: "Comrades, tonight we commemorate the seventeenth anniversary of the March on Rome: a redemptive event, a holy event! . . . Fascism is not only the redeemer of Italy but of the entire world." For this speaker, the 1939 military occupation of Albania — he used the word liberation — was an act of redemption. "Today," the orator claimed, "even the Albanian people cry: 'Hail, oh Duce, redeemer of the oppressed . . .' Comrades!" Tenisci continued, "let us restore our spirit with vibrant and passionate faith in the 'Duce Magnifico,' founder of the Empire and an apostle of Christianity . . . let us remember and exalt the thousands and thousands who died for the Great Fascist Revolution." Defiant and even inconsiderate of the many young Canadians who were then at war, he continued his bombastic speech by quoting Mussolini, "we forge ahead . . . Peace is Roman . . . Against all odds and all nations Ethiopia is ours for ever." In the orator's wishful thinking, Mussolini's "powerful strength and his unbending will destroyed the egoistical and monopolistical coalition of Jews, Masons, and communists." All those present cheered this high-sounding speech.[19]

In the spring of 1940, on the eve of Italy's entry into the war, *L'Eco* published three leading articles (on 13 April, 18 May, and 8 June 1940 respectively) two of which dealt with the readiness of the Italian army and one with the "Four Years of the Empire." In these articles the paper addressed the question "What is Italy going to do?" — a question which was then on everyone's mind. The answer, the paper claimed, lay in the logic of things. Since the war was between the old world and the new order, there was no doubt which side Mussolini's Italy would choose and on this point the newspaper was right. "The new order, the order of tomorrow shall be our order: the fascist order of justice and work."[20] *L'Eco*'s readers knew that this was the order for which Hitler was fighting.

The military readiness of Italy was presented in the context of an ample commentary on a speech that had been delivered by General Soddu, Italian Under-Secretary of War. *L'Eco* pointed out that Soddu's speech was "a highly interesting page of history on Italian military preparation in the present state of Europe." In view of the sensitive nature of the subject the paper noted, General Soddu was "prudent" with regard to his discussion of weaponry. He described however, how well-trained and ready the armed forces were, both troops and officers, in every one of the three major components of Italy's military force on land, on sea, and in the air. "With these forces," the paper confidently boasted, "if a military intervention is necessary, victory will certainly be achieved."[21]

In parallel with these pompous fascist speeches which were laced with military demagogy, *L'Eco* reported profusely, as already noted, on initiatives undertaken by leading Italians to "show Canadian authorities the loyalty of citizens of Italian origin." Angelo Branca, Marino Culos, and Mrs. Enedina Fabbri — who had distinguished herself in the Red Cross campaign during the First World War — together with other men and women, created an Italian Red Cross Committee to help Canadian soldiers at war; these included many Italian Canadians who had enrolled to fight fascism. In fact, *L'Eco* reported that the first Canadian soldier to die overseas was Belvino Basso of the Royal Canadian Artillery, son of Italian parents from Trail, B.C. On 23 January 1940, artilleryman Basso was killed in England as the result of a collision between his motorcycle and a military truck.[22]

In the campaign to help Canadian soldiers at war, Enedina Fabbri in Vancouver appealed to all women of Italian origin who "have always helped their Mother Country, to do now the same for their adoptive Homeland where their families live."[23] Similarly at a meeting held in Trail, B. C., "Italians unanimously decided that each would contribute $1.00 a month to the Red Cross for the duration of the war." Further, in the same settlement, a large meeting of Italian Canadians was addressed by Mr. Blaylock, President of the Consolidated Mining & Smelting Company. Over 500 people attended this meeting held in the town's Colombo Hall. The Master of Ceremonies was Father Balò who had recently been transferred from Toronto. Mr. Blaylock spoke to those assembled and warned them of the imminent danger which threatened all of them. He said, "There is a probability that, at any time now, Italy enters the war perhaps against England. This would put you in a tragic situation. I shall do my best to keep you on the job."

Then, anticipating what actually happened shortly after, he added, "Some Italians have been involved in [fascist] politics, for these people there is a good possibility that they are going to be interned as soon as Italy enters the conflict.[24]

The internment began on 10 June 1940, and in the evening of that same day Angelo Branca and his collaborators in the Red Cross Committee in Vancouver held a meeting over which Branca himself presided. In introducing the reason for the meeting he said, "the world has been shocked by an act of perfidious cowardice. This declaration of war by Mussolini will be recorded by history as one of the most cowardly and traitorous actions since the beginning of time."[25]

On the same day Alberto Boccini, owner and editor of *L'Eco,* was arrested and then interned, causing the demise of this newspaper. Ironically, in its last issue (8 June 1940), *L'Eco* published the following appeal:

> Italian Canadians, who for a long or short time work and live in these always generous lands, must answer all the appeals of the Dominion Government to citizens. This is the best form of loyalty that Ottawa requires: Give to your adoptive Homeland what you can — give it now, give it promptly.

Several other Italian Canadians from Vancouver were arrested with Alberto Boccini for their fascist affiliation and all of them were interned first in Kananaskis (Alberta), and then they were taken to Camp Petawawa, Ontario.

CHAPTER FIVE

ANTI-SEMITISM IN ITALY AND THE ITALIAN-CANADIAN FASCIST PRESS

The anti-Semitic measures that were promulgated by Italy's fascist government in 1938 occurred in three stages. They began in 1937 with the publication of Paolo Orano's book, *Gli Ebrei in Italia*. Then on 16 February 1938, the *"Informazione diplomatica N. 14"* appeared, followed by the *"Manifesto degli 'scienziati' razzisti"* (Scientists' Manifesto on Race) on 14 July. Finally on 17 November, the *"Provvedimenti per la difesa della razza italiana"* (Provisions for the Defence of the Italian Race) were *legalized* by the Italian Parliament. The first and second phases served to prepare the ground-work for the third and operative phase.

Taken together, the measures invoked severely curtailed the social, professional, and economic freedom of Italian Jews: they were prohibited from marrying (Aryan) Italians; Jews who had settled in Italy after 1 January 1919 were ordered to leave the country within six months; Italian Jews were fired from their positions in the school system, including the universities, the civil service, and the army; and Jews could not hold developed-property that exceeded a value of 20,000 lira or land valued at more than 5,000 lira. Moreover, they could not own industries which produced military equipment or employed more than one hundred workers.[1]

The introduction in Italy of draconian, anti-Semitic measures "surprised and shocked Jewish and Gentile Italians" as well as the free world.[2] In the first and second stages of the campaign, Italian-Canadian fascists and their press (*L'Italia* and *Il Bollettino*) refused to believe reports from Italy and charged anti-fascists with slandering Italian fascism. Then, after a period of denial, as information arrived from the Italian government in Rome directly, the fascists and their press fell meekly into line with fascist policy but they tried to minimize what was happening to Italian Jews. All three of the local fascist newspapers, however, subscribed to the anti-Semitic campaign to varying degrees.

The Vancouver-based *L'Eco* abstained from editorialized comments and limited itself to reporting only the news; the Montreal-based *L'Italia*, as far as the surviving issues of the paper allow us to see, followed the anti-Semitic fascist line diligently and added a touch of its own anti-Semitism; but the Toronto paper, *Il Bollettino*, under direction of the self-proclaimed "fascist and Catholic" Tommaso Mari, gave vent to its own hitherto repressed anti-Semitism by publishing the vilest slander it could find in both Italian and North American anti-Jewish publications.

Mussolini's anti-Semitism provoked a wave of indignation across Canada, more intense than that caused by the assassination of Matteotti in 1924. The Matteotti case occurred during a period of social turmoil in Italy and although Mussolini was suspected of being involved in the affair he firmly denied such accusations. In 1938, however, the persecution of Jews was a cynical, political expedient born from his own mind and "one of those word-breaking about-faces for which he is now famous," according to a statement by Louis Palermo, then business agent of (Italian) Local 274 of the Amalgamated Clothing Workers.[3]

By this time, fascism had become a threatening force in Canada as well, with several thousand adherents in Quebec, Ontario, and the Western Provinces:

> There is a Fascist movement in Canada and it is growing. Whether it is a mighty force destined to turn the Dominion from a democratic into a totalitarian state, as its impassioned leaders assert; or whether it is nothing more than an ephemeral out-break of anti-Semitism, blown into unmerited prominence by the mouthing of a few crackpots, as some of its critics declare, it exists. It is here. It is a Fact.[4]

In the late 1920s and early 1930s, Italian blackshirts marching in military formation were considered an exotic curiosity. By 1938, under the auspices of Adrien Arcand's National Social Christian Party (NSCP) and Joseph Farr's Nationalist Party, hundreds of young Canadians wearing browns shirts and displaying swastikas drilled in Montreal and Toronto. Many leading Canadians had become aware of fascism's menace to the country. A CCF leader, M. J. Coldwell, who thought that fascism "can't happen here," changed his mind: "When I read the *Gazette* and saw those pictures of fascists in uniforms drilling under army officers, I knew that those who said it might happen here were right."[5] The future liberal Premier of Quebec, Adélard Godbout, confirmed Coldwell's fears: "Le fascisme est plus dangereux que le communisme chez nous, car il a de nombreux adeptes et des moyens d'action perfectionnés."[6]

Anti-Semitism was well entrenched in some sectors of Quebec nationalist intellectuals who saw the Jews as the "symbol of the evil totality incarnated by capitalism, democracy, and modernity."[7] At the same time, anti-Semitism was denounced in many quarters. Bishop John Farthing, for example, "in April 1938 . . . denounced the anti-Semitism of the NSCP as 'neither Christian nor British' and asserted that it threatened 'the very root of our liberties.' "[8]

Mussolini's unexpected change of heart regarding the Italian Jews exacerbated the tense situation that existed in Canada. A week after the publication of the infamous *"Manifesto degli 'scienziati' razzisti,"* the *Toronto Daily Star* published an editorial, "A Knotty Nazi Puzzle," which ridiculed German anti-Semitism but which was also mindful of its Canadian and Italian off-shoots. It reads:

> The medical dictionary discloses a profound Nazi puzzle. The decrees purging Germany of all Jewish influences forbid music produced by Jewish composers, books by Jewish authors, plays by Jewish playwrights, and so on. It is possible to exist physically without hearing certain music or seeing specific plays. But curiosity is aroused as to what a good nazi German does when he is ill, since the treatment for a number of common diseases was discovered and initiated by Jewish scientists. What, for example, does a Nazi do when he has heart disease? If he is to obey the anti-Jewish decrees, then he must not use digitalis, since it is the discovery of the Jew, Ludwig Traube . . .

The editorialist continued with a long list of similar cases, then concluded:

> To be consistent the Nazis will need to invent purely Aryan diseases which only Nazi doctors may treat. So far they have revived an ancient disease, social strife and hatred. And as for this unhappy ailment two Jews, Jesus Christ and Karl Marx, have prescribed treatment.[9]

In another editorial titled "Who They Are," *Toronto Daily Star* (26 September 1938) addressed Italian fascists squarely by quoting from Ignazio Silone's *Fontamara*. The paper gave a chilling picture of black shirts:

> We knew these men in black shirts. They had come at night; otherwise they wouldn't have had the pluck. Most of them stank of wine, and if you looked them in the eyes they didn't like it, but looked away. They were poor folk, too, but a special kind of poor folk; landless, not brought up to any trade, or knowing too many trades, which is the same thing. They were the type that disliked hard work... On various occasions the so-called Fascists had beaten, wounded and even killed people against whom the law had no complaint, and those who had done these things had been rewarded by the authorities. We could not protest. The whole thing was legal, perfectly. The one thing that would have been illegal would have been for us to make a protest.

This editorial provoked *Il Bollettino*'s usual tirade of slander against *The Star*: "Calumniators! Cowards! Liars! The spittle that you attempt in vain to fling at someone else's face returns to yours."[10]

The Globe and Mail, through its Rome correspondent, Arnaldo Cortesi, emphasized the contrast existing between the Pope and Mussolini on racism. Some of the headlines for those reports are quite instructive: "Pope Lashes Race Theories" (25 July), "Pope Opens War on

Racism: Race Policy for Italy Denounced" (30 July), and "Il Duce Defies Papal Warning on Race Issue" (1 August). In the 3 August 1938 issue, under the title "Pope Warned: He Can't Win Over Fascism," Cortesi reported:

> The extreme right-wing Fascist Leader Roberto Farinacci ... today fires the first broadside at the Pope in the war between the Fascist regime and the Catholic Church over the race question ... Signor Farinacci begins by saying that French atheists, Communists, Freemasons, democrats and Jews are hoping that the Catholic Action Associations may frustrate the designs of the Fascist Regime since the Catholic Action Associations represent the Church and cannot be attacked without attacking the Pope himself ... "Perhaps," ended signor Farinacci, "the Pope expects ... Italian Catholic youth to take up a decided attitude against fascism. Such a hope would be puerile, since Italian youths remain faithful to the State and Fascism; whereas Catholic Action Associations would be irreparably damaged by the conflict with Fascism."

Mussolini artificially created a Jewish Question in order to solve what he perceived to be two converging political problems: namely, his desire to make Italians a "master" race given that Italy had acquired an empire,[11] and to align his own policy with that of his axis partner, Hitler.[12] It was a cynical expedient because Mussolini himself, and most fascists — except perhaps for a very small number from the "Movimento Nazionalista" like Giovanni Preziosi — did not believe in racism.[13] Louis Palermo rightly pointed out that "Anti-Semitism in Italy will never go beyond the Fascist threshold of official Fascist circles because Italians have already learned at their own expense the lessons of intolerance and racial and religious hatred."[14]

In fact, not even the ducetto Roberto Farinacci,[15] editor of the anti-Semitic sheet *Regime Fascista,* believed in the racial theory. He was of the opinion that anti-Semitism was a "purely" political problem. Three weeks after the publication of the "Racial Manifesto," Farinacci made his disbelief on the race issue clear in a letter to Mussolini to whom he claimed that "he did not believe in the racial theories on which the anti-Jewish policy was allegedly based."[16] Further, while fomenting an anti-Jewish campaign, he had a personal secretary, Jole Foà, who was not only Jewish but also a fascist from the very beginning.[17] Moreover, in 1944, when the Germans dominated Northern Italy, Farinacci saved "fifty 'Semites' from Cremona, his home city, from being arrested by the nazis."[18]

In Italy, Jews numbered one per one thousand of the population and were well integrated. According to Antonio Gramsci, one of the most incisive Marxist thinkers of this century, Italy was free of anti-Semitism because Jews contributed to the development of an Italian national consciousness and to the development of a lay culture in concert with the rest of the Peninsula's populations.[19] And Benedetto Croce in his magisterial *History of Italy, 1871-1915,* said of Italian anti-Semitism:

> Fortunately enough, there was no sign of that folly which goes by the name of anti-semitism, which consists in first strengthening by persecution the solidarity of the Jews and their separation from all other races, and then trying to overcome the consequences of persecution by more persecution.[20]

Italian Jews were so well integrated into every aspect of national life that a renowned rabbi, David Prato, called them "Hebrews of Italian religion,"[21] meaning that their real religion was Italian national identity. Indeed, being Jewish in Italy was as different or as similar as being Sicilian, Calabrian, Tuscan, Roman, Friulian and so forth. In fact, the French writer Max Nordau, even accused Italian Jews of having "forgotten their origin."[22] That Italian Jews were first of all Italians is confirmed by the fact that not even after the persecution did they seem to feel different from other Italians. Italian Jews did not create, for example, as Jews did in many other European countries, an autonomous anti-fascist movement. Instead, they joined existing anti-fascist Italian parties and within them fought in the Italian Resistance movement.[23]

Further, during the period when fascists thought that zionism might be a means to penetrate into the Middle East, Mussolini was friendly with both Italian and world zionist leaders. He received zionists of the calibre of Chain Weizmann (in 1926 and 1934), Nahoum Goldmann (1934), and Nahum Sokolov (1927), to mention only a few. Italian Jewish leaders like Angelo Sacerdoti, head Rabbi in Rome, Felice Ravenna, President of the Union of the Italian Israelite Communities, David Prato, Dante Lattes, and many others were in regular contact with the Duce. Margherita Sarfatti, a Jewess, was Mussolini's lover, co-editor of the periodical *Gerarchia* and one of his biographers. Jews were members of the Fascist Party and some even occupied high positions in Mussolini's government.[24]

Furthermore, Mussolini allowed the formation of the "Italy-Palestine Committee" in 1927,[25] and gave legal status to the Jewish communities in the country: Italian Jews were, in fact, the only group in the country enjoying the privilege "of freely voting for their own representatives in the Union of the Israelite Communities, which was recognized by the Government."[26] From 1933 on, Mussolini helped Jews fleeing persecution in Germany and other European countries and further, hundreds of young zionists of the "Betar" group (which was led by Wladmir Jabotinsky) received military training at the Navy School of Civitavecchia. Later, these men became the "nucleus" of Israel's Navy.[27] In turn, Italian and international Jewish leaders praised Mussolini and fascism publicly.[28]

The Jewish Question, then, was an artificial creation and as such a betrayal of Italy's tolerant tradition; and it was also a betrayal of Mussolini's own words and deeds up to 1937. Cynically, on the eve of the anti-Semitic legislation, in June 1937, Mussolini told Generoso Pope, editor of *Il Progresso Italo-Americano* of New York:

> As soon as you return to New York, I authorize you to inform American Jews that they have no other reason to worry for their brothers living in Italy, but malevolent information. I authorize you to say clearly that in Italy Jews have received, receive, and will continue to receive the same treatment accorded to any other Italian, and that I don't have in mind any type of racial or religious discrimination. I remain true to a policy of equality for all before the law and freedom of religion.[29]

Soon after Hitler rose to power in Germany, Mussolini wired Italian diplomats abroad, including the Consul General in Ottawa, Luigi Petrucci, the following dispatch which was dated 16 May 1933: "Send me immediately a report on the Jews' demonstrations against Hitler."[30] Unfortunately, efforts to secure Petrucci's answer to Mussolini have failed but two letters from Petrucci to Mussolini referring and relating to that report are available.

In one of these letters, Petrucci discussed the Pastoral Letter against communism issued by Cardinal Villeneuve, Primate of Canada, and published on 21 November 1933. Petrucci explained that the Pastoral came at a crucial moment, "right when the Jewish and Masonic press has hailed with pleasure the recognition of the Soviets by the United States . . . This has highlighted the secret affinities among Masonry, Jewry, and communism, so much so that it has provoked a veiled anti-Semitism particularly among Franco-Canadian Catholics."[31]

The other letter was a report on a motion against the emigration to Canada of Eastern and Central Europeans — a motion that had been passed by the Montreal City Council on 19 October 1933. That decision, Petrucci argued, "stated that it was not wise to let into Canada people who, because of their subversive doctrine, were undesirable in their native countries. These people would definitely harm Canada." The motion was, according to Petrucci, an "anti-Semitic statement."[32] Anti-Semitism in Canada, he explained, has been stimulated by Hitler's fight against Jews in Germany, although "at present it is platonic and limited to the Franco-Canadian Province . . ."[33]

Hitler's victory stimulated nazi supporters in Italy as well. Instigated by nazi agents and perhaps, by Mussolini himself who played both sides of the issue, they initiated an ambiguous anti-Jewish and/or anti-zionist campaign in the extreme right-wing newspapers; namely, *Il Tevere* edited by Telesio Interlandi, *La via italiana* of Giovanni Preziosi, and Roberto Farinacci's *Il Regime Fascista*. This vociferous crusade reached its apex in the spring of 1934. In March of that year, an anti-fascist cell was discovered in Turin and fourteen men, mostly Jews, were arrested.

It was alleged that one of the conspirators, the Jew Mario Levi, while escaping to safety in Switzerland, had shouted at the police chasing him, *"Cani di italiani, vigliacchi"* (You Italian dogs, you cowards).[34] Later, this affair was revealed as an exaggeration[35] but at the moment it created much excitement and triggered negative reaction in the major national newspapers, like *Il Giornale d'Italia* in Rome, *La Stampa* in Turin, and *Il Corriere della sera* in Milan. This episode created strong reactions even among Italian Jews themselves.[36]

To calm the anxiety that the campaign created among Jews in Canada and the United States, the International Italian radio service transmitted a declaration on the position of Italian Jews which was assumed to have been "inspired by Benito Mussolini himself,"

> The Jews in Italy enjoy equal rights with all other citizens and therefore they also share the same duties as all Italians. Italy had not known any anti-Semitism, and even today it knows no prejudice against the Jews. On the contrary, the Jews proved loyal and reliable Italian citizens; they fought bravely in the War at the side of their Italian comrades. Therefore, the Jews, like all other citizens are given the highest positions in the administration of the state, and the army. The Jews in Italy are granted the highest honours; so, for example they are also members of the Italian Academy. Italian Jews are very patriotic and they are loyal adherents to Fascism which knows no racial discrimination.[37]

On this subject, the fascist *Il Carroccio* of New York intervened with an article titled, "Mussolini and the Jews." It was very critical of Hitler who, the editor stated, had fallen morally and politically short of his Italian mentor.

Hitler with his racial policy was "not a star pupil of Mussolini's, but a miserable bungler." This was also true, continued *Il Carroccio,* of "those pupils of Mussolini's who theoretically affirm the equality of the Jews," but in practice discriminate against them. Instead, Mussolini's political genius, concluded the paper, stands on "the beautiful harmony of theory and practice, of word and deed."[38] The anti-Semitic campaign was echoed even in *Il Bollettino.* On 2 March 1934 the Toronto paper published an article titled *"Gli ebrei e Il fascismo,"* in which the author sided with the Italian Jew-baiter. Tommaso Mari repeated all the common slanders used against Jews, disguising his calumnies under the paternalism of Mussolini's bombastic pro-Jewish words. Mari argued that international Jewry's stand against fascism was not a reaction to Hitler's anti-Semitic policy, but "the consequence" of the internationalism of Jewry. According to Mari, the nazi policy only triggered the Jews' anti-fascist nature, "the Jews, after Hitler rose to power, have found their, should we say, natural attitude towards fascism: that is anti-fascism."

Mari made a distinction in his tirade, he referred only to "those Jews who, though naturalized citizens, are not integrated into the nation as happens in Italy and in many cases even here [in Canada]." Because they have been discriminated against, explained Mari, Jews are opposed to any "racial, religious, and social prejudice." Therefore their struggle for freedom leads them to embrace the most radical theories which aim at subverting the social order, "Marx and Lenin . . . are Jews." Further, Mari said, Jews have always favoured unlimited freedom which for them "too often means *'fregare il prossimo'* (to cheat one's fellow man)."

"As the Duce said," concluded Mari by way of a conciliation, "the Jewish question is not resolved by expelling the Jews from one country to another, but by giving them a nation: create it for them if they don't have one." Once they have their own nation, prophesied the editor, "Jews will be more fascist than any other people ... because ... they are both shamefully greedy and, at the same time, the most passionate dreamers that history has ever recorded."

Often in *Il Bollettino,* seldom in *L'Italia,* and never in *L'Eco,* one finds innuendo and insinuation linking the Jews to bolshevism, international finance, and immoral behaviour, even before the racial legislation was introduced in Italy. For example, Mari's articles on the "Free Press" and on *"Ludi cartacei,"* which were discussed above, constantly allude to the Jews as those guilty of corrupting the press and degrading democracy. The allusions became open remarks during the Ethiopian conflict: Jews were behind both the manoeuvring of the League of Nations and Britain's plots against Italy. Ironically, however, the British "Imperial Fascist League" (IFL), not to be confused with Sir Oswald Mosley's movement, accused Mussolini of waging war on Ethiopia on behalf of the Jews who paid for it in the hope "that the Negros in Africa will be stirred up to rebellion against the Whites."[39]

In the Italian fascist press in Canada, anti-Semitism was kept under control in view of Mussolini's public position on the subject, for fear of the reaction of Canadian Jews, and because, in Canada as in Italy, Italians and Jews got along well together both socially and at work. Many Italians and Jews worked in the needle industry or garment trades both in Montreal and Toronto and both communities experienced discrimination by Canadian nativists, Anglo-

Saxon right wingers and the militant Orange Order. In the Sault Ste. Marie area, the Ku Klux Klan was particularly active against Roman Catholic Italians and Jews.[40] Further, in Toronto, Italians and Jews had been living together in the city's "St. John's Ward" for many years and, in the 1930s, both groups had moved westward to the area bounded by Dundas, Bloor, Brunswick, and Ossington.[41] As neighbours, they got along well. Jewish and Italian women often baby-sat for each other and, thus, some Italian-Canadian children could function in Yiddish and similarly Jewish kids were able to speak some Italian. Mixed marriages between these two groups occurred occasionally.[42]

A splendid example of their good relations was the Italian participation on the side of Jews in the Christie Pits Park riot in 1933. Stimulated by Hitler's anti-Semitism in Germany, some right-wing Canadian youths created a Swastika Club in Toronto and practised discrimination and sometimes even engaged in violence against Jews. Christie Pits Park at the junction of Bloor and Christie Streets on the city's west side was the threatre of violent fights between boys of the Swastika Club and Jews in the summer of 1933. Scores of Italian boys went to help their Jewish friends and one of the participants recalled that he was the only Jew in a truckload of Italian boys rushing to Christie Pits.[43]

On the other hand in Canada, as in Italy, some Italian Jews were fascists. At least one Jewish woman, Elisa (Rebecca) Palange, was married to Pasquale Palange, a tailor who was actively involved in the Toronto Fascio Principe Umberto. Elisa was indeed the first trustee of the Italian Fascist Women's Club of Toronto.[44] By order from

Rome, however, she was removed from that position, when she returned from Italy where she had accompanied a group of young Italian female fascists to a fascist camp in 1934. Rome ordered the Italian Consul to replace Mrs. Palange and, according to a leading figure in the Toronto fascio, Rome reproached fascists in Toronto with the question: "Didn't you have anyone else to send? Only a Jew!"[45] In the following year, Elisa Palange was replaced by Etelvina Sartini Frediani.[46]

The official policy from Rome was that a "Jewish Question" did not exist in Italy. Perhaps, as a way of complying with this policy, *Il Bollettino* dropped its Winnipeg correspondent, G. S., after only three reports from that city. His reports had emphasized the participation of Italian Canadians in the meetings of the Nationalist Party and the reporter was too indulgent with the anti-Semitic tirades of Mr. William Whittaker, President of the Nationalist Party, and a certain Mr. Davis.[47] Reporting on a meeting held on 29 April G. S. wrote:

> An important meeting of the Canadian Nationalist Party was held at the Columbus Hall of our city. The large hall was crowded with chosen people mostly Italians... Signor Scinocca, a hearty fascist, expressed the need to stop communism.[48]

Further, among the many fascist groups active in Toronto, *Il Bollettino* maintained contact with the Canadian Union of Fascists (CUF) which, following Mussolini's official teaching, was not anti-Semitic.[49] Articles by an officer of the CUF, Charles Brandel (alias Charles Crate[50]) its national organizer, W.F. Elsey, Secretary of the Woodstock

Branch;[51] and Magistrate Alfred Jones,[52] all appeared in *Il Bollettino*.

Canadian Jewish leaders, for their part, were careful not to disrupt the good relations that existed between Italians and Jews as the following example shows. In 1936, a visiting Rabbi, Jesse J. Schwartz, in a radio program and in an interview with the *Time Journal* of Fort William, Ontario, charged that the Italian government mingled in Middle East affairs because it "wished . . . to embarrass England." In a letter to the newspaper in question, Mr. Marino, the Italian Consular Agent of Fort William, accused Rabbi Schwartz of "cheap" shots because "no proof was offered, and for which no proof existed."

Dr. M. L. Stitt, a leading Jew of Fort William, on 20 June 1936, wrote to the Jewish Congress:

> I think it will be well advised if any future Jewish speakers are on tour, utmost caution should be advised, especially against Italians . . . We are trying to avoid any undue controversy, and are hoping by further interviews with Italian leaders in this community to settle this matter.[53]

In the fearful atmosphere of the time, created by German persecution of the Jews and reports of atrocious violence in the Middle East, Rabbi Schwartz's activity made Canadian Jews nervous and worried even for their Italian brothers.

Probably to calm the agitated Jewish community, *Il Bollettino* published, in three instalments, a booklet titled *The Jews in Italy* which was written by Swiss Rabbi Eli Rubin under the pen name Sozius. In the presentation of the booklet Italian readers were asked to advise their Jewish friends to read it:

> We would like our readers who are in contact with Hebrews (and there are many) to suggest Jews to read the words of a person beyond suspicion... In Italy, Jews have always been treated better than any other country. They receive now under the Fascist Regime the same treatment. ... This should clear the minds of many Jews who live here fearing that their brothers in Italy may suffer the same persecutions that have fallen on the German Jews.[54]

The booklet in question was an apologia for fascism and an indictment of nazism for the way these two parties treated the Jews. The following is an example of the tenor and content of *The Jews in Italy:*

> Considering the torment and the humiliations Jews are suffering in so many Countries of Europe, well acquainted with the incessant German fight to annihilate the Jews, we must ask ourselves upon examining the position of the Jews in Italy: "Is this the same Continent? Is this the same Century?" The spirit of liberty and liberality which surrounds the Jews in Italy ... is the same by which the Jews in the United States are surrounded. As to the religious and human tolerance Fascist Italy is rising like a beacon of light over the stormy sea of religious and racial hatred prevailing in the greater part of European Countries.[55]

Local fascists were proud of the fact that there was no anti-Semitism in Italy: Italian fascism and Mussolini were not equivalent to German nazism and Hitler. For example, the young philo-fascist intellectual, Frank Molinaro, speaking to a "Jewish Youth Club," described his 1934 visit to Italy and high-lighting the meeting he had there "with the Minister of Finance, the Jew Guido Jung, and other Italian Jewish personalities, in Rome. They all praised the Regime and *il Duce*," Molinaro said.[56] On one occasion even *The Catholic Register* intervened on this subject with an editorial, "Word or Stinkbomb?" in which the Roman Catholic paper lamented that in Canada "anti-Semitism is now called fascism though fascist Italy has had no more trouble with the Jews than has Canada herself."[57]

In this atmosphere, the incredulity of Italian Canadian fascists and their press was understandable when the Montreal *Canadian Jewish Chronicle* published a report "An Italian 'Stuermer'," in its 18 February 1938 issue, stating that Italy was soon to inaugurate an anti-Semitic policy. That editorial declared that "it is beginning to look as if the Duce has thrown off his mask and has joined Hitler in his wild Jew-hunting chase." This editorial took its cue from the Jew-baiting *Il Giornalissimo* and the publication of the infamous *"Informazione diplomatica N. 14"* of 16 February 1938 which officially marked the beginning of anti-Semitism in Italy. Apropos of this note, Galeazzo Ciano, Minister of Foreign Affairs, wrote in his diary: *"Il Duce* personally edited the Informazione diplomatica N. 14 on the Jewish question. *Il Duce* himself defined it as a master piece of anti-Semitism, since in its form it is almost conciliatory."[58] The following week, 25 February, *The Canadian Jewish Chronicle* published an editorial, "Italy's Utopia for Jews," which states:

> It is a pity that the Duce is so vague about the territory he has in mind [for a Jewish State], although there is no doubt that such a State will come under the direct jurisdiction of Italy. Fortunately, an inkling of the new paradise has crept into the press, and according to a dispatch from Vienna, it

would seem that the Duce has in mind Tripoli, his province in Norther Africa.

L'Italia nuova and its French section *Le Canada Latin* polemically answered the *Canadian Jewish Chronicle*, charging that it was a smear campaign created by anti-fascists who "would give anything to be able to prove that there is racial discrimination and lack of religious freedom in Italy."[59] *L'Italia nuova* continued, "American anti-fascists know well that part of the American Hebrews, which was not led astray by communistic and bolshevik aberrations, had on many occasions openly shown sympathy for the fascist regime. If for nothing else, for the reason that under the present regime, in spite of some lone and discordant voices, a racial question never existed in Italy."[60]

In an article which is, for the most part, the English translation of the *"Informazione diplomatica N. 14,"* Le Canada Latin wrote:

> Recent journalistic utterances may have created in some foreign minds the impression that the Fascist Government is about to inaugurate an anti-semitic policy. In responsible Roman circles one is in the position to unqualifiedly state that such an impression is absolutely wrong, and these would-be anti-semitic utterances are caused principally by the fact that foreign, anti-fascist currents of thought are nearly always traced to Jewish sources . . . The law which governs and regulates the life of the Jewish communities has proven its merits and will remain unaltered.[61]

The *"Informazione diplomatica"* touches upon the formation of a Jewish State: "The responsible Roman circles are of the opinion that the universal Jewish problem may be solved in one way: by the creation of the Jewish State in some part of the world, but not in Palestine."⁶² It was the phrase, "not in Palestine,"⁶³ that caught the attention of the editor of the *Canadian Jewish Chronicle* who seemed to be well-informed on the Italian situation. His answer to the arguments expressed by both *L'Italia nuova* and *Le Canada Latin* went right to the point:

> As for the proposed Jewish state outside Palestine which the Duce is advocating, it is strange that this proposition should come up just at a time when he has eyes on a new Mediterranean alignment. Why is he so panicky about a Jewish Palestine? The pro-Palestine committee of the [British] House of Commons put its finger on the right spot when it declared that "because the Duce wants to get Britain out of Palestine, it is the best reason why Britain should stay there." As far as we are concerned, the rumors about Tripoli, Libya or Abyssinia as colonization lands for Jews need not be taken seriously. The important warning to us is that the Duce emphasizes a Jewish state outside Palestine, which indicates that he is more concerned about a Jewless Palestine than he is about a Jewish State. He is not sure where the Jewish State can be but he is at least sure that Palestine must be *judenrein*.

The editor concluded by brushing aside the fascist papers' reassuring words: "We would very much like to believe that the Italian governmnet is not anti-Semitic, but in a country which permits such violent anti-Jewish fulminations as those expressed by Roberto Farinacci and Virginio Gayda — remembering always that the press in Italy reflects nothing but the thoughts of the government — it would require more that the bland assurance of our contemporary to believe othervise."⁶⁴

While *L'Italia nuova* was disputing the truth of the news about anti-Semitism in Italy, *Il Bollettino* was on the anti-Semitic trail. In its 7 April 1938 issue, the Toronto-based paper published an article, "The Wandering Jew," which had a clearly anti-Jewish tone. It was taken from *Il Crociato,* the paper of the Italian fasci abroad and printed in Rome. The article is a list of "folk-legends" about the Jewish diaspora, implying that at the core of the tales there is a profound truth: God's malediction, the old charge against the Jews made by Christian bigots. It also linked these myths with what was happening in Palestine and Austria at that time:

> In Austria! Right there, nazism repeats to Israel the cry of the legend, "Go, go, walk!" So the painful odyssey goes on. Even at their ancient seat, by the Dead Sea, Jews are hounded (pitiless ostracism). England herself, which would like to establish Judaism in Palestine, intends to keep Jerusalem for herself.

In conclusion *Il Bolletino* repeated the anathema, which was the statement that seemed to interest the paper most: "'Go, go, walk!' It seems that friends and enemies alike collaborate in making obvious the despair of the people who killed the Son of God." But in the following week, 14 April 1938, *Il Bollettino* published an editorial which stated that "the official position of fascist Italy towards Jews has always been and continues to be absolutely indifferent before the so called *problema ebraico.* This should be the position of every Italian fascist wherever he lives." This editorial appeared perhaps because Jewish advertisers complained to the paper's management. A memo dated 8 June 1938 which is currently found in the Ontario Jewish Archives states that, "the files of *Il Bollettino,* Italian weekly newspaper, were examined today with a view to ascertaining if anti-Semitic articles published by that paper had been continued or if they had ceased, as had been promised to advertisers by the manager."[65] Optimistically, the memo continued, "it is my opinion arrangements could be made with *Il Bollettino* to omit any anti-Jewish articles in the future. Mr. Perley [read Perilli, manager and owner of the paper] already promised to do this and indicates his willingness to print an editorial correcting impressions which may arise out of the articles that we deem to be injurious to the Jewish community."[66]

While *Il Bollettino* and *L'Italia* were interested in events in Italy and Canada regarding anti-Semitism, the western Canada newspaper *L'Eco* ignored them. In fact, the first time that *L'Eco* mentioned Jews was in its 10 September 1938 issue, when some measures against the Jews had become a reality; and it mentioned the Jews by simply publishing an item from a press agency. The report noted that the Italian Royal Academy had nominated a "scientific" committee to "study what has been the Hebrew influence in Italian life, from ancient Rome to the present."[67]

Two weeks later, on 24 September, the Italian-Jewish question reappeared as a news item. *L'Eco* informed its readers that the Italian government had undertaken "measures" to remove Jewish university professors from their positions. Such measures were justified by the "fact" that "from 1909 to 1938, Jewish professors had increased both in number and percentage, going from 41 to 174, that is from 4.8% to 12.2%."

In another agency dispatch published by the paper, we read that of the 15,000 Italian Jewish families, 3,522 enjoyed all rights except being able to teach (Aryan) children. These families deserved special treatment because they belonged to people who had special patriotic merits: "406 families had one member who died in war; 721 families had a man who volunteered for the war; 1,577 families belonged to decorated war veterans; 3 were families of people who died for the fascist cause; 20 had an invalid in the fascist cause; 724 were families of fascists before the March on Rome or in the second half of 1924; and, finally, 51 families had each given a legionary for the Fiume expedition."[68] Contrary to its eastern counterparts *L'Italia nuova* and *Il Bollettino, L'Eco* never indulged in Jew-baiting. It never published an editorial denigrating the Jews, but the paper also never once dissociated itself from this or any other of Mussolini's policies.

Undoubtedly, Branca's influence on the paper and on the Italian community of Vancouver was a determining factor in steering *L'Eco* away from explicit anti-Semitism. Angelo Branca was "the only Canadian other than John Diefenbaker to have been honoured with the President's Medal of the State of Israel."[69] One could also infer that the lack of visible anti-Semitism was not entirely attributable to Branca's influence. The editors, Alberto Boccini and his predecessor Bruno Girardi, were not anti-Semitic. The news and agency items that Boccini chose to publish presented Jews in a good light; they presented Jews as reliable Italians, some of whom were even good fascists. It can be argued that the editor left the intelligent reader to make his or her own judgement regarding the Jewish question in Italy.

This was not the case with the eastern newspapers. After the publication of the *"Manifesto della razza"* on 14 July, *L'Italia nuova* no longer denied what was taking place in Italy, it only down-played the severity of the decrees and their consequences. In the 6 August 1938 issue, the title of an article read, "Italy Is not Anti-Semitic: plain words do not need explanation." According to the editorialist, it was merely an exaggeration of some North American newspapers which artfully implanted in the public mind the idea that "Italy [was] implementing anti-Semitism like Germany." The proof against this, continued the paper, "consists in the fact that all Jews who live there are calm and quiet."

A month later, *L'Italia nuova* returned to the argument. It minimized the lot of the Italian Jews again but for the first time admitted that certain restrictions were applied against them. The measures were simply an "equalization of the size of the Jewish population with the number of positions they held" in the country.[70] The editor of *L'Italia nuova*, Giulio Romano, blamed the Jews themselves for the treatment they received by reporting from an article written by Samuel Rosen, a Jew: "Let us be frank. Before we blame anybody for recent anti-Jewish decrees why shouldn't we first blame those irresponsible radical groups among us who are responsible for what is happening?"[71]

To calm the growing criticism and to avoid Roman Catholic defections in particular because Pius XI had been very critical[72] of fascist racial policy,[73] *L'Italia nuova* added that "the Vatican itself had rightly revised its own attitude on this matter and has had to admit that there is no relation between Italian racism and the racism of other countries."[74]

Against growing criticism in the community, *L'Italia nuova* deployed its sarcasm: "The tender crying hearts affected by philo-Semitic humanitarianism did they ever ask themselves what destiny and how many positions would be reserved to 44 thousand Catholics in a nation of 44 million Jews? The answer is in Tel Aviv: in a population of 156 thousand inhabitants you find not even one gentile."[75] To further convince its readers how it was that Roman Catholicism went hand in hand with racism, *L'Italia nuova* emphasized the "illustrious" example of St. Stephen. According to the paper St. Stephen, first King of Hungary, neither recognized Jews as legal citizens of his country nor did he allow them to own property. As one can see, concluded the paper, "the Saints of the Church do and have engaged in *vero e proprio* (actual) racism."[76]

By the end of October, *L'Italia nuova* no longer minimized the lot of the Italian Jews. It was the scientific activities surrounding the newly discovered racial "discipline" that now interested the paper: "intense research is taking place to invigorate racial awareness in every stratum of the population . . . it is understood now as never before that no country could rise to great power and have a spiritual mission in the world when the divine spark of its origin is obscured . . . from this supreme necessity derives another: not to allow the Jewish forma mentis to infiltrate our spiritual substance through books and education."[77] This was necessary, according to *L'Italia nuova,* because the essence of the two races was profoundly different: "The Aryan race enjoys building, creating; the Semitic race lusts for possession."[78]

On 14 and 15 July 1938 the Canadian press reported in detail on the *"Manifesto degli scienziati razzisti,"* a manifesto which had been published in Rome with a great amount of clamour in all Italian national newspapers. This document, which was prepared by a group of fascist university professors for the Minculpop, essentially proclaimed or, better, invented the existence of an Italian race,[79] which was European and Aryan whereas, Jews were Asiatic and Semitic:

> Jews do not belong to the Italian race . . . of the Semites who in the course of centuries landed on the sacred soil of our Patria nothing in general remains . . . Jews are the only people that have never assimilated in Italy. This is so because they are Asiatic, absolutely different from the European race to which Italians belong.

Despite this crude Manifesto, *Il Bollettino* hypocritically repeated that there was no anti-Semitism in Italy; rather, it was the Associated Press and the French Agency Havas that distorted words and facts with the obvious intention of creating the impression that "Italy is on the verge of an anti-Jewish program."[80] This view was also stated in a letter to the *Globe and Mail* by Frank Molinaro. Ignoring reports on the Manifesto, he wrote: "Much is made of articles written by Roberto Farinacci, Paolo Orano, and Oreste Gregorio which appeared in the *Regime Fascista* and Mussolini's own paper, *Il Popolo d'Italia.* These were not anti-Semitic, but aimed rather at a clarification of the political status of Italian Jews with reference to Italian foreign policy."[81] It is obvious that Molinaro had in mind the polemic which had stirred the Italian press the year before in 1937, when Paolo Orano's book, *Gli ebrei in Italia,* appeared.

On 4 August and 1 September, however, when the first decrees against the Jews were promulgated,[82] the Italian fascist voice in Toronto no longer needed to, nor could it continue to dissemble. Indeed, *Il Bollettino* became disturbingly anti-Semitic, collecting the most vile slander against Jews and printing it without fear, shame, or decency. It even published, in weekly instalments, an English-language version of the "Protocols of the Meetings of the Learned Elders of Zion," an obviously apocryphal work[83] which in 1938 only an obtuse and evil mind could put into circulation as a valid document. Significantly, *The Catholic Register* asked: "Are not those who charge Jewish leaders with having written the 'Protocols' morally bound to prove them to be Jewish in origin?"[84]

In their behaviour, in particular in their anti-Semitism, the editors of *Il Bollettino,* and Mari in particular, conformed to what Renzo De Felice said of the young fascist hierarchs in general: "They thought with the head of propaganda and felt with the heart of their career."[85] Mari was, in fact, an employee of the Italian Consulate and who knows what type of reward he expected to receive in Italy when, on 10 June 1940, he and his wife Giuseppina Gatto repatriated with the Vice-Consul Francesco Barboglio. As events transpired, most of his comrades who were taken to a security camp in Petawawa, Ontario, were luckier than he was.[86]

Dante Colussi Corti, editor of the anti-fascist weekly *Il Messaggero italo-canadese,* produced, long before the Semitic question, a penetrating sketch of Mari's psychological make-up. It is useful for an understanding of the intense anti-Semitic crusade that *Il Bollettino* undertook in the months following the publication of the racist Manifesto by the Italian government. Colussi wrote:

> The "magnum" mouth piece of the Fascio has spoken: short of positive facts and plausible arguments as usual, he has displayed a series of more or less fantastic conjectures,

> distorting, in his customary way, truth and facts. Following the whim of his distorted logic, Mari presents his abortive arguments which are made up of strange suppositions and incongruent conclusions, in a pseudo-scientific language. In reality, he only reveals the megalomaniac character of a little man posing as a superman.[87]

From August on, almost every issue of the paper carried three or four and sometimes even five articles about Italian racism.[88] All of these articles may be divided into three basic groups: 1. articles explaining what was taking place in Italy and why; 2. news and agency items aimed at distinguishing Italian racism from German racism; and 3. writings like the "Protocols" which were intended to defame Jews and Jewry. Essentially, Jews were portrayed as responsible for everything base and evil which was happening in the world:

> We shall not be deterred from pointing to the Jew as the inspirer, the instigator and the beneficiary of this dreadful catastrophe [the Spanish Civil War]. Behold the World Enemy, the wrecker of civilization, the parasite among the nations, the son of chaos, evil incarnate, the ferment of dissolution, the plastic demon of every decadence.[89]

The personal and collective moral standard of the Jews was very low, according to *Il Bollettino*. It reported that insurance companies refused to insure Jewish firms against fire because of the large number of dubious claims.[90] Moreover, Jewish women were considered licentious. "Masquerading" as French, Italian, and so forth, promiscuous Jewish women spread "licentiousness into the lives of the leading men at the head of nations."[91] The paper reported further that even the eminent American statesman and scientist Benjamin Franklin was an anti-Semite because he believed that Jews lowered the morality of nations they live in and that the Jews were social "vampires."[92]

The articles that *Il Bollettino* dared to print were unspeakable and the reaction of a Mr. I. Davis of Sault Ste. Marie gives a faithful idea of the typical response they provoked. In a letter to the Toronto branch of the Canadian Jewish Congress, Mr. Davis wrote: "I cannot remember ever seeing anything as horribly filthy as the quotations in this article, taken verbatim from the *Italo-Canadese Bolletino* (sic), and I feel certain this filthy sheet has gone entirely beyond all decency and beyond any newspaper's reights (sic)."[93] The alarmed Jewish Congress engaged a "staff of legal experts" to determine if they had a case against the paper.[94]

The measures taken against the Jews, *Il Bollettino* explained, were a consequence of reborn Italian Imperialism: "It is more than natural that a people which has a millenarian civilization should guard its biological purity that generates the forms of its genius . . . For it is the primordial and fundamental quality of the race, not the environment or history that generates the unmistakable traits of a nation as imprinted in its thought, art, and culture."[95]

The measures of 1936 which prohibited marriages between Italians and people of colour were the first steps taken by Italian racism (see appendix No. 12). It was only a matter of time, continued *Il Bollettino* in another article, that the Jewish question would necessarily follow from an act taken to prevent the production of a mulatto race. According to the newspaper, the fact that "sceptical people" and "imbeciles" did not see the Jewish question as imminent was irrelevant. "If Mussolini were a Prime Minister of any democratic government," who had to overcome parliamentary opposition, he would think and act in this way. "But Mussolini is the leader of a people who think like Romans thought and, like the Romans, would build for posterity... Mussolini does not wait for events to occur in order to act; he foresees them and acts in advance, modifying and dominating them."[96] Further, Italy was a Roman Catholic country in which the faith was practised by both the Church and the State. "The State cannot tolerate Jewish agnosticism and atheism."[97] These doctrines may be tolerated in England, which is not a Christian country, since her "people accept Darwin's theory . . . making the book of Genesis a big lie."[98]

With regard to anti-Semitism, the interpretation which held that Mussolini was a pawn of Hitler and which was expressed by the world press (and even by German newspapers)[99] was vigorously rejected by Mussolini and his Canadian parrots. Anyone who said that fascism was following in nazism's foot-steps was a liar in *Il Bollettino*'s opinion. Any reader could see, simply by skimming Mussolini's speeches and writings, that he had posed the "Jewish Question" at the beginning of fascism in 1919. Furthermore, stressed the local fascist paper, there is a drastic difference between German and Italian racism: Italians do not speak of "race superiority" as the Germans do, but of "separation."[100]

Italians, argued *Il Bollettino,* simply point out the differences among races which God himself had created and which men certainly do not dare to change. Ironically and unintentionally, *Il Bollettino* engaged in a polemic with no less an authority than the Pope himself who had forcefully stated that "humanity is one single universal, Catholic race."[101] "If God," wrote *Il Bollettino,* "in his divine and boundless wisdom thought necessary to populate the earth with groups of people biologically and unmistakably different from one another, we do not see why mere mortals should not keep intact such differences. But, instead, we end up obeying a misunderstood concept of 'universality' and let races mix and muddle." Fascists believe, this article continued, that "to practice racism as Mussolini does — that is trying to maintain and reinforce God-given differences — leads to God rather than to the devil."[102]

The profound ideological differences on racism between Pius XI and Mussolini were reflected in *Il Bollettino* as a mere difference of opinion between Catholic Action and the Fascist Party — differences that could be resolved with a frank discussion:

> The different views between the National Fascist Party and Catholic Action are the object of negotiations between the appropriate organs of the Party and Catholic Action. The exaggerations of foreign correspondents, who had foreseen even a schism between Italy and the Vatican, are baseless [here, the allusion to Arnaldo Cortesi, correspondent of *The Globe and Mail* is obvious].[103]

After all, wrote *Il Bollettino,* Pope Pius XI did not condemn racism but rather its "extreme" positions.[104]

Il Bollettino's quibbling and bursts of rage were the result of frustrations caused by the progressive isolation in which the paper and its supporting comrades increasingly found themselves after their delirium of the Abyssinian victory faded away. As a consequence of the Pope's firm condemnation of racism, most Ontario Roman Catholics who had been supporting fascism during the Ethiopian war turned against it and they thereby irritated Mussolini's local pawns.

The crisis between the fascist regime and the Catholic Church created by the Italy-Germany axis, the racial campaign and the growing rivalry between Catholic Action and fascism, reached its peak with the Papal locuzione or speech of 28 July 1938. Speaking to students of the "Propaganda Fide," Pius XI confirmed that "Catholic means universal not separation as racism or nationalism indicate."[105] Spurred on by the Pope's words, some Roman Catholics did make the connection between both "fascism and communism" as "forms" of the lay culture,[106] projecting onto fascism and racism all the negative feelings that communism conjured up in a Roman Catholic mind.

From the summer of 1938, the influential paper of the diocese of Toronto, *The Catholic Register,* assumed a more critical distance from fascism. *Il Bollettino* acknowledged this change and it revealed in an ambiguous tone, humble and defiant at the same time, its awareness that a powerful friendship was in jeopardy. "With stubborn insistence," wrote the Elm Street paper, "the editor of the *Catholic Register* publishes every now and then something against fascism."[107]

Il Bollettino charged H. Somerwille, editor of the *Catholic Register,* of being "ignorant" because he printed a passage from a speech that Cardinal Hinsley delivered in Birmingham, England. In that speech the Cardinal accused fascism of paganism and added, "because the Church is anti-Communist she is not therefore pro-Fascist."[108] According to *Il Bollettino,* the Roman Catholic paper of Toronto should have known that the passage in the Cardinal's speech in which he quoted Mussolini in fact misrepresented the Duce's ideas. On the basis of this misrepresentation the *Catholic Register* noted, "whatever good has been done by Fascism there is underlying that movement a great danger."[109] Mari concluded, in the customary fascist style and mentality, "people writing for the Catholic press should not be allowed to publish similar foolishness."[110] A postion similar to that of Cardinal Hinsley was also expressed by the most reverend Carrell, Bishop of Calgary. Bishop Carrell defined anti-Semitism as "a vile race theory" and his definition was duly reported in the *Catholic Register.*[111]

Whether the *Catholic Register*'s position toward fascism reached the Franciscan priests serving the Italians in Toronto and elsewhere is not known. It would be comforting to believe however, that at least some Italian priests cooled the zealous pro-fascist enthusiasm that had been displayed during the Ethiopian conflict. The only available indication regarding this cooling is Father Balò's recommendation that Italian Canadians in Trail, British Columbia, where he was transferred from Toronto in 1939, comport themselves as loyal Canadians.[112]

Sensing that support of fascist anti-Semitism had been the last straw, *Il Bollettino* burst into a tirade against those Roman Catholics who, it claimed, misunderstood the Pope:

> Some hostile Catholics hustle to condemn everything and everyone: interpreting the Pontiff's thought in their own way, they surely condemn the racial policy of the Italian Government. In their heroic furore, they do not realize that

> the Holy Father has only condemned the excesses of racism. The Italian racial measures do not suffer from extremism ... the one who writes this is a devout Catholic and a fervent fascist and in his own conscience has found a perfect synthesis of God and Country and therefore cannot be accused of being one-sided.[113]

Mari went on to note that Father Gemelli, Rector of the Milanese Catholic University of the Sacred Heart, had understood quite well both Mussolini's policies and the Pope's teaching. Father Gemelli had a medieval view of the relation between Church and State. He, says Renzo De Felice, used the commemoration of a medieval scholar, Gugliemo da Salicento, as a pretext "for praising fascism and *il Duce*," and for expounding the traditional core of right-wing, religious anti-Semitism as suggested by the following:

> Undoubtedly those people, who because of their blood and religion cannot be part of our beautiful Patria, are in a tragic and sorrowful situation — a tragic situation in which, once again as in many other occasions in the past centuries, they are sought out by that terrible curse that, as deicides, they brought upon themselves. Haunted by such a curse, they wander through the world unable to find peace. Punishment for their horrible crime follows them everywhere for ever.[114]

Apart from the position taken by the *Catholic Register*, the Ontario section of the Canadian Jewish Congress began an effective boycott campaign against *Il Bollettino*. To better monitor its editorial activity and perhaps to have a complete list of firms advertising in this anti-Semitic paper, the Ontario section of the Canadian Jewish Congress subscribed to the paper. On 8 September the Executive Secretary, Oscar Cohen, sent *Il Bollettino* the following letter:

> Enclosed herewith is a postal note for $2.00 for which kindly send us *Il Bollettino* for one year . . . Kindly start our subscription with the first issue in August, 1938. We would appreciate receipt of the back copies.[115]

The effect of the Jewish campaign was felt immediately by *Il Bollettino,* as it quickly complained:

> It is sometime now that Jews take every opportunity to stand against Italians, against people belonging by birth or origin to an anti-communist nation. We have the proof right here in our own office. For weeks now, Jewish firms no longer place ads in our paper. The few that have remained because they found a particular material gain let us candidly know that they have been asked, almost coerced with threat of economic (and perhaps even material) reprisal by Jewish organizations, to cancel their ads.[116]

Strangely, *Il Bollettino* lamented the fact that Jewish firms no longer placed their ads in the paper! In reading this whining article which appeared beside a vicious, anti-Semitic piece titled *"Variazione sul Problema Integrale della Razza"* (Variation on the Fundamental Racial Problem), one wonders whether the editor expected Jews to send *Il Bollettino* roses and a thank-you card?

Moreover, during the municipal election, the Canadian Jewish Congress proceeded with a campaign to dissuade candidates from placing advertisements in *Il Bollettino,* a Jew-baiting paper. Several municipal candidates received a letter similar to the following:

Dear Alderman Shannon:
We note that an advertisement for your election to the city council appeared in the last edition of *Il Bollettino* . . . We wonder if you are aware that this paper has been consistently publishing fascist and anti-Semitic propaganda. As a matter of fact the issue in which you have advertised contains an instalment of the "Protocols of the Elders of Zion" . . . We feel sure that you were not aware of this information and we hasten to draw it to your attention. Unfortunate inferences may be drawn as a result of your advertisement . . . We would appreciate hearing from you in this regard.

Sincerely yours,
Oscar Cohen, Executive Secretary.[117]

Alderman Shannon answered that he "was pleased" to receive the letter and stated that he was "entirely unaware of this information."[118]

On 15 January 1939, *Il Bollettino* returned to the problem again with an article titled "Our Firm and the Jews," in which it accused Jews of attempting to defame and starve the paper. Jews and their firms and their friends, who not only placed advertisements in the paper but also commissioned printing work (invoices, business cards, bills, leaflets and so forth) from the Italian Publishing Company which owned *Il Bollettino,* had redirected their orders elsewhere. This hurt the firm's business and *Il Bollettino* charged that "the Jews of Toronto, following a (secret) decision taken in their Congress held recently in Toronto, initiated a strong campaign to strangle the Italian Publishing Co. and *Il Bollettino* which informs our readers of all their shady actions against Italy and fascism, in Italy and abroad."

In its typical style, the paper intended to imply more than it said as is suggested by the parenthesis round a word in the phrase "(secret) deliberation." There was nothing secret about either the deliberation or the decision taken; Mr. Cohen wrote to anyone who happened to do business with the Italian Publishing Company. The Salada Tea Company was the last to remove its advertisement from *Il Bollettino* perhaps as a consequence of a letter that Secretary Cohen sent to the firm's advertising agent, Mr. Thornton Purkis.[119]

At the same time that the *Catholic Register* condemned pagan fascism and the Jews carried on their boycott, most Italian Canadians, including a very patriotic association, dissociated themselves from *Il Bollettino*'s suicidal anti-Semitic course. The defection of Italian Canadians reached even to the core of local fascism once it was clear that Italy had broken away from her traditional friendship with England. In fact, some local fascists even sent a telegram to Mussolini begging him to break away from German domination and to stick with England.[120]

The powerful Lodge Ontario of the Order Sons of Italy gave voice to the growing resentment in the Order in a motion in which the Lodge condemned anti-Semitism:

> WHEREAS the anti-Semitic policy of the fascist Government is neither approved by the Italian people nor by the Italians abroad and it is particularly despised by the Italians in Canada . . . the Lodge Ontario protests in the most energetic manner against such a policy of persecution and condemns a certain Italian press in Canada that sustains and expresses anti-Semitic sentiments. The Lodge Ontario condemns also the principle on which religious and racial hatred is based. Being aware that Italians in Canada are themselves a national minority and some day they might

become victims of such principles, the Lodge Ontario REAFFIRMS once again its will and purpose to live in harmony and peace with all the nationalities which make up the Canadian population, regardless of race, religion and language.[121]

Moreover, some Italian-Canadian professional and business people now took a stand against fascism. The manifesto published in the first issue of the anti-fascist *Voce degli italo-canadesi* was signed by many influential patrons from Toronto, Hamilton, and Montreal.[122]

Reacting to the isolation, *Il Bollettino* accused those who challenged fascist authority of being communists. This charge was most effective before the Ethiopian war, but after the war such a charge in the fascist paper become meaningless since *Il Bollettino* used it blindly: *The Toronto Daily Star, The Globe and Mail,* Mayor Day of Toronto ("Is Mayor Day a Communist, or is he paid by . . . ?"[123]), Reverend Domenico Gualtieri, and many others were all labelled as communists or communist supporters! Others, like Giuseppe Ricci, founder of Lancia and Bravo Pasta Factory, cut the weak link they had had with the fascist Dopolavoro. In his autobiography, Ricci wrote:

> Our firm had a four-man bocce team participating in a tournament sponsored by the Società Dopolavoro . . . At the end of the tournament [in the summer of the 1938] in which our team came second . . . we returned home. From then on, we never participated in the Dopolavoro's activities nor did we go to Casa d'Italia.[124]

By the summer of 1939, the winds of war were blowing. The hopes that Italy would revitalize her friendship with

England had vanished and the Mussolini-Hitler axis had produced the "Steel Pact." *Il Bollettino* and *L'Italia nuova* had become shadows of those golden years, when publicity, the fascist grants, and a growing readership had seemed to promise a great future. With a reduced number of pages, a dwindling readership, and almost no advertising and with an identity crisis even within the fascist ranks, the papers were moribund. Once in a while, they expressed their frustration in outbursts of bombastic hallucinations of superpower:

> Fascism, *il Duce,* Italy are too great and powerful to need us to defend them against vulgar provocateurs and subtle, shady political meddlers. We defend ourselves by speaking of Italy's present greatness which is greater than what it was in the past, albeit it had been very great.[125]

In September 1939, the German invasion of Poland was the last blow to the black-shirt press, bringing it to its knees. Its final demise occurred on 10 June 1940, when Mussolini declared war on France and England and by extension, on Canada. As an employee of the Italian Consulate, Tommaso Mari was repatriated.

His colleagues at *Il Bollettino, L'Eco,* and *L'Italia nuova* were taken to security camps. Attilio Perilli, in the camp at Petawawa where Italian Canadian fascists were interned, gave life to a ghost; he produced an underground edition of *Il Bollettino*.[126] He gathered news from newspapers and radio, and hearsay and rumours brought in by those inmates who went to work outside of the compound. With the help of a "second-hand typewriter and carbon paper," he put together *Il Bollettino,* making as many copies as there were barracks: twelve. In the evening, it was read aloud in those same barracks, before inmates went to sleep.[127] In the first months of internment, the underground *Bollettino* helped to keep alive the dream, or rather the illusion that Mussolini would do to France and England what he had done to Ethiopia. As the months went by and the years lapsed, that mirage faded away and with it Perilli's phantom *Bollettino,* the last vestige of the Italian-Canadian fascist newspapers.

Epilogue

We have followed the route of the Italian-Canadian fascist press from its first attempts in the 1920s to success and decadence in 1930s, and its demise in the early 1940s. This trajectory follows the reception fascism received in Canada and in the English-speaking world in general; that is to say, in Britain, the United States of America, and Australia. The Ethiopian war was the turning point for the Protestant and lay people in English-speaking Canada. Many Roman Catholics remained staunch supporters of fascism throughout the Ethiopian campaign and during the Spanish Civil War. Both fascism and the Roman Catholic Church remained side by side fighting — according to the propaganda of the time — against slavery in Abyssinia and bolshevism in Spain, in defence of Western civilization.

However, when Mussolini decided to introduce anti-Semitic measures in Italy to harmonize his policy with that of his German allies, the Roman Catholic Church became alarmed. In nazi Germany there had been a pagan revival and many priests and bishops had been beaten or jailed. In Italy, the anti-Semitic measures prohibited marriage between (Aryan) Italians and Jewish Italians, modifying the 1929 Concordat which had given the Church legal power over marriage. But above all the anti-Jewish measures challenged the Church's basic postulate which was and is that all human beings are children of God and, therefore, siblings.

These practical and theoretical confrontations added to the perennial controversy between fascism and the Church over the movement known as Catholic Action, through which the Church claimed the right to educate Italian youth. Pope Pius XI took a firm stand against the Italian government's racial legislation, awakening within the Roman Catholic Church a current of thought which opposed fascism. Before the Pope's outspoken criticism and because of the official position of the Church on fascism, anti-fascist Roman Catholics felt inhibited, if not muzzled, in their efforts to criticise and oppose fascism and its agents. When they were released by the Pope's stand, anti-fascist Catholics became confident and vocal. Hence, in Canada, a strong opposition was mounted against fascism by both the Roman Catholic anglophone clergy and their parishioners. In the tense political atmosphere highlighted by the impending war, *L'Italia, Il Bollettino,* and *L'Eco* became increasingly isolated until they lost their only remaining powerful allies in the middle of 1938.

Were those Italian Canadians who stood by these newspapers until the end, only expressing their patriotism as the interlocutor, who was mentioned in the forward, maintained? Certainly, if "patriotism" was involved it must have been a very perverted sentiment which trampled on every human value, freedom and decency. A sound conservative, Henry Corti (Enrico Corticelli), who stood firmly against local fascists, warned both the Consul General Luigi Petrucci and his hot-headed cohorts of the dear consequence of importing fascism to Canada and among the Italian Canadians.

Commenting on a speech that Consul Petrucci delivered at a banquet given to him by fascists and World War One veterans, Corti pointed out the anachronistic situation in which Canadians of Italian origin would find themselves in — as they actually did in June 1940 — if they joined fascism or any other association depending from a foreign power. Addressing the consul, he wrote:

> You ask and demand that we shall be . . . loyal to fascism and its leader, though you know that we swore loyalty to the British Crown . . . Your and your satellites' task aims, as you have announced, to make of Italians abroad fascist recruits, followers of a party which is perhaps the best in the world, but as Canadian citizens we cannot be members of a party whose principle, good or bad whatever, are foreign to our new country . . . We have taken an oath of allegiance to Canada, a representative democracy, and we . . . cannot take a new oath to an authority which in the future may be on the opposite side of our new country.[1]

He concluded this lucid editorial by addressing the presidents and officers of the Italian Canadian associations in general; though, he had in mind the officers of the Order Sons of Italy. "Regarding our Associations," he wrote, "a good number of them are legally constituted and would become illegal every time they pass at the dependence of fascism for, whether the Italian consul wants to admit or not, fascism as an institution emanating from a foreign government is illegal in Canada."[2]

Hard-core fascists were deaf to these reasonable words inspired by realism and continued blindly to follow Mussolini's slogan "we'll forge ahead." This led them to the Petawawa internment camp.

There was, however, among Italian Canadian fascist ranks and their supporters some frustration with events unfolding from 1938 on. Mussolini's alliance with Hitler and consequent breaking away from France and Great Britain created fear and resentment among some fascists and their supporters, in the two main communities of Montreal and Toronto.[3] This resentment was never as openly expressed as it was in British Columbia. In Vancouver, for example, leading figures like Angelo Branca initiated a movement to re-assert the Italian Canadians' loyalty to their adopted country and to defend them from mounting Italophobia. A similar initiative was taken by Italian left-wing groups. Of this, however, we shall speak in a forthcoming book on the Italian Canadian anti-fascist press.

In Ontario and Quebec, unsatisfied fascists and their friends did not find the strength and courage to openly oppose Mussolini's policy and challenge the consuls' authority — consuls were revered far beyond what their offices warranted and what they personally deserved. The unsatisfied fascists did not dare to take a stand and expose themselves one way or the other. In Toronto, for example, when, in 1939, Massimo Jacopo Magi resigned, the new leader of the Fàscio Principe Umberto became Ruggero Bacci, a worker, because "no one, among the professionals, including the five local physicians (R. Invidiata, D. Sansone, P. Fontanella, G. Glionna, and Scandiffio) who were best equipped to lead, accepted the office."[4] Dissidents in the Montreal fascio sent Mussolini a telegram, begging him to remain an ally of Italy's traditional friends, France and Great Britain. This wishy-washy position became a good alibi which helped many of petit bourgeois professionals to get out of the internment camp as soon as their case was heard by a judge.

Supporting the short-sighted and arrogant editorial policy of *L'Eco, L'Italia nuova,* and *Il Bollettino,* there were the hard-core fascists who believed that Mussolini would do to France and England what he had done to Ethiopia. This was not too hard to believe considering the war situation of 1940: continental Europe was occupied by the axis troops; and England was under the menace of invasion. The fifth column fear, sweeping Canada and the other English-speaking nations, was a convincing proof that nazi-fascism was about to dominate the world.

These hard-core fascists were proud to be taken to the concentration camp when on 10 June 1940 the RCMP rounded up about 600 Italian Canadians. Pictures show some of them smiling as the police are taking them away. Their naive and insolent smiles reveal their blind faith in Mussolini, whom they thought to be the infallible Duce, as was asserted by the fascist press in general and the local one in particular. Apropos of the *Duce infallibile* (infallible Duce), *L'Italia nuova* once wrote: "In the supreme hour, it is beautiful to give up thinking and believe in the Duce as one believes in God."[5] The belief that Mussolini soon would win the war, free the internees from the constraints of the camp, proclaim them heroes, and compensate them for their courageous stand, was shared by many faithful fascist internees in their first months at the Petawawa camp. The following passage from an internee's letter, which is dated 7 October 1940 and addressed to his wife in Toronto, clearly expresses this common belief:

> Dear E. . . . Be calm, when the war is over, my *avvocato* (lawyer), who has no equal throughout the Americas, will

settle all accounts and you can be sure that he knows how to do it.[6]

In an interview, this internee said that he used the word *avvocato* (lawyer) instead of Mussolini in order to evade censorship; and, certainly, in the context its meaning is obvious and clear.

Further, in looking at the essential elements of fascist policy toward Italians abroad a disturbing element becomes clear. The two peoples most despised by fascists were Jews and Anglo-Saxons. Fascists and nationalists in particular accused Jews of being a supra-national people, of placing Judaism above the country in which they were born and had been living, for many generations. The sense of brotherhood amongst Jews, which was more than religion and rather a strong sense of belonging to each other as a people, disturbed fascists and nationalists: "Mussolini can only strike the Jews in Italy, while the Jews can retaliate from every corner of the globe."[7] At the same time, fascists tried to emulate the Jews in the realm of national identity by attempting to create among emigrants (or Italians abroad), including the third and fourth generations, a sense of belonging to Italy. The *"Colonie estive, marine e montane"* (mountain and seashore Summer camping) which, the Italian government sponsored every year throughout the 1930s, gathered tens of thousands of youths, boys and girls, from all over the world each year in Italy in an effort to make them feel part of and belonging to the new Italy. (See appendix No. 14 for the effect of such camping experience on a young Italian-Canadian woman.)

Further, the fascist press continuously instilled in the minds of emigrants and their offspring the idea that they were guests in and not an integral part of Canada. Ironically, their emphasis on the idea of belonging elsewhere was exactly what they accused Jews of. A charge which was closely associated with betrayal. This was the essence of Paolo Orano's book, *Gli ebrei in Italia,* of 1937: "Since the [Jewish] communities are allowed, they cannot have any other activity, but the practice of religion. Only fascism teaches and proclaims who are the great men, who are the wise ones, the sages, the heroes, and the deserving people for every Italian. The *Patria* is unique and does not admit adulteries."[8]

In regard to the British, fascism and Mussolini envied and despised the sense of superiority displayed by their upper and middle classes. At the same time, fascist propaganda tried to make Italians feel superior. In reality, Italians in general, and emigrants in particular, did not feel that they were a part of a superior race. Because of their long history of submission to foreign domination, they identified with the poor and the oppressed as they themselves had always been. Notwithstanding the official rhetoric for which he was often directly responsible, Mussolini, in private, despised his compatriots for this attitude, as Indro Montanelli has recently pointed out in the *Corriere della sera*. He wrote that when "Flandrin, who had been for few day in Italy, went to say good bye to Mussolini, the French guest lamented that fascists behaved like masters with the Italian people. And Mussolini, who from the balcony called the Italians a people of heroes, navigators and Saints, answered him thus: 'How else one can behave with a population of servants.'"[9] On the other hand the British, who had experienced centuries of democracy and had a long history of colonial successes, felt confident that they were entrusted with a mission towards other peoples and nations. Mussolini and fascists, especially those coming from the nationalist movement, attempted to instill in all Italians but particularly in the country's emigrants a sense of national superiority. They did so with the aid of the myth of ancient Roman glory, strength, and power which Italians were supposed to have inherited. "You are the new Roman legions," Cesare Maccari said to the Italians of Hamilton, Ontario, who went to hear him speak.[10]

Consciously or unconsciously, this was the policy that the Italian-Canadian fascist press actively pursued throughout its existence. Each of the three newspapers we have studied presents a different approach to the implementation of this policy. *L'Eco* was the most moderate of the three, while *Il Bollettino* was the most extreme, bold, and reckless. This and the wishy-washy position of the community's petit bourgeois leaders probably explains why on 10 June 1940, in Ontario and in Toronto, where *Il Bollettino* was widely distributed, the reaction against Italians was the "most truculent," whereas in the Western provinces "reports of violence directed at Italians were non-existent."[11]

The nightmarish fascist experience among Italian Canadians as it appeared in the local fascist press was perceived either as a nationalist *ubriacatura* (intoxication)[12] by Reverend Gualtieri or as "a nice [patriotic] dream" by an unrepentant fascist.[13] These interpretations still persist and divide Canadians of Italian origin.

APPENDICES

APPENDIX NO 1

L'ITALIA, 7 JUNE 1924.
COLONIAL PROBLEMS:
OPPOSING FACTIONS IN THE ORDER SONS OF ITALY.

The harmonious understanding that reigned among us, leading the community to progress and social affirmation, has been replaced by a fractious spirit which brings within the Order, one against the other, two hostile tendencies and two different aspirations. Some people call this contrast Italy versus anti-Italy; others call it futurism and passivity.

It is time for the members to decide if the Order should be a socio-political-patriotic institution or, on the other hand, a large and empty mutual benefit association which simply looks after sickness and mortuary benefits.

The constitution states that the intention of the founders of the Order was to create a patriotic institution. In our opinion, then, the Order, because it is a collective and eminently political association, should impose above all the concept and the cult of the Fatherland. This should, however, be done without invading the field of the militant political parties and by respecting all members' beliefs and differing opinions.

To this end, the Order should prepare, help, and stimulate Italians to become Canadian citizens, in order to use their votes for the affirmation of our community.

There are some people who would like to see the Order become an instrument of fascist propaganda. Others would give their soul away a thousand times in order not to hear the cry of Evviva Mussolini. And a third group, which has no personal view, is attracted and repulsed by the one or the other, from right and from left, in a confusion of ideas, proposals, and odd resolutions which moves the onlooker to pity.

Some members remonstrated against the Supreme Venerable and the Supreme Orator, Liborio Lattoni, because they saluted in the Roman [fascist] manner and allowed the band to intone [the fascist song]

Giovinezza during the inauguration of the Order's Grand Lodge of Quebec.

For the celebration of Mazzini's anniversary, which shall take place on next 22 June [1924] at Ville Émard, other members have already ordered the band not to play the Royal March or any other hymns which might offend the hyper-sensitive soul of those without a Fatherland [anarchists] and provoke disorder. Is there a reason for the existence of an Order which is deprived of its patriotic virility and made an eunuch by subtle subterfuge of those few intriguers who, perhaps unknowingly, are victims of ideas that are hatched at night by internationalist Jews?

It is the Order's duty to launch heavenward with faith and enthusiasm the loud and vibrant cry glorifying that man [Mussolini] and to sing the Italian national hymn in his honour. It is its duty to cry with all its strength Viva Mussolini! . . . That someone should believe that he can not agree with this or that others should want to make the Order a field of communist manoeuvring are questions which the membership should deal with once and for all.

Appendix No 2

L'Italia, 7 March 1936.
ALWAYS AHEAD

The Italians in Canada should be proud because, through the voice of their leader, the representative of the Royal Government in Canada, they have proclaimed in this part of the world that the ignominious sanctions would not stop the Italian people from its destined goal. They also denounced the League of Nations for being an active instrument of those nations which, being well fed, pretend to freeze humanity in the present state.

The persons involved are secondary to this loud protest against attempts to strangle Italy and relegate her to the role of a small power.

Even the person of the Canadian Prime Minister becomes secondary. In order to please the international social democracy, the Masonic anti-Catholics and anti-Italians and his friend, the poor leader of the CCF (a party which stands between socialism and Bolshevism or the second and third international), the Prime Minister attacked the man whose duty was to point out to sound Canadian citizens the injustice against Italy and the dangers involved in these perpetrations. We Italian Canadians do not hold a grudge against the Hon. Mackenzie King who certainly cannot ignore the formidable influence of the English and anti-fascist propaganda that overwhelms this country. Unintentionally, however, he rendered a great service to our cause by bringing to the country's attention our protest against the sanctions.

Though the Canadian Press, which is clearly and completely subjected to English and masonic interests, tried to place on a second plane the anti-sanction and anti-League speech of last sunday, the large Canadian public has learned that someone raised in this county a voice against the inequity of the sanctions and, maybe for the first time, can earnestly question if it wouldn't be better for Canada to free herself from her obligation towards the Geneva Society and, taking a North American view, support that Pan-America policy which is promoted by President Roosevelt.

This would break the propaganda circle and the interests that control the press and the Clubs of this country which keep Canadians ignorant of the real scope of the League of Geneva, masking their intentions with humanitarian theories in the name of international justice.

We, Italo-Canadians, are happy to have made our modest contribution to the great cause which Italy is fighting for in the world, the triumph of the true civilization which must be based on a superior sense of International justice.

While as every day passes, our army adds new glory to a preceding one. Our soldiers now have no enemy before them except the hardship of the inaccessible African land. We must intensify our struggle against the social-democratic enemy that tries, with all its power, to take from us the fruits of our victory. Our enemy is insidious because it prevents people from learning the true reasons which led Italy to undertake this hard trial.

It is necessary to illuminate for foreigners the ideal beauty of this great civilizing task that Italy has undertaken with enormous sacrifices.

Courage brothers, the masses of sound-thinking citizens, the respectable people, shall be with us even in Canada.

Appendix No 3

L'Italia, 16 October 1937.
LOCAL POLITICS

This is an argument which requires a long discussion and we must, by necessity, return to it in order to clarify our ideas before reaching a definite conclusion.

For the time being, let us confine ourselves to some general observations. Right from the start, let us state that we have no political ambitions. Our task and aspirations are not in this thorny field in which, we believe, only young Italian Canadians should compete. Being born and educated in this Canadian land, their way of thinking makes the young generation best qualified to represent us in the municipal, provincial, and federal assemblies.

But the paper — as an organ of public opinion and as an expression of the collective sentiment — has the duty to tackle certain issues even if, during this disinterested action of clarification, it must go against some electoral interests or tread on someone's toes.

We affirm the Italians' actions in every field and even, naturally, in the political one which has an extraordinary importance for the activity of the Italian community.

Our situation in relation to the Canadian political movement is not rosy.

We do not have a serious, efficient, and powerful organization. The Italian Canadian voters are disoriented, dispersed, ill-treated. Politicians when they need use them by employing some prominent people who take personal advantage of the situation. They create groups and gangs in this or that Ward to serve the cause of Councillor X or M. P. Y. The results are minimal, insignificant, and sometimes even negative.

Everything must be done again. We must start from scratch. We must create a solid foundation on which we can build, piece by piece, the Italian Canadian political organization which is independent, strong, disciplined, and uniting all.

We must find the courage to eliminate those amateurish politicians and lackeys who want to represent everyone but represent nothing.

The Italian Canadian voting mass must have a central and single direction by which talented and noble-hearted leaders are chosen; they are the ones who, because of their prestige, trust and consensus in the community, have the highest possibility of success.

Only in this way are we able to create amongst the masses of hard-working Italian Canadians a trust which has been lacking until now. In the past, interplay between parties and competition among candidates attempted to capture the Italian votes without considering the collective interest.

Appendix No 4

Il Bollettino, 5 January 1934.
I LUDI CARTACEI (THE PAPER GAMES) OF MONDAY.

Last Monday municipal elections revealed once again that these Ludi cartacei are a mirage for the wretched masses searching for relief from today's misery.

Fraud against the most needy part of the society is always the dominant note of every election.

Men of moral rectitude are disgusted to see the many deceits which are carried out during an election. It disgusts them to see the so highly praised principles of democracy trampled on. It disgusts them to see the electoral herd which passively follows any leader holding a jingling bell.

The electoral herd passes silently and mute and with lowered heads as though it were a funeral procession. The shepherd with his stick in hands and crossed arms says to himself: "You have grazed enough on the meagre field, you have enough in your belly to give me milk and wool, so vile a herd rushes to your fold." Barking and arrogant politicians dog the herd's steps. They bite the sheep who dare to lift their heads, even if it is to express their satisfaction. They run and bark for no other reason than to justify their work as the pall-bearers in a funeral.

There are people who dare to call this scene the "march of freedom." It is a march of slaves who are exchanged between masters.

We have seen the masters of the CCF consort with the conservatives; conservative leaders share out their spoils; communists (even if they call themselves differently) litigate with socialists. The press without character, dignity and decorum serves. Who? Public interests? Ohibo? It is pretending too much. It serves the more or less confessable interests of more or less obscure gangs or clients. This is called freedom of the Press. If someone tries to bring the translation of this article to the local daily papers (people with a small brain do it often) you'll see whether they dare to protest. Not on your life, "Their order is to snore."

Political degradation has reached this lowest stage. We are living in a period of complete decadence of the democratic institutions, which does not mean that these institutions theoretically cannot be good, no. They have degenerated. We have exceeded in the basic principle of democracy. This excess created evil. If you drink daily, a little it does not harm you; but if you drink too much even once in a while it damages your organs.

We are witnessing the ruin of democracy as it was conceived and practised in the last century. Now it is necessary to create a new democracy — a democracy which is strong, energetic, vital, and just — one that truly guards people's interest, the real interests and not the mirage, the ghosts, the dust of drugs which stupefies you like opium stupefies the Chinese.

We must go toward the people without election: we must go to the people to assist them, and guide them, and feed them without promising the garden of Eden which is, by now, lost without a trace. Nor must we go towards people with the dictatorship of the proletariat which is nothing else but the same yoke by a different name.

It is necessary that the people give those who lead them their support. People must trust its leaders. Force must be used only infrequently and only temporarily. Then, it is necessary that people give its consent to the leaders. Consent is not expressed with the arithmetic of election numbers, no. If my vote or consent is so great and strong that it allows me to endure any sacrifice, then it is not right that my vote is worth as much as the vote of a drunkard who does not even know how to read the names of the candidates but goes to vote anyway because someone put a piece of paper in his hands.

No! My vote is a more precious commodity and I have the right to ask for a higher price. This is the democracy of the chosen; the democracy in which the best men are chosen to lead the people and to provide for the needs of a nation.

To this type of democracy people adhere enthusiastically. They choose it because they are aware that with facts the leaders work for its moral and material well-being.

T. M. [Tommaso Mari]

Appendix No 5

Il Bollettino, 8 June 1934.

THE DOMINANT ELECTION NOTE

In the Ontario electoral campaign, the dominant note of this week is the news that forty CCF candidates are ready to contest the election and another twenty-five will be ready shortly.

This news has been received with joy by the rank and file of the Conservative Party and with disgust by the Liberals.

The Liberals have based their campaign on the need to change the provincial administration and re-organize the deplorable conditions of Ontario's affairs. If a third party gets into the race it divides those who want a change and diminishes their possibility of success, giving advantage to those who are for the status quo, the conservatives.

Ontario has never had a struggle as fierce and decisive as this one ending on June 19th.

By dividing the unsatisfied voters, the pseudo-socialist CCF, an indefinite and incongruent party, plays in the hands of the conservatives who through this move see their possibility of a victory tremendously increased. Is there a secret accord between conservatives and CCF? It would surprise no one. In politics, power grabbing has become a speculative transaction as at the stock-exchange: the immoral principle "business is business" applies even to elections.

Nominating candidates even in those ridings where they have no chance to win, the CCF knows that it helps the Conservative Party. These signs of political corruption soil further the CCF's tainted reputation. However, no one is surprised. The CCF behaves as a pseudo-socialist party does. What surprises, instead, and provokes the disgust of sound-thinking persons is this Party's pretension to save Canada from the ruin in which Conservatives are leading it, though the CCF itself is instrumental in helping them.

The leaders of the CCF would profit from studying the history of Rome and learn from the lives of the Gracchi's.

We are witnessing intriguers plotting a classic political manoeuvre.

There is a want of political as well as social consciousness. This creates an ambiguous situation while a most shameful deceit is consumed. The June 19th election will once again reveal that elections are an enormous fraud which the leading classes perpetrate against the population.

By lending itself to this deception, the CCF betrays the workers for the second time — the first time was at the [founding] Regina Congress. From a third party people expect a moral and material resurrection. They have received, instead, a shameful and atrocious deceit.

The dawn of a Canadian resurrection is too far away yet; though its first signals might be seen in some nationalist candidates of Northern Ontario. They affirm that between the Conservatives who are supported by England, the Liberals who are supported by the United States, and the CCF which is supported by Russia and, maybe, even Japan, should rise a party supported by Canada.

Politics is a strange affair: in the habit of favouring one or the other foreign powers, Canada is forgotten.

Appendix No 6

Il Bollettino, 23 November 1934.
THE ROYAL VICE CONSUL'S MANIFESTO TO TORONTO'S ITALIANS

I publish today the first list of pledges that I have collected for the Casa d'Italia which will soon be built in Toronto.

The sum pledged represents an eloquent response to those who are still sceptics of the outcome of this splendid initiative.

I feel it is my duty to thank and applaud those who first supported the idea and I signal them to be admired by all of Toronto's Italians.

I am certain that they are followed by all those countrymen who have kept intact the cult of their Patria of origin and whose names may appear on the next list.

All the people listed have participated with large and small sums of money or days of work and building material. Thus, the Casa d'Italia of Toronto will soon be a reality and a splendid monument, a symbol of the patriotic passion of our race.

FIRST LIST OF PLEDGES

ITALIAN Government $5,000.00
FASCIO of Toronto $1,000.00
Ass. Na. COMBATTENTI $150.00
BACCI Ruggero $20.00
BADALI Giovanni $100.00
BADALI Salvatore $10.00
BADALIS S. $100.00
BERNARDO MICHELE $500.0
BIFOLCHI Domenico $15.00
BREGLIA Achille e Gentilina $100.00
BRUNETTI Mariano $10.00
CIRA Joe $200.00
CAMASTA Francesco $1.00
CANZANO Carmela $5.00
CARUSO Guglielmo $10.00
CARUSO Umberto $10.00
CIARFELLA Raffaele $20.00
CIAMPOLILLO Luigi $20.00
COMELLA Giacomo $50.00
DI CRESCE Domenico $5.00
DILILLO Nicolantonio $12.00

LAUDADIO Romolo $20.00
MAGI J. Massimo $1,000.00
MANDALFINO Antonio $10.00
MICLET Arnaldo $100.00
MORANDI Luigi $10.00
MISSORI Marco $50.00
MORANDI Pietro $12.00
ORLANDO Maria $100.00
ORLANDO Eliseo $200.00
PALANGE Pasquale $200.00
PANTALEO Felice $10.00
PAOLUCCI Domenico $25.00
PARISI Giuseppe $50.00
POLENTA Romano $20
PETRUCCIANI Gino $25.00
PORTOGHESE Giuseppe $25.00
QUARANTA. Pasquale $50.00
RE Frank $50.00
REZZA G. $25.00
RUFFO Raffaele $25.00
ROMEO Francesco $25.00

DE BIASIO Angelo $20.00
DARRIGO Stefano $25.00
DE RUBERTIS Mario $50.00
DELL'ANGELO Vittorio $10.00
D'AMICO Alfonso $10.00
V. F. $15,000,00
FREDIANI Francesco $50.00
FIORAVANTI Eugenio $25.00
GUERRA Domenico $20.00
GRITTANI Nicola $20.00
GATTO Antonio $200.00
GRITTANI Giambattista $25.00
GRITTANI Giuseppe $500.00
INVIDIATA Dott. Rosario $100.00
LIMA Pietro $50.00
LIVORIA Giovanni $2.00
LONGO Giuseppe $10.00

SANSONE, Dot.Donato $100.00
SCANDIFFIO Raffaele $50.00
SPERAPANI Ruggero $60.00
SAVOIA Giovanni $100.00
SUBRANNI Nicola $25.00
SCANGA Francesco $30.00
SAVOIA Egle $30.00
SCOCCIA Mariano $5.00
TEOLIS Angelo $20.00
TOMASICCHIO Giuseppe $200.00
TEDESCO Giuseppe $50.00
TOMASONI Antonio $10.00
TROMBETTA Michele $25.00
VINCE Rocco $50.00
VALOPPI Augusto $50.00
VATTOLO Corrado $20.00

Totale Prima-lista 26,307.00

WORK-DAY PLEDGES

Teolis Angelo $380.00 in painting and decoration work
Quattroviocchi Luigi 6 days of work
Bacci Giuseppe 6 days of work
Lavoria Giovanni 12 ' '
De Blasio Angelo 6 ' '
Cappuccietti Agos. 6 ' '
Rosano Giuseppe 12 ' '
D'Amato Giovanni 6 ' '
Muraca Antonio 6 ' '
Ianniziello Anton. 6 ' '
Notari Giuseppe 6 ' '
Bianchi Antonio 6 ' '
Amendola Salvatore 6' '
Mizzoni Giovanni 12 ' '

Cuscania Emanuele 10 days
Cialo Luigi 10 ' '
Aloisi Antonio 10 '
Belisario Donato 6 '
Dini Arduino 6 ' '
Fava Ulderino 6 ' '
Fava Guido 6 ' '
Missori Alessandro 6 '
Pinto Bernardino 12 '
Vizzaccaro Orazio 6 '
Zanussi Giuseppe 6 '
Carollo Prof. Pietro art work
Danese Primo art work plaster

Appendix No 6A

Il Bollettino, 21 December 1934.
SECOND LIST OF PLEDGES PRO-CASA D'ITALIA

We publish the second list of the Italians who had pledged to contribute for the Casa d'Italia.

After the Christmas and New Year holidays, the campaign will start again with renewed impetus.

Every passing day, the number of those who understand the usefulness of the magnificent task undertaken by the Italian colony is growing and the enthusiasm for the assured success grows as well.

Amount of the preceding list $ 26,307.00

Ferrari G. $20.00	Goggio Prof. Cav. Emilio $100.00	
Vistorino Vincenzo $500.00	Molinaro Pasquale $10.00	
Turano Salvatore $100.00	Scorsone Vincenzo $100.00	
Culotta Leonardo $25.00		
Collected by Mr. R. Ciarfella		
Lupo Gioacchino $20.00	Nicoletti Marino $5.00	$25.00
Collected by Mr. G. Parisi		
Basilio Nino $5.00	F. D'Onofrio $18.00	
B. Gismondi $5.00		$28.00
Collected by Mr. Valoppi		
Guglielmo Biagio $2.00	Contini Fioravanti $20.00	
Stoangi Augusto $20.00	Lucciola G. $15.00	
Frank Mora $10.00	Contini Tommaso $25.00	
Verdon A. $10.00	Conzanese Joe $10.00	
Medora G. $10.00	Zeppieri R. $5.00	
Binelli M. $5.00	Calci Bernardino $5.00	$137.00
Collected by Mr. R. Scandiffio		
Schiralli V. $5.00	Volpe Francesco $25.00	
Cavalluzzo G. $5.00		$35.00

Collected by Mrs. Orlando
Campagna G. $5.00   Di Pietro J. $12.00
Laiola Teresa $15.00 $32.00

Collected by Badali, Lima & Comella
Sanci Sam $50.00   Cusimano S. $25.00   Liotta Vincenzo $25.00
Amodio Sam $25.00   Comella Ant. $20.00   Calderone S. $20.00
Battaglia Joe $10.00   Comella S. $10.00   Grimaldi Santo $10.00
Amodeo Ant. $10.00   Zucchero Gius. $10.00   Cusimano Gius. $10.00
Amodeo Agostino $10.00
                                                          $235.00

Calderone F., Badali Leo, Scolaro Giacomo, Concilla Agostino, Mannoni
Sam, Gioffré Joe $5.00 each $30.00

Collected by the Ontario Lodge, O.F.d'I.
Ontario Lodge $60.00   Sguigna Dante $60.00   Velocci Isidoro $60.00
Zambri Teodoro $50.00   Mari Tommaso $50.00
Rev. Sauro Libero $25.00   Gianvecchio Rocco $25.00   Costarella N. $12.00
Mandalfino R. $12.00   Grieco Francesco $10.00   Tammaro S. $5.00
Iona Giuseppe $5.00   Grieco F. fu Pietro $2.00   Iagallo Giacinto $0.25

                                                          $426.25

                                        Total Collection $28,126.25

Pledge of Working Days

Collected by Mr. Valloppi
Conforzi Pietro 20 bags of cement   Innocenti R. 1 week work
Formenti Abramo 1 week work   Michelin Walter 1 week work
Colautti Domenico 1 week work   Toboni Giulio 1 week work
Snoidero Carlo 1 week work   Colacci Angelo 1 week work
Fafaretto F. 1 week work   Guerra Angelo 1 week work
De Nino P. 2 days work   Colamartin S. 1 week work
Ciambini G., building material for $50.00 value.
Tambosso A., tile work with two workers for $100.00 value.
Collected by Mr. R. Scandiffio
Regina G. building material for the value of $25.00
Morra L. 5 days of work   Risimini O. 5 days of work
Curletta Angelo 1 week of work   Guadagno Dominic 1 week of work
Angelony Tony 2 weeks of work
Collected by the O.F. d'Italia
Lo Franco M. 1 week work with a truck   Iacovino P. 1 week of work
Di Falco Domenico 1 week of work   Collected by P. Parisi
A. Romano 2 days of work   L. Perfetti 1 week of work

APPENDIX No 7

IL BOLLETTINO, 10 APRIL 1936.

SALUTE TO THE VOLUNTARY COMRADES

The desired number of Italians living in foreign lands who enrolled for the East-African campaign has been reached and no more volunteers will be accepted. These volunteers manned two black-shirt legions, which are now on the front-line ready to fight. The large enlistment of Italians living abroad manifests in all its splendour their patriotism; and reveals their awakened sentiment of devotion and solidarity towards the Patria. Italians wherever they live have understood the importance of the historical moment and the civilizing mission that Italy is undertaking.

At the front, our black-shirts who came from foreign lands are organized in two legions — 221st and 321st — and they will certainly prove their patriotism and their bravery.

Even the Italians of Toronto are represented there.

Many more would have desired to serve their Patria; however, they did not have the privilege of being accepted.

While we send a salute with our heart full of emotion and pride to those who are at the front, we say to those who could not join our fighting comrades that they should be proud and feel satisfied for having nourished and expressed such virile purpose and for which they have the recognition of all the con-nationals living in Canada and of the Italian Royal Authorities.

Appendix No 8

Il Bollettino, 8 May 1936.
ETHIOPIA IS ITALIAN

We Are There and There We Will Stay
— The Worst to Those Who Touch Us.

Italians, Victory Is Ours!

That which the military experts of every country of the world considered to be an impossible task was accomplished by the Legions of Rome.

The Black shirts and the young eagles, the *bersaglieri*, the infantrymen and light cavalry, with the help of the valorous colonial troops — Ascaris, Dubats, and Libyans — have began where the legions of the Roman Empire had left off and have gone beyond, reaching the Ethiopian plateaus which ancient Romans had never conquered.

Led by Badoglio's and Graziani's military genius and by expert commanders of the army corps, they have accomplished in the course of seven short months what the Pharaohs and all the successive conquerors could not accomplish in millennia.

At this moment our humble, grateful, and reverent thoughts go to those who fell on the battle field with the name of Italy on their lips, the image of our tricolour in their eyes, and the vision of our strength and unfailing victory in their strong hearts.

Let us not forget that this was done despite the usual Nations which, jealous of our greatness, did everything to torture the Italian people. Had those Nations not organized and instructed the savage Abyssinian tribes with their officers and agents and had they not given them moral and financial help and furnished them even with Dum Dum bullets, much of our loss would have been spared. Were it not for these Nations, which encouraged the fury of our barbarian adversaries, many of our brothers would have been alive today.

But their sacrifice has not been and will not be futile!

Fifty millions of Italian hearts who live within the country and abroad intone today the paean of victory, hymn of joy, and song of gratitude.

Joy and gratitude because their unshaken faith in their Leader has been justly recompensed, because their sacrifices and their inexpressible passion has today obtained the hardly contended reward.

It is not only a victory against the Abyssinian hordes and against the natural obstacles of the land which contrasted the proceeding of our legions.

It is a victory against the long history of domination and abuse of power which Italy had to endure throughout the centuries. This fascist Italy allows NEVER AGAIN.

It is a victory against the tortuous sophism and the jealous objections of self-declared judges of international morality who hide themselves on the shores of a Swiss lake; it is a victory against the POLICEMEN that protect the store-room (*dispenza*) of the wealthy nations; it is a victory against shady international congregations which — disguised in clownish religious, masonic, or communist costumes — have always in the centuries stood in the way of our Motherland and have strangled her development and taken away the fruits of her victories and of her sons' hard labour.

With this victory of the new Italy, the complicated and unstable structure of those decrepit institutions is collapsing.

The first powerful blow to bring down the disfigured face of the family of Nations has been made by the pick of the man who towers over friends and enemy alike, the creator of that faith that has transformed Italians into heroes or saints, the man for whom the crowds cheer in our sunny piazzas filled with flowers. The man who the adversaries fear and respect and whom pygmies attempt to smear with that venom which, in the end, turns against them.

During the millennia Italy has produced colossal figures of emperors and popes, of saints and generals, artists and apostles, poets and leaders, statesmen and philosophers, scientists and navigators.

Today Italy has produced the man who, anticipated for fifteen centuries, has completed the Risorgimento: Italy was made; he made the Italians.

We Italians look at ourselves and are surprised to be what we have always been and at the same time feel different, conscious of our individuality, more serene and strong.

The miserable adversaries of the new Italy will not surrender soon. They continue to prick, scorn, and spread their venom and their defeatism. But their attempts are destined to fail. Our strength will force them to fry themselves in their own shell, as viscid snails.

Italy, which was never a turbulent nation and has always loved peace, will never allow any one to block her progress but will continue on the road laid down by her destiny. Guided by the strong and never failing Duce BENITO MUSSOLINI, she will be faithful to her Soldier King.

The Italians of Toronto and Ontario, in this period dense with events and sombre with preoccupations, have never lost their faith in the destiny of their Motherland, have shown, with their offering of money and jewels and even with armed men, their ardent patriotism and their intense faith in fascism. To them I give a deserved praise which gives me pride and satisfaction.

Viva Italy: Viva the King: Viva il Duce: Viva the Revolution of the Black Shirts!

Appendix No 9

The following is the list of money collected for the Red Cross, city by city, as it appeared in *Il Bollettino*, 29 May 1936. The reader should note that in the Ontario list, Hamilton, London, Niagara and other cities and towns with sizeable populations of Italian Canadians, are not included. We do not know how much money those cities collected.

Donations for the Italian Red Cross and Gold for the Motherland

Ontario		British Columbia	
Toronto	$6,410.43	Vancouver	$2,158.85
Timmins	$3,118.90	Fernie	$129.85
Ottawa	$1,400.00	Prince Rupert	$128.50
Sudbury	$1,000.00	Trail	$105.00
North Bay	$665.35	Kamloops	$34.60
Sault Ste. Marie	$553.64	Powell River	$24.50
Kirkland	$115.00	Penticton	$23.00
South Porcupine	$208.50		000.00
Fort William	$123.90		000.00
Total	$13,595.72		$2,604.30

Alberta		Manitoba	
Coleman	$173.85	Winnipeg	$427.00
Calgary	$171.45		
Nordegg	$61.35		
Edmonton	$43.95		
Lethbridge	$42.75		
Cadomin	$40.00		
Blairmore	$34.25	Senneterre, Quebec	$2.00
Drumheller	$30.60		
Venice	$24.55		
Bellevue	$22.75		
Mountain Park	$21.50		
Banff	$20.00		
Hylo	$17.00		
Total	$704.00		$429.00

Ontario $13,595.72
British Columbia $ 2,604.30
Alberta $704.00
Manitoba $429.00
Total $17,333.02
From gold collected $ 3,492.23
Grand Total $20,825.23

Appendix No 10

L'Eco italo-canadese, 3 September 1938.

RELIGION AND FASCISM

Subversive doctrines discrediting religion and its ministers, spreading errors and lies, lead nations, soon or later, to their demise. World nations and, specifically European nations, may be divided into two groups: communist nations and fascist nations. Regarding the communist group, we know what their program is and what their social and moral conditions are. Stalin in these days has sent a letter to the communist youth of Riga. In this letter he says: "I have been an atheist from my youth and I continue to remove God from the mass of the Soviet citizens and particularly from the youth so that atheism will forge ahead."

Regarding the fascist nations or nations of fascist sentiments: how many of them pretend to follow the decalogue [ten commandments]. How many of them profess openly to have God as their protector? Only fascist Italy.

Only one Dictator has recognized that above him there is the Dictator of Dictators, Christ-King; only the Duce Benito Mussolini has understood well that to have peace among the nations of the earth it is necessary to have cannons, but to have peace within a nation it is necessary to have God and his religion. As a good Leader he has understood that Napoleon ended his triumph as soon as his pride caused him to rebel against the Roman Pontiff, God's representative on earth. Let us remember that Napoleon on the rock of St. Helen wrote: "who goes against Rome is never too far away from ruin!"

The Duce and the Italian people have accepted the supreme law of Religion and, in fact, we see that in the entire world Italy is the most peaceful and happy nation. She has the most pure population. Her economy is truly a mystery and a continuing miracle.

How can this be explained? The Duce has tried to give his people wealth, not with utopian words but with genuine equality, real freedom, and true brotherhood: deeds and faith are the sole foundations on which an orderly nation stands.

He has understood that the reign of justice belongs to the Church and to the Church he has entrusted his people. He leads the nation from triumph to triumph by means of faith which is destined to triumph! His political, economical, military, and social successes have been unsurpassable. His diplomatic achievements have astonished the world. The nation follows him. Divine Providence guides him. The Duce undertakes his high task with faith repeating: "Write this. Be happy. To such superb height he never bent!" If he "forges ahead" he will be inexpugnable, because heaven's blessing descend on him and on Italy as a whole.

Let us hope that he continues to keep this conduct and eliminates the extremist from his party [Farinacci?] those men who, more than once, gave his enemies the chance to attack him, charging him of limiting and destroying freedom in Italy.

His enemies say that there is neither freedom of the press nor personal freedom of movement in Italy. This is the biggest lie that the reds could invent. Certainly, the reds no longer can preach their utopian ideas, they cannot publish lies about what is immortal; but they find in the Italian press, in the political and social life of Italy, all that is beneficial to the entire Italian people — Italian Fascism is the party of order, not of revolution.

—F. R.
Trail, B. C., August 1938

Appendix No 11

L'Eco italo-canadese, 25 November 1939.
CONFERENCE ON THE MARCH ON ROME
BY F. TENISCI
COMRADES!

Tonight we commemorate the seventeenth anniversary of the March on Rome: a redemptive event, a holy event! Let me remind you of the great and very beneficial changes that this historical event have brought and shall bring forth in shaping the destiny of the world.

Seventeen years ago, Italy was infested by a congregation of renegade vultures who came from the international underworld. The incompetent Government tottered. It was made up of traitors and of those who had dodged the war. Our beautiful Italy was about to lose her crown of shining pearls with which our Caesars, our Saints, and our valorous warriors adorned her. Rome was in peril. Until one of her genial sons, prophet and innovator, the predestinated Benito Mussolini rushed to her aid.

On 28 October 1922, on Italian soil, the valorous Black shirts, led by our infallible Duce, initiated the battle for the redemption of the world!

Believe, obey, combat was Mussolini's motto! And his Black shirts believed, obeyed, fought, and gave Rome a new Italy, a purified Italy. They gave Italians the real Rome: Rome with Christ's cross! On that 28 October, the hard toil for the reconstruction of the State began. It was built on the debris of the masonic and demo-liberal State.

Three months after, on the prophetical day of 12 January 1923, the Fascist Grand Council met and decided on the constitution of the Voluntary Militia for National Security. An army-corps of willed and faithful men felt the audacious spirit of the heroic vigil. On the following 10 February those fearless Black shirt squads became a Militia — the armed garrison of the Nation.

On 12 May 1924, the National Council of the Corporation was created. Later, the Duce defined it as "the thinking brain which prepares and coordinates the economic activity of the Nation."

On 3 January 1925, Mussolini made a decisive break with the past and compromises once and for all. He initiated the construction of the true fascist State.

The *"Carta del Lavoro"* (Labour Charter) came into being on 21 April 1927, the recurrence of the foundation of the Great Rome. The

Charter has been the living expression of the highest social justice. The Charter confirmed the growing of the Corporative State, stone by stone, the symbol of fascism. The revolution marched on. The renewed Italy resisted and victoriously reacted to the economic crisis that engulfed the nations in the depression years.

Italy has won. Italy has been saved. On 11 February 1929, the genial Duce reached an accord which is engraved in golden letters in the history of our Mother Country. He obtained a peace that no government, King, or Minister was ever able to obtain: He gave Italy and the Church the Lateran accord. With the formula "free and sovereign Church and free and sovereign State," he put an end to the long-standing Roman Question. He gave the Italian nation political and religiose unity.

At dawn of the Ninth Year [1931], the Duce solemnly affirmed the universal function of the Fascist Revolution which opened the way to a fascist Europe — a Europe which models her own institutions after the practice and theory of corporatism. On the 25th of March of the Twelfth Year [1934], a plebiscite, extraordinary in human memory, endorsed the corporation.

The Thirteenth Year [1935] was the year of the military power and the war of the Nation. Inaugurating the city of Littoria, the Duce said: "Ploughs cut furrows, but it is the cannon which defends them." And on 2 October [1935], the cannons echoed the Duce's powerful appeal . . . the shining Divisions of the undefeated Royal Army and the battalions of the Black shirts sailed for East Africa . . . Europe, preoccupied and in commotion, protested and condemned such an action. But Italian people united as one heart and one will, believing in their reasons and certain of their rights, forged ahead and answered the sanctions, imposed by the Geneva organization, by displaying a tricolour flag in every home.

On 18 November 1935, the Italian nation accepted the economic war which was imposed upon her by her former friends. Standing alone but led by a powerful leader, the Italian people shattered the barriers of the diplomatic merchants; and on May 9, 1936, with unsatiable faith, the Italians acclaimed the "Empire of Rome" reborn.

From the balcony of the Venice Palace, the Duce proclaimed: "We forge ahead . . . Peace is Roman . . . against all odds and nations Ethiopia is ours for ever." His powerful strength and his unbending will destroyed the egotistical and monopolistic coalition of Jews, Masons, and communists.

Though defeated, this coalition attempted to revive itself in Spain. But Spain is a sister to Latin Rome and from Rome the shining legions of volunteers went to war again. The Duce could not keep silent in this new attempt to strangle a nation. He had to obey its doctrine: "Rome, always Rome is at the bottom of any audacious evolution . . . go towards the people . . . save people from marxism . . . elevate the people" are the most obvious aims of fascism.

Benito Mussolini, a latin genius, made an imprint on the new Spanish history. Sustained by strong revolutionary and holy ideals, his legionnaires, made up of invincible leaders and followers, re-invigorated the Spanish nation and led her on the right path originally opened by the ancient great Roman generals. During the second punic war, the Roman Publio Cornelius Scipio liberated Spain from the Carthaginians. Julius Caesar defeated Mario and Silla; it was the Roman Caesar Augustus who united Spain under Rome's protection. And now it is a Roman, Mussolini, who with his doctrine and military might gives freedom and Christianity to that oppressed nation.

Later, from the other side of the Adriatic sea, the plea of another people oppressed by a tyrannical government reached Rome. And Rome answered . . . on 7 April 1939: "Down with tyrants . . . and peace to you Albanian brothers." Today, even that people cry: "*Hail oh Duce,* redeemer of the oppressed . . ." The celebration of the March on Rome in this grave and decisive moment for the destiny of Europe has a more profound and human meaning . . . working vigilantly in silence . . . and silence is gold; and even us, Italo-Canadians, should observe this principle.

COMRADES!

We must be proud that today our Mother Country has replaced the negative theory with realism, destruction with construction, atheism with religion, hatred with love. These are all strongholds of fascism which our brothers profess and we Italians abroad should admire as splendid ideals. Fascist doctrine not only teaches us to love the land in which we were born or where our parents, who emigrated in less prosperous years, were born; but fascism teaches as to love and respect even our second Patria which gives us the privilege of citizenship.

COMRADES!

Let us elevate our minds and our hearts in immutable devotion to his Majesty the King, who has been three times victorious, Roman Emperor . . . Let us restore our spirit with vibrant and passionate faith in the Duce Magnifico, founder of the Empire and apostle of Christianity . . . In our humble and thoughtful mind, let us remember and exalt the thousand and thousand men who died for the Great Fascist Revolution

— EIA!

Appendix No 12

Il Bollettino, 25 August 1938.
RACISM IN ITALY

Through recent events, fascist Italy's stand on race policy is becoming clear.

A positive racist policy in Italy began just after the proclamation of the Ethiopian Empire. Italy took several steps to determine the juridical position of the indigenous population. These measures absolutely prohibited marital and extra-marital relations between white people and indigenous populations. Crossbreeding of races is a serious plague which the fascist government wants to avoid and stop, opportunely, right from the beginning. In the majority of cases, individuals produced by cross-breeding of races reveal the defects of both races which generated them. They are unhappy and consequently constitute a social danger. This same principle guides the racist policy in Italy today in relation to other elements who are not of the Italian race and whose mingling with Italians is not desirable.

Italian Jews have never ceased to consider themselves Jews. That is they are different from Italians in blood, ancestry, nature, and tradition. Some Italian Jews have often vocalized the typical assertion that the Jewish people are superior to all other peoples. Some Jews have even committed the very serious mistake of expressing sympathy for the Jewish-mason International which, as every one knows, in Italy as in every other country, is a separated group which is and must be identifiable and identified.

All the uproar of lies that the anti-fascists cry regarding projected persecution are going to end in the wastepaper basket together with the other lies, equally vain and equally vile, that have been there for the last sixteen years.

"Forging ahead" Mussolini's Italy with great wisdom will keep pure for all future generations that Italian blood which gave life to twenty-five centuries of history.

Appendix No 13

L'Italia nuova (in Le Canada Latin section), 5 March 1938.*

"THE JEWISH SIUATION [SIC] IN ITALY"

Under the title, "Italy's Utopia for Jews," the *Canadian Jewish Chronicle* published an article not only misleading in its heading (since Italy has never nurtured any idea on an "utopia" for the Jews), but that also errs in facts and conclusions.

The writer in the *Canadian Jewish Chronicle* states for example, that the Fascist Government has not yet decided upon its policy towards the Jews in Italy . . . that Mussolini, having declared that the Jewish problem can be solved by the creation of Jewish State . . . that a dispatch from Vienna would seem to indicate that the Duce has in mind Tripoli as the new State . . . that Italy has failed to colonize Tripoli, so much so, that there are as many Italian government officials in the land as there are private citizens.

First. It was inaccurate to state that the Fascist Government had not decided upon a policy towards the Jews resident in Italy. In fact, *"L'Informazione Diplomatica"* (which is the official organ of the Italian Government for public and international news), published as follows in the 14th number:

"Recent journalistic utterances may have created in some foreign minds the impression that the Fascist Government is about to inaugurate an anti-semitic policy. In responsible Roman circles one is in the position to unqualifiedly state that such an impression is absolutely wrong, and these would-be anti-semitic utterances are caused principally by the fact that foreign anti-fascist current of thought are nearly always traced to Jewish sources.

The responsible Roman circles are of the opinion that the universal Jewish problem is to be solved in one way: by the creation of the Jewish State in some part of the world, but not in Palestine — State which in the fullest meaning of the word, is to be in the position to care for the Jewish masses scattered in many lands through diplomatic and consular channels.

"Though Jews live in Italy, it does not necessarily follow that there is an Italian Jewish problem. The Jews in other countries number millions, while in Italy there are only about from 50 to 60 thousand Jews in a population of 44 million people.

"The Fascist Government, however, reserves the right to watch the activities of the Jews who have only recently landed in Italy in order that the Jewish element, with regard to the general life of the country, does not prove disproportionate to the intrinsic merits of the individuals, and to the numeric importance of their communities.

"The Fascist Government, further, is absolutely contrary to any direct or indirect pressure to obtain religious abjurations. The laws which govern and regulate the life of the Jewish communities has proven its merits and will remain unaltered."

It would seem that one could not be more clear, more precise, more categorical, than what, the Italian Government has been in this note.

Second. It is for this reason that citing the supposed telegram from Vienna (after all, it is not quite clear how Vienna could regulate the relations between the Italian Government and the Jews) that the idea of putting the thought in the mind of Mussolini to offer Tripoli to the Jews is senseless. The above mentioned note specifically states that is necessary to give the Jews (not in Palestine but elsewhere) a State in the full significance of the word with its own diplomatic and consular representaives, etc. Then, how could Italy offer Tripoli, which is part of Italy, to create another State? Would it want to create a State within a State?

The fact that the statement, was made that such a "State" should be created elsewhere that in Palestine does not mean at all that it has to be created in Tripoli.

Third. But the writer in the *Canadian Jewish Chronicle* does not miss the opportunity to subtly insinuate that Mussolini wants to give "us" Tripoli because during all the years that Italy has had this territory she could not persuade her own people to go there. This is similar to the old wives' tale which followed the foreign press during the Italian expedition to Ethiopia when it sought to show that Italy did not need any colonies, that the Italians do not know how to colonize, and, moreover, that colonies do not enrich a nation, but make them poorer.

The truth is altogether different. More that 30 thousand Italians live already in the Mediterranean region of Tripoli to the east and west of Tripoli, and about 20 thousand live in Cyrenaica.

These Italian citizens (who are not part of the government officials referred to by the writer in the *Canadian Jewish Chronicle*) have transformed Tripoli into one of the most beautiful cities on the northern coast of Africa. Tripoli is the capital of a region that only twenty years ago was nothing but wasteland, but where today slowly but surely, grows 2 million olive trees, 2 million orange and tangerine trees, and 18 million grape vines!

Such are the true facts, which we hope the *Canadian Jewish Chronicle* will lay before its readers.

* This article was reprinted in the *Canadian Jewish Chronicle*, March 11, 1938.

Appendix No 14

L'Italia nuova, 15 October 1938.

IMPRESSIONS OF A YOUNG ITALIAN WOMAN

Montreal, 10 Oct. 1938-XVI
Prof. Giulio Romano
Editor of the *Italia nuova*
City:
Dear Sir,

I just returned from Italy where I was happily visiting as a member of the G.I.L.E. (Gioventù Italiana Littorio Estero) of the Montreal group. I feel the need to send you this letter in which I attempt to summarize my impressions and express my feelings of gratitude for the inestimable gift of my trip to the delightful Madre Patria.

I remember the fatherly words directed to us before our departure published in the column of this newspaper:

> Italy is waiting for you. She will receive you as a beloved mother. You will see incomparable visions of beauty and greatness which will do more than inspire your admiration they will astonish you. It does not matter how wild your fantasy may be, you cannot imagine the immensity of wonders which you will have the chance to see once you are on the enchanting soil of Italy.

Dear Sir, it was just so. We began to sense the first impression of the beautiful, of the new and grandiose which attended us, as soon as we got on board the ship *Rex*. On that magnificent ship, which openly attests to Italy's renewed greatness, we breathed a new air; the life on board was a pre-taste of the sweetness of our Italian stay.

Arriving in Naples, before that picture of unbelievable heavenly beauty, we were truly astonished. It was like dreaming. And our dream continued to fascinate us when we reached Rome. We learned to know her by visiting, day in and day out, its monuments, its temples and palaces, flowers, parks, galleries, and art exhibitions. We finally became aware of the splendours and glories of that city which is rightly called Eternal.

But, among all the memories, the one that remains most vivid in my mind is the day that we saw *il Duce* for the first time. I confess that standing before that Great Man who has done so much good for Italy and who is adored by the entire nation, my eyes were filled with tears and my hear with emotions. The Duce smiled tenderly and kindly. The man who looked at us was not a severe leader, grave and thoughtful; he was the tender, good, and affectionate father who showed his pleasure in seeing his children who came from so far away, and he offered them that unique smile, caressing, unforgettable . . .

Oh, if all Italians living abroad could see that smile! I tell you frankly that if I had seen nothing else, the Duce's smile and the words he spoke at the final gymnastic display on September 10 (a date indelibly impressed on my memory) would have been enough to make that trip a happy experience.

All my gratitude goes to the Duce for the happiness that I felt and it goes also to all those faithful interpreters of his thoughts and executors of his will, who did everything necessary to make our too short stay in the smiling Peninsula pleasant.

With my return to Canada the enchantment is broken. The memories will, however, never leave me and I particularly cherish the Duce's words in his speech to us: "As you leave Italy remember that the Tricolour of the Patria is always your companion." I feel a new faith and a certainty which mingles with the hope to return to Italy, and to cry loudly again before the most beloved *Capo* (leader), his immortal name: *Duce! Duce!*

Saluti Fascisti.
Ersilia Sauro

ENDNOTES

INTRODUCTION

1. Kenneth Bagnell, *Canadese: A Portrait of the Italian Canadians,* Toronto: Macmillan of Canada, 1989; Mario Duliani, *The City Without Women,* Antonino Mazza trans., Oakville, Ont., Mosaic Press, 1994; National Congress of Italian Canadians, "A National Shame: The Internment of Italian Canadians," A brief by the National Congress of Italian Canadians, January 1990, unpublished submission to the Government of Canada.
2. Angelo Principe, "Video," *Eyetalian,* Summer 1997, p. 97, a review of Nicolas Zavaglia's documentary, *Barbed Wire and Mandolins* which aired on the Canadian Broadcasting Corporation.
3. It is useful to compare, for example, Principe's report of the behaviour of the then Grand Venerable of the Order Sons of Italy of Ontario, Vittorio Sabetta, in the polemic around the "castor oil" threat issued by the editor of the Bolletino, with how he is presented in Antonino Mazza's introduction to Duliani, ibid., p. xiv.
4. I consider some of my own work in this field to be of this type, as in my work on the Order Sons of Italy of Ontario, *Within Our Temple: A History of the Order Sons of Italy of Ontario,* Toronto: Order Sons of Italy of Canada, 1995, p. 4. Better efforts to analyze contemporary conditions are provided, for example, by Bruti Liberati, *Il Canada, l'Italia e il fascismo: 1919-1945,* Roma, Bonacci Editore, 1984.

FOREWORD

1. Kenneth Bagnell, *Canadese. A Portrait of the Italian Canadians,* (Toronto: MacMillan of Canada, 1989), p. 75.
2. *Il Bollettino,* 22 December 1933; *Il Cittadino italo-canadese,* 14 December 1933. Pancaro claimed to have discovered a haemostatic serum which could stop any type of haemorrhage. See, "Dr. Pancaro Returns From Italy with the Confirm of his Scientific Discovery," *Il Bollettino,* 18 May 1934. On the 8 June 1934 issue, *Il Bollettino* published another article related to Pancaro's medical discovery: "Bishop O'Brien Saved by Dr. Pancaro's Serum." In 1930 Pancaro authored a booklet titled *L'anestesia spinale* for which he was congratulated by Mussolini himself;" *L'Araldo del Canada,* 31 January 1931.

3   See *Il Bollettino,* 29 November 1936. This and every other translations appearing in this book, unless otherwise stated, are the author's.
4   Translation by Celestino DeJulis.
5   Angelo Tasca, *The Rise of Italian Fascism* (New York: Howard Ferting, 1966: first edition 1938), p. 36.
6   G. A. Borgese, *Goliath: The March of Fascism* (New York: The Viking Press, 1937), p. 215.
7   The use of the term Casa d'Italia, literally Italian House or Centre, can be somewhat misleading to contemporary readers. The institution which is described, in particular in the 1930s, was the exported version of what was called in Italy the Casa del Fascio or Fascist House or Centre, which is the translation which will be used in the current study.

CHAPTER ONE

1   Renzo Santinon, *Fasci italiani all'estero* (Roma: Edizione Settimo Sigillo, 1991), p. 257.
2   Giuseppe Bastianini, "I Fasci italiani all'estero: Il valore di un Congresso," in *Gerarchia,* October 1925, p. 635.
3   For a concise view of these problems, see *Fascismo e società italiana* (Torino: Einaudi, 1973) edited by Guido Quarza: in particular, see "L'esercito e il fascismo," by Giorgio Rochat; "La magistratura e il fascismo," by Guido Neppi Modona; and "Il potere economico e il fascismo," by Valerio Castronovo.
4   Matteotti was abducted on 6 June 1924. His body was found two months later riddled with bullets. Two fascists were held responsible — Americo Dumini and Amleto Poveromo — and they were sent to jail for a few years. They were charged again after the liberation and along with Giuseppe Viola (fugitive) were condemned to 30 years in prison. See "Fascism between Legality and Revolution, 1922-1924," in *The Axe Within,* edited by Roland Sarti (New York: New Viewpoints, 1974), pp. 15-31.
5   Giovanni Amendola (Salerno, 1886 – Cannes 1926) led a protest of 123 liberal Members of Parliament against Mussolini who was suspected of being involved in the murder of Matteotti. Fascists assaulted and violently beat Amendola twice. As a consequence of the assault he died in France soon afterward.
6   Renzo De Felice, *Intervista sul fascismo* (Bari: Laterza, 1976), p. 29.
7   Quoted by Edwin P. Hoyt, in *Mussolini's Empire* (New York: John Wiley & Sons, In., 1994), pp. 9, 109.
8   According to fascist propaganda, *corporazioni* or corporations were supposed to harmonize conflicts among the productive forces of the country for the supreme interest of the nation. In practice, it was the PNF which regulated labour-management conflicts by imposing decisions which, most of the time, favoured industrialists.

9   In *Mussolini il Duce, Gli anni del consenso, 1929-1936* (Torino, 1974), p. 330, Renzo De Felice quotes from *Il Corriere della Sera*, 21 January 1927, the following statement by Winston Churchill, who visited Italy in 1927, "If I were an Italian I am sure that I would have been with you [Mussolini] from the beginning to the end of your victorious struggle against the bestial appetites and passions of Leninism . . ."
10 David F. Schmitz, *The United States and Fascist Italy: 1922-1940* (Chapel Hill & London: The University of North Carolina Press, 1988), p. 4; Alexander De Conde, *Half Bitter, Half Sweet* (New York: Scribner's Sons, 1971), p. 184.
11 Kathleen McMillan, "Fascism in 1925-26," in *Fascism*, by Giuseppe Pezzolini, translated by Kathleen McMillan (London: Methuen & Co. Ltd, 1926), p. 182.
12 *Ibid.*, p. 186.
13 See *L'Italia* (Montreal), 16 March 1935; in "I fasci italiani all'estero;" in *Ricerche sul fascismo* (Urbino: Argalia Editore, 1971, p. 119), Enzo Santarelli writes, "if not exactly at the beginning, at least in the first stage of the fasci, some merchants and manufacturers in particular considered the emigrants abroad (work and capital) as a channel and instrument of economic expansion, a real and potential market."
14 It is interesting to remember here to what lengths Dr. Gustavo Tosti, Acting Consul-General of Italy in New York, went in 1905 to dispel the preoccupation of Mr. Sergent, Commissioner-General of Immigration of the United States, with the Italian Government's effort "to colonize [its] subjects who come to this country [the United States] for the purpose of maintaining in them a love of their mother country." See Gustavo Tosti, "Italy's Attitude Toward Her Emigrants," *The North American Review* (vol. 153, 1905), pp. 720-726; Alexander De Conde, *op. cit.*, pp. 193-194.
15 See Silvano M. Tomasi, "Fede e patria: the Italica Gens in the United States and Canada, 1908-1936. Notes for the history of an emigration association," in *Studi Emigrazione/Études Migrations* (Rome: Centro Studi Emigrazione, Anno XXVII, September 1991), pp. 319-340; Matteo Sanfilippo, "Monsignor Pisani e il Canada (1908-1913), *Annali Accademici Canadesi* (Ottawa, VI, 1990), pp. 61-75.
16 See Roberto Cantalupo, *Racconti politici dell'altra pace* (Milano: Istituto per gli studi di politica internazionale, 1940-XVIII), p, 304. Fascism began as a movement in 1919 and was formed as a political party in 1921. At the founding convention, held in Rome on 6 June, the assembly decided that emigrants or "italiani all'estero" that is, Italians abroad, should have their representatives in the Parliament. In an interview with Carrol Binder, Rome correspondent for the *Washington Daily News* (14 March 1928), however, Mussolini declared that "the Italian Government never thought to give a place in Parliament to American citizens of Italian origin," *Opera Omnia di Benito Mussolini*, Vol.

XXIII, a cura di Edoardo e Duilio Susmel (Firenze: La Fenice, 1957), pp. 124-25.
17 See Giuseppe Bastianini, "Fasci italiani all'estero: il valore di un Congresso," *Gerarchia* (October 1925), p. 636. Fascists were aware of what a well-organized group of people could achieve in the North American political system where every elected individual from the highest office down was sensitive to voter pressure. In mentioning Jugoslavia, Bastianini indirectly refers to President Wilson's position on Dalmatia during the Paris Peace Conference of 1919. President Woodrow Wilson's stand dashed the hopes of Italian nationalists for Dalmatia and provoked D'Annunzio's expedition to Fiume, capital city of that region.
18 Camillo Pellizzi, "I fasci all'estero," *Gerarchia* (April 1929), p. 181.
19 For an interesting study of the development and different meanings of the myth of the Grande Italia, see Emilio Gentile, *La Grande Italia: ascesa e declino del mito della nazione nel ventesimo secolo* (Milano: Mondadori, 1997), in particular see the Third Part, "La nazione dei fascisti."
20 Quoted by Gianfranco Cresciani, in "Italian Fascism in Australia," *Studi Emigrazione/Études Migrations*, no. 90 (June 1988) p. 238.
21 See Enrico Boni, "Giovanni Caboto," *Rivista d'Italia e d'America*, Anno II (June-July 1926), p. 84; Roberto Perin, "Making Good Fascists and Good Canadians: Consular Propaganda and the Italian Community in Montreal in the 1930s," in *Minorities and Mother Country Imagery*, edited by G. Gold, (St. John: Memorial University of Newfoundland, 1984), pp. 142-46.
22 *Il Cittadino italo-canadese*, 28 December 1933.
23 *Il Messaggero italo-canadese*, 28 January 1933.
24 With reference to the Fronte Unico Morale, Charles Bayley over-estimated the extent of the penetration of fascism into the Italian community of Montreal; see his M.A. Thesis (McGill, 1939). Since then, this factual error has been accepted by scholars — for example, Luigi Bruti Liberati, *Il Canada, l'Italia e il fascismo, 1919-1945* (Roma: Bonacci, 1984); John Zucchi, *Italians in Toronto* (McGill-Queen's University Press, 1988); and Martin Robin, *Shades of Right: Nativist and Fascist Politics in Canada, 1920-1940* (Toronto: University of Toronto Press, 1992). For a redress of the figures produced by Bayley see Angelo Principe, *The Concept of Italy in Canada and in Italian Canadian Writings from the Eve of Confederation to the Second World War*, Ph. D. Dissertation, University of Toronto, 1989, pp. 257-259.
25 *L'Italo-Canadese* (of which we have a copy of the first issue) was, probably, the first Italian newspaper in Canada, not *il Corriere del Canada* as Filippo Salvatore says in "Il fascismo e gli italiani in Canada," *Storia contemporanea*, a. XXVII, n. 5, ottobre 1996, pp. 833-863. *L'Italo-Canadese* appeared in Montreal in 1894 and it was edited by Pietro Catelli. In Toronto, Joe Saporita published *Lo stendardo* in 1898; see Duncan

McLaren, *Ontario Ethno-Cultural Newspapers, 1835-1927* (Toronto: University of Toronto Press, 1973), p. 107.

26 See *Il Progresso italo-canadese*, 7 August 1930; Costantino Lozima, "Gli Italiani nella provincia dell'Ontario (Canada)," *Bollettino della Reggia Società Geografica Italiana*, Serie VI, Vol. IV (gennaio-febbraio 1927) p. 25. In the middle of the 1930s, *L'Italia* became a supporter of the Liberal Party.

27 The first functioning fascio was created in Montreal in 1925. The following year (1926), the "Fascio Principe Umberto" was organized in Toronto. The men behind it were Camillo Vetere of Montreal, who was the fascist trustee for Canada, the painter Vittorio dell'Angelo, Francesco Gattuso, and Dr. Pasquale Fontanella. Gattuso was chosen as secretary of the fascio. In 1927, Nicola Selvaggio, delegate of the fascio of Toronto, was received by the Duce. He brought Mussolini a gold medal embossed with the maple leaf emblem which was a gift from the fascists of Toronto. Mussolini reciprocated the gift with an autographed photograph of himself for the comrades of Toronto.

28 The thesis of a "nascent inferiority complex" was advanced first by John P. Diggins, *Mussolini and Fascism*, p. 80, and the argument was accepted by John Zucchi, *op. cit.*, p. 168, and Martin Robin, op. cit., p. 209.

29 *The Mail and Empire* (Toronto), 1 November 1926.

30 See John E. Zucchi, *op. cit.*, pp. 103-117, 141-165.

31 See *Il Carroccio* (New York), February 1923, p. 265; Interview with R. B., author's collection; Angelo Principe, "Note sul radicalismo tra gli italiani in Canada dalla Prima Guerra Mondiale alla Conciliazione," *Rivista di studi italiani*, vol. 7, no. 1-2 (June-December 1990) p. 117; John Zucchi, *op. cit.*, p. 171.

32 See Gabriele Scardellato, *Within Our Temple: A History of the Order Sons of Italy of Ontario* (Toronto: Order Sons of Italy of Canada, 1995); John Fainella, "The Development of Italian Organizations in Calgary," *Alberta History*, vol. 32, no. 1 (1984) p. 22.

33 A. Principe, "The Difficult Years of the Order of the Sons of Italy (1920-1926)," *Italian Canadiana*, Vol. 5 (1989) pp. 104-14; Taped interview with Bortolotti; Souvenir Programme: 50th Anniversay (sic) of the Order of Italo-Canadians (Ottawa, 1976); Spada, *The Italians in Canada* (Ottawa: Canada Ethnica, 1969) pp. 98-100.

34 Spada, *op. cit.*, 113.

35 *Ibid.*, p. 109.

36 John G. Fainella, *op. cit.*, p. 22.

37 Marino Culos, *Souvenir* (Ricordi) (Vancouver: The Author, 1935).

38 *Il Progresso italo-canadese* (Toronto), 7 August 1930; *La Tribuna canadese*, 2 August 1930.

39 See *Il Progresso italo-canadese*, 31 July 1930.

40 In Toronto's Ward 5 there were 4,264 Italian residents in 1931. See Appendix B, Tables 1 and 9, in Cyril H. Levitt and William Shaffir, *The Riot at Christie Pits* (Toronto: Lester & Orpen Dennys, 1987), pp. 294, 298.
41 See "Viaggio in Canada cinquant'anni fa," *Mosaico* (September 1975), p. 34.
42 Costantino Lozima, *op. cit.*, p. 25.
43 Taped interview with Attilio Bortolotti; regarding left wing radicals, Father Joseph Longo of St. Mary of the Angels Catholic Church on Dufferin Street in Toronto, wrote to Archbishop James McGuigan: "This parish may be rightly compared with an african [sic] Mission; greediness, the war, the depression and communism made many Italians [not] only to forget their religious duties but to hate the priests," quoted by John Zucchi, *op. cit.*, p. 122.
44 See *Documenti Diplomatici Italiani,* Settima serie: 1922-1935. Vol. I (Ministero Degli Affari Esteri, Roma MCMLIII), pp. 10-11; "Europe's New Peril," *The Globe,* 29 October 1922; "A Menace to Peace," *The Toronto Daily Star,* 31 October 1922.
45 See *Il Grido della stirpe* (New York), 24 April 1926.
46 See *Il Corriere Italiano* (Toronto) Year 1, No. 1 (23 March 1929).
47 See memo to the Minister of the Interior from the Direzione Generale di Pubblica Sicurezza (Public Security) dated 12 January 1915, *Archivio Centrale dello Stato, Casellario Politico Centrale* (ACS CPC) f. 1168, Giovanni Leone Castelli.
48 A copy of this letter is preserved in Castelli's file, see above, No. 47.
49 In Castelli's file in the *ACS CPC,* there is a three-way correspondence among L. Bissolati, the Office of the Minister of the Interior, and the Prefect of Foggia. Because of the deletion of Castelli's record, there is nothing in the Casellario Politico Centrale at the State Central Archives for Nanni Leone Castelli between 1918 and 1926, the years during which Castelli was in the army and then in North America, both in the United States and in Canada. In 1926, he moved to Mexico and again came under surveillance as noted below.
50 *Il Martello* (New York) 28 June 1924. According to *Il Martello,* which quotes Miss Ingrassia's parents, Castelli initiated *Le Fiamme d'Italia* with his wife's savings.
51 Castelli did publish a short monograph on his experience in D'Annunzio's expedition: *L'opera di Fiume* (Albany: La Capitale, [n.d.]). Unfortunately, all attempts to locate a copy have failed.
52 For further details see Angelo Principe, *The Concept of Italy in Canada and in Italian-Canadian Writings . . . ,* cit., p. 218.
53 See Angelo Principe, "The Difficult Years of the Order of the Sons of Italy (1920-1926)," *cit.,* p. 109.
54 *Il Martello,* 28 June 1924.
55 See "Connubio Castelli/Vetere nella Suburra Coloniale," *Il Martello,* 16 August 1924.

56   *Ibid.*, 29 December 1923.
57   *Ibid.*, 28 June 1924.
58   *Il Grido della stirpe*, 24 April 1924.
59   According to *Il Martello* (22 November 1924), Castelli's father said to Miss Ingrassia: "My son had always been a bad character (pessimo arnese). He made my wife, his mother, cry and even beat her to rip from her the money I was sending. He was not satisfied with a five lira note, he wanted the hundred. He never worked; he never liked to work... Even his first wife, poor woman, loved him but when she realized that she had made a mistake she asked for a separation. She lives with her father and is happy, now."
60   See *El Universal*, 6 May 1929; *Excelsior*, 16 May 1929; *La Prensa*, 16 May 1929; *Grafico*, 16 May 1929, various newspaper clippings from Castelli's file no. 1168 at the *ACS CPC*.
61   *Il Martello*, 16 August 1924.
62   In Mexico, Castelli published *Dos naciones y un destino* (México: Edizione de Genio Latino, 1932); *La stafa de San Lázaro* (hecho y documentos) (México: D. F., edizione de Genio Latino, 1944), and in Italy, he published a 44-page booklet titled, *Tullio Murri: Profilo di un grande uomo di fede* (Bologna: Edizioni di Aristocrazia, 1925). The booklet was reviewed in *Giovinezza*, 26 December 1925.
63   *ACS CPC*, f. 1162. This very long letter was sent from Mexico City, on 16 April 1926 to His Majesty King Vittorio Emanuele III.
64   See the letter dated 24 December 1940, from Castelli to Armando Mazza, editor of the Bolognese newspaper *Il Resto del Carlino*. Castelli declared that he never knew of such a sentence and that he left Italy in 1921 and in 1926 with a regular passport. He concluded his letter saying, "I remind you that when Mussolini formed the government, a decree was issued regarding the trials against Fiuman legionaries. Could you send me a copy? Could you tell me to whom at the Military Tribunal I should write to obtain specific information?" *ACS CPC*, f. 1168.
65   "Tuesday 20 March, in the Hygeia Hall, prof. F. M. Gualtieri held the announced conference on Papini. He spoke with competence on the life and works of the renowned Italian writer," *La Favilla*, March-April 1928; *Calabria letteraria*, vol. 37, nos. 1-3 (1989), p. 68.
66   See *La Favilla*, May-June 1927.
67   Francesco M. Gualtieri, *We Italians: A Study in Italian Immigration in Canada* (Toronto: Italian World War Veterans' Association, 1929), p. 3.
68   *La Favilla*, October-November 1928.
69   *Il Messaggero italo-canadese*, 18 November 1933; *Il cittadino italo-canadese* (Montreal), 23 November 1933.
70   Gaetano Salvemini, *Italian Fascist Activities in the United States* (New York: Center for Migration Studies, 1977), p. 19.
71   See Mackenzie King's Diaries, 25, 26, and 27 September 1928 (Transcript 63, Film F, K54), pp. 5233-5234.

72 *Il Bollettino*, 26 June 1936.
73 *Ibid.*, 18 December 1936; *The Telegram*, 8 October 1935.
74 *Le Devoir* (Montreal), 13 February 1929.
75 *Ibid.*, 20 February 1929.
76 Quoted by Martin Robin, *op. cit.*, p. 208; *Il Bollettino*, 6 November 1933; Luigi Bruti Liberati, *Il Canada, l'Italia e il fascismo: 1919-1945*, *cit.*, p. 240, n. 76.
77 Giuseppe Tomasicchio was once expelled from the fascio. Even Giuseppe Federici, the leader of the Fascio Principe Umberto, was removed from his position because he and his executive boycotted a speech delivered in Toronto by Domenico Trombetta, the editor of *Il Grido della stirpe*, in 1929. See *Il Bollettino*, vol. 1, no. 1 (20 September 1929); *Il Grido della stirpe*, 2 November 1929. Giuseppe Federici was the nephew of Nicola Masi, the Italian Consular Agent in Hamilton and of the convicted Flavio Masi. Flavio had been "sentenced to two years in Kingston Penitentiary" for his part in defrauding Italians by selling counterfeit immigration permits for $200.00 each. For a detailed account of this affair see, James Dubro and Robin Rowland, *Undercover: The Case of the RCMP's Most Secret Operative* (Markham, Ontario: Octopus Publishing Group, 1991), pp. 105-128.
78 *Il Bollettino*, 2 February 1934.
79 *Il Progresso italo-canadese*, 21 December 1929: Consul Ambrosi was accompanied by Rev. Father Truffa, Rev. Father Auad, Rev. Father Rutolo, Dr. G. Glionna, Dr. R. Invidiata, Dr. P. Fontanella, Dr. D. Sansone, Sir (Cavaliere) V. E. Giannelli, Antonio Gatto, president of the Comitato Inter-sociale, Angelo Teolis, G. Grittani, and P. Molinaro. For an analysis of the collaboration of fascists and Italian Catholic priests in Toronto, see Luigi G. Pennacchio, "The Torrid Trinity: Toronto's Fascists, Italian Priests and Archbishops During the Fascist Era, 1929-1940," in *Catholics at the "Gathering Place": Historical Essays on the Archdiocese of Toronto, 1841-1991*, edited by Mark George McGowan and Brian P. Clark (Toronto: Canadian Catholic Historical Association, 1993), pp. 223-253.
80 *Il Bollettino*, 22 February 1935.
81 See Kenneth McNaught, "The 1930s," in Part One of *The Canadians: 1867-1967*, edited by J. M. S. Careless and R. Craig Brown (Toronto: MacMillan of Canada, 1968), p. 239.
82 Kenneth McNaught, *A Prophet in Politics* (Toronto: University of Toronto Press, 1963), p. 246.
83 Kenneth, McNaught, "The 1930s," *cit.*, p. 248.
84 For a detailed account of extreme right-wing movements in Canada, see Martin Robin, *op. cit.*, and Lita-Rose Betcherman, *The Swastika and the Maple Leaf* (Toronto: Fitzhenry & Whiteside, 1978), and a more recent analysis of right-wing movements in Canada by Stanley R. Barrett, *Is God a Rascist?* (Toronto: University of Toronto Press, 1987).

85 See "Fascists Seek Stevens for 'Duce' of Canada," *The Evening Telegram*, Friday 27 September 1935.
86 *Ibid.*
87 Article 2 of the "Nuovo Statuto dei Fasci Italiani all'Estero" prohibited fascists from getting involved in the politics of the host country, ". . . non partecipare a quella che è la politica interna dei paesi dove i fascisti sono ospitati," Mussolini, *Opera Omnia*, Vol. XXIII, *cit.*, p. 89.
88 The Padlock Law gave police the power to close buildings and even private houses throughout the province, which the authorities might consider to have been used for communist activities. Michael Oliver, "Quebec and Canadian Democracy," *Canadian Journal of Economics and Political Science*, vol. 33, no. 4 (November 1957), p. 509. H. A. Logan, *Trade Unions in Canada* (Toronto, 1948), chap. XXV; L. J. Rogers, "Duplessis and Labour," *Canadian Forum*, October 1947.
89 It suffices here to mention "La settimana italiana" or Italian Week that was observed across Canada in January of 1934. Fascist speakers came from Italy to extol the virtues of fascism. These included men like the aristocrat Don Mario Colonna, the journalist Luigi Villari, and women like the author Amy Bernardi. Scores of local intellectuals like the President of the University of Toronto, Professor Cody, and Professor Emilio Goggio of the Italian and Spanish Department of the same university, the young Frank Molinaro and many others were always travelling on speaking engagements to different societies, clubs and associations across the country.
90 See "Mussolini giudicato dalla Sig.ra Eaton," *Il Bollettino*, 1 August 1930.
91 Alfred S. Jones, "Fascism," in *Addresses of the Empire Club of Toronto* (1934), p. 418.
92 Renzo De Felice, *Interpretations of Fascism*, translated by Brenda Huff Everett (Cambridge, Mass.: Harvard University press, 1977), p. 4.
93 Lita-Rose Betcherman, in her fine work *The Swastika and the Maple Leaf, cit.*, p. 81-82, reaches the same conclusion: "At mid-decade, Mussolini . . . was widely regarded as an economic statesman, and his abolition of parliamentary democracy and civil rights was, if anything, approved by his Canadian admirers . . . Judges and university professors, as well as big business and the press, were attracted by Mussolinian ideas."
94 Roberto Perin, *op. cit.*, p. 151; Luigi Bruti Liberati, *op. cit.*, p. 76.
95 See *Il Bollettino*, 2 March 1934.
96 See *Il Messaggero italo-canadese* (Toronto), 21 October 1933.
97 Spada, *op. cit.*, p. 127.
98 The title of Perin's article itself is appropriate, "Making Good Fascists and Good Canadians: Consular Propaganda in the Italian Community in Montreal in the 30s," *cit.*
99 See *L'Emigrato* (Toronto), vol. 2 no. 5, 30 March 1932.
100 Luigi Bruti Liberati, *op. cit.*, p. 65; ACS CPC, f. 905.

101 Archivio Nazionale dello Stato: Casellario Politico Centrale, F. 905; *The Toronto Daily Star*, 15 August 1935; "Entretien avec Antonino Spada," in Filippo Salvatore, *Le Fascisme et les Italiens à Montréal* (Toronto: Guernica, 1995), p. 274.
102 Gaetano Salvemini, *op. cit.*, pp. 8-9.
103 Filippo Salvatore, *op. cit.*, p. 152.
104 See "Survey of Italian Fascism in Canada," 2 September 1937, p. 14, enclosed in letter of F.J. Mead to Commissioner, RCMP Security Service Records, quoted by Martin Robin, *op. cit.*, p. 226.
105 Watson Kirkconnell, "European Canadians and their Press," in *Canadian Historical Association*, 1940.

Chapter Two

1 The Italian population of the Province of Quebec was concentrated mostly in the Montreal area which had an Italian population of 20,871. Toronto was the next largest concentration with a population of 13,015 Italian Canadians: Ward 1, 742; Ward 2, 999; Ward 3, 1,395; Ward 4, 1,070; Ward 5, 4,264; Ward 6, 2,637; Ward 7, 1,105; Ward 8, 690. See, *Census of Canada 1931*.
2 See *Il Carroccio* (New York), February 1922, no. 2, p. 425.
3 In 1926, and in 1932, Camillo Vetere directed *L'Araldo* for a few months before he returned to edit *L'Italia*. In 1938 he moved from Montreal to Sydney, N.S., to occupy the vacant office of Italian Vice-Consul but he stayed there only a few months. Long enough, "per estorcere denaro" (to extort money) from several people before returning to Montreal. On this point, see Vittorio Restaldi, "Memoriale sul trattamento degli italiani al Canada dopo la dichiarazione di Guerra" presented to the "Direzione Generale Italiani all'Estero, Affari Transoceanici" in 1942 (ASAE, Canada, b. 12, f. 7), p. 9; Restaldi's Memoir was published by Luigi Pautasso, *Quaderni canadesi* (Toronto, January-February 1976) pp. 5-8.
4 *Il Carroccio* (New York), February 1924, p. 242.
5 See Angelo Principe, "The Difficult Years of the Order of the Sons of Italy," *Italian Canadiana*, vol. 5 (1989), pp. 104-116.
6 *L'Italia* (Montreal), 7 June 1924. For the entire text, see appendix No. 1.
7 *L'Araldo* (Montreal), 14 February 1925; "Entretien avec Antonino Spada," in *Le Fascisme et les Italians à Montreal*, edited by Filippo Salvatore (Toronto: Guernica, 1995), p. 270; Antonino Spada, *The Italians in Canada, cit.*, p. 111. In the years 1929-1931, *L'Araldo* was edited by Ottorino Incoronato, secretary of the Montreal Fascio Luparini, first and by Camillo Vetere later. In the 1929-1932 period the paper was the "Organ of the Montreal Fascio." See No. 3 above.
8 See *Il Carroccio*, September 1925, p. 279.

9 *Loc. cit.*
10 *L'Italia*, 4 May 1935.
11 The General Committee meeting in Montreal on 12 July 1931, announced that on "October 4, the Monument to Giovanni Caboto would be inaugurated," *Il Progresso Italo-Canadese*, 18 July 1931. Two years later the Monument had not yet been erected because the Montreal City Council denied a place where it could be installed. Against the General Committee, *Il Messaggero* (24 June 1933) wrote, "It [was] deplorable that those who lately have thrown themselves into the laudable initiative to claim one of our Italian glories did not know how to spare the Italian community such a humiliation. A litle more seriousness would have helped a great deal the good cause and have avoided, after so much pompous and often useless propaganda, ridicule on themselves and all fellow countrymen;" see also "Discorso del Vice-Console alla Riunione Pro Monumento A G. Caboto," *Il Progresso Italo-Canadese*, 11 December 1930.
12 Roberto Perin, "Making Good Fascists and Good Canadians: Consular Propaganda and the Italian Community in Montreal in the 1930s," in *Minorities and Mother Country Imagery*, edited by G. Gold (St. John, Nfld.: Memorial University of Newfoundland, 1984), pp. 142-46; Luigi Bruti Liberati, *Il Canada, l'Italia e il fascismo: 1919-1945* (Roma: Bonacci Editore, 1984), pp. 68-72.
13 *Il Messaggero Italo-Canadese* (Toronto), 23 December 1933.
14 *Il Bollettino*, 5 January 1934, translation by Celestino Dejulis.
15 *L'Italia*, 18 May 1935.
16 *Loc. cit.*
17 *Loc. cit.*
18 *Loc. cit.*
19 Charles M. Bayley, *The Social Structure of Italian and Ukrainian Immigrant Communities, Montreal 1935-1937*, unpublished M. A. Dissertation, McGill University, p. 194n.
20 See Dr. William Sherwood Fox, "Mussolini and the New Italy," paper delivered at the Empire Club of Canada (Toronto), 25 February 1932, p. 88.
21 Luigi Bruti Liberati, *op. cit.*, p. 122.
22 See "Entretien avec Dieni Gentile," Filippo Salvatore, *op. cit.*, p. 139.
23 See Nicoletta Serio, "L'emigrato va alla guerra: i soldati italiani nel corpo di spedizione canadese (1914-1918)," in *Il Canada e la guerra dei trentanni*, edited by Luigi Bruti Liberati (Milano: Edizioni Angelo Guerini, 1989), p. 116 n.
24 *L'Italia*, 4 May 1935.
25 Philip Morgan, *Italian Fascism 1919-1945* (London: The McMillan Press Ltd., 1995), p. 143.
26 *L'Italia*, 20 July 1935.
27 *Ibid.*, 21 March 1936.
28 *Ibid.*, 20 July 1935.

29 Luigi Bruti Liberati, *Il Canada, l'Italia e il fascismo: 1919-1945*, cit., p. 122.
30 *L'Italia*, 7 March 1936. It was not the first time that Petrucci's behaviour was the object of a question in the House. The year before, Humphrey Mitchell (East Hamilton) had asked a similar question of Sir George Perley, Acting Prime Minister. In a speech on Corporatives, delivered at the Château Laurier in Ottawa, the Ottawa Citizen reported that Petrucci had said, "I can safely say to the Canadian citizens of Italian origin that to them is reserved the great task of explaining to their fellow citizens the real meaning of the Fascism of Mussolini so that it will be much easier for the Canadian people to adapt themselves gradually to the new economic and political system which is hardly avoidable." Canada. House of Common, Hansard, 1935, p. 1276 and 1364.
31 Grace MacInnis, *J. S. Woodsworth: A Man to Remember* (Toronto: The MacMillan Company of Canada Limited, 1953), p. 240.
32 *L'Italia*, 8 February 1936.
33 See *Il Lavoratore* (Toronto), 19 September 1936; Luigi Bruti Liberati, *Il Canada, L'Italia e il fascismo*, cit., p. 133.
34 *L'Italia*, 19 September 1936.
35 Charles M. Bayley, *op. cit.*, p. 161.
36 *L'Italia*, 7 March 1937.
37 *Ibid.*, 25 September 1937.
38 Guglielmo Vangelisti, *Gli Italiani in Canada* (Montreal: Firenze, 1958), p. 212.
39 *Ibid.*, p. 214.
40 *L'Italia*, 9 October 1937.
41 *Loc. cit.*
42 *Ibid.*, 16 October 1937.
43 *Loc. cit.*
44 *Loc. cit.* See the entire text of the article "Local Politics" in appendix No. 3.
45 *Ibid.*, 9 October 1937.
46 *Ibid.*, 2 October 1937.
47 See Roberto Perin, *op. cit.*, pp. 153-154, where Brigidi is described as "the real puppeteer;" Luigi Bruti Liberati, *op. cit.*, p. 153-54.
48 Herbert F. Quinn, *The Union Nationale: Quebec Nationalism from Duplessis to Léveque* (Toronto: University of Toronto Press, 1979), p. 70; H. F. Quinn, "The Bogey of Fascism in Quebec," *Dalhousie Review*, vol. 28 (1938), now in *Quebec in the Duplessis Era, 1935-1959: Dictatorship or Democracy?* edited by Cameron Nish, (Toronto: The Copp Clark Publishing Company, 1970), p. 22.
49 F. Rose, *Fascism Over Canada* (Toronto: New Era Publishing, 1938), p. 17.
50 *L'Italia nuova* (*Le Canada Latin* section), 25 December 1937.
51 *Ibid.*, 29 April 1939.
52 Roberto Perin, *op. cit.*, p. 151.

Chapter Three

1. *Il Bollettino*, 22 November 1929.
2. *Ibid.*, 14 February 1930.
3. *Ibid.*, 6 June 1930.
4. Luigi Sturzo, *Italy and Fascism* (New York: Harcourt, Brace and Company, 1926), p. 129.
5. *Il Bollettino*, 12 October 1934.
6. *Ibid.*, 19 October 1934.
7. Luigi Sturzo, *op. cit.*, p. 130.
8. Consul Ambrosi in *Il Bollettino*, 4 May 1934.
9. *Il Bollettino*, 3 August 1934.
10. For a view of fascism as religion, see the interesting work by Emilio Gentile, *Il Culto del littorio: la sacralizzazione della politica nell'Italia fascista* (Bari: Editori Laterza, 1993).
11. *Il Bollettino*, 21 February 1930.
12. *Ibid.*, 23 May 1930.
13. *Ibid.*, 16 May 1930.
14. *Ibid.*, 21 February 1930.
15. *Ibid.*, 15 June 1934.
16. See Danelo Veneruso, *Il seme della pace: la cultura cattolica e il nazionalimperialismo fra le due guerre* (Roma: edizioni Studium, 1987), pp. 187-203. Until 1936, *Civiltà Cattolica*, the monthly publication of the Jesuit Order, supported fascist economic policy because it stemmed from the Roman Catholic doctrine as expounded by two Popes, Leo IX and Pius XI in two famous encyclicals on the social problem, *Rerum Novarum*, and *Quadragesimo anno* respectively.
17. *Il Bollettino*, 28 September 1934; see also, "Esperienza Corporativa," 5 October 1934.
18. *Ibid.*, 1 March 1935.
19. *Ibid.*, 24 May 1934.
20. Professor Cody said these words in a conference delivered to the Italian-Spanish Club on 5 March 1935, reported in *Il Bollettino*, 8 March 1935.
21. *Il Bollettino*, 24 May 1934.
22. *Ibid.*, 22 December 1938.
23. *Ibid.*, 5 January 1934. Appendices Nos. 4 & 5 are two articles discussing democratic election from a fascist point of view. Particularly negative is Mari's judgement of the newly formed CCF Party.
24. *Loc. cit.*
25. *Ibid.*, 5 January 1939.
26. *Ibid.*, 12 January 1934.
27. *Ibid.*, 26 January 1934.
28. *Ibid.*, 31 January 1937.
29. *Ibid.*, 22 February 1935.

30 For example, a special election issue of *Il Bollettino* for 15 June 1934, the last before voting day on 19 June carried thirty-five advertisements: nine political, fourteen commercial, eight professional, and four social. The nine political ads were: two for Mrs. Joshua Smith, independent, Bellwoods; one for Tom Bell, Conservative, Bellwoods; one for E. F. Singer, q.c., Conservative, St. Andrew; one for Edward J. Murphy, q.c., Conservative, St. Patrick; one for Dr. Dalrymple, Liberal, Dovercourt; one for Arthur W. Roebuck, Liberal, Bellwoods; one for Ernest C. Bogart, Liberal, Bracondale; and one for F. H. Avery, Liberal, Lincoln, a constituency located outside of the city boundaries. The fifteen commercial advertisements were: Angelo Restaurant; Progress Cigars; Perfect Electric Co.; Bloor Flower Shop; Paris Taxi; George Coles [confectionary]; Cabot Macaroni, Hamilton; Agenzia di Navigazione, M. Missori; Studio Fotografico Moderno; Marini Monumental Art Co.; Columbus Coal; L. Perfetti, Elettricista; City Dairy; and Wrestling, Maple Leaf Garden, Social. Eight were professional advertisements: Dr. Donato Sansone, surgical doctor; Denton & Denton, lawyers; N.F.A. Scandiffio, B. A., lawyer, Italian notary; Meyer Rotstein, lawyers, collectors, notaries; Dr. V. Cosentino, dentist; G. F. Sansone, optometrist; Dr. P. Fontanella, surgical doctor; Dr. M. C. Cosentino, dentist. There were four social: 15 Luglio, Grande Picnic del Fascio e Combattenti, two ads; 17 June, Festa Campestre: James Franceschini invita tutti gli italiani di Toronto e d'intorni, two ads.

31 Once the fascist regime had consolidated its grip on Italy, it set about the task of building in every Italian city and town a so-called Casa del Fascio or Fascist House or Centre. These Centres provided facilities for and control over all political, social, recreational and sport activities for their respective communities. For obvious diplomatic reasons, the name Fascist Centre could not be used abroad, instead for immigrant enclaves, they were called Casa d'Italia or Italian Centres. Of course, they served the same function abroad as they did at home and it is a misnomer to call them Casa d'Italia — the more appropriate name, given their importance for the promulgation of fascist ideology, is Fascist Centres.

32 On the Salesian brothers' work in Toronto, see Luigi Pautasso, "I Salesiani a Toronto (1924-1934)," in *Italian Canadiana*, vol. 9 (1993), pp. 115-139.

33 *Il Bollettino*, 12 January 1934.

34 "Toronto's Italians Play Large Part in City's Life," *The Toronto Daily Star*, 2, 6, and 12 January 1934.

35 Some of the people mentioned were: the renowned tenor Edoardo Fontana, a friend of Mussolini; Dr. Pasquale Fontanella, Giuseppe Grittani, the Salesian Father Peter E. Truffa, Dr. Rosario Invidiata, Professor Cav. E. Goggio, Antonio Gatto, Jacopo Magi, E. Fattori, Dr. George A. Glionna: "in 1909 he was the first Italian to graduate in Medicine from the University of Toronto," Maestro Domenico, Angelo Carbone, leader of the Fascio Principe Umberto (1931-1934), Tommaso Mari,

and many others. Among all these men there were three women: the Cuban born Mrs. Ferrari Fontana, Miss A. Iannuzziello, teacher of the Italian School, and the latest arrival, Mrs. Fantechi-Tavanti, possibly a singer.

36 *Il Bollettino*, 2 February 1934.
37 Taped interview with R. B..
38 See "Manifestini antifascisti al comizio Parini" (Anti-fascist leaflets at Parini's meeting), *La voce operaia*, 10 February 1934; Il Bollettino, 3 August 1934.
39 *Il Bollettino*, 3 August 1934.
40 *Ibid.*, 25 January 1935.
41 *Ibid.*, 23 November 1934.
42 *Ibid.*, 26 October 1934.
43 One of the questions reported by *Il Bollettino* (30 November 1934) was although "we have to pay for it but the House will be owned by the Italian government rather than being ours?"
44 Antonio Gramsci wrote: "It always happens that an individual belongs to more than one particular Association and often to Associations which are in contrast between them. A totalitarian policy aims exactly at: 1. that members of a given party find in it all the satisfaction that they found before in multiple organizations, that is that they break all the links that hold them with organisms and extraneous cultural organizations; 2. to destroy all other organizations or to incorporate them in a system in which the Party is the only regulator," quoted by Emilio Gentile, in *La via italiana al totalitarismo* (Firenze: La Nuova Italia Scientifica, 1995), p. 11.
45 See "Un'indegno atto di rappresaglia," *Il Messagero italo-canadese*, 25 March 1933. It seems that professor Antonio Sabetta went to his home town of Ururi, in the Province of Campobasso, for a brief vacation. At Ururi he was arrested and taken to Rome where he learned that Ottorino Incoronato, the Secretary of the Montreal Fascio, who was from the same town, had denounced him to the Italian police as an anti-fascist because he did not want to be involved in community affairs.
46 In an interview by the author with Father Balò, he reported the following, "I went to see the consul and I asked him this: 'do you intend to build Casa d'Italia? If you do, I won't renovate my church. He said go ahead. But after about a month they, the fascists, initiated collections for the Casa d'Italia." This seems to contradict the actual behaviour of Father Balò as reported in *Il Bollettino* (5 February 1935) at a meeting presided over by Consul General Luigi Petrucci, "Rev. Balò expressed his satisfaction for the project [Casa d'Italia] and assured us that he will give his maximum support."
47 The following are the titles of articles on the Fascist Centre which appeared in *Il Bollettino* from 26 October to 9 November 1934: "The Colony Answers Enthusiastically the Consul's Appeal for the Casa d'Italia;" "To Whom Is Destined the Casa d'Italia," October 26; "The

Casa d'Italia Will be Built"; "Parini Keeps His Word: $5,000.00 from the Government for the Casa d'Italia;" "What Is the Situation with the Casa d'Italia," 2 November; "How Will the Casa d'Italia be Maintained;" "Casa d'Italia Will Have no Debts;" "In Favour of the Casa d'Italia," 9 November.

48 *Ibid.*, 30 November 1934.
49 *Ibid.*, 26 October 1934.
50 *Manifesto of the R. V. Console.* See appendix No. 6.
51 See, in the Toronto Land Registry Office, details of the legal transaction between George W. Beardmore (owner) and Toronto Casa d'Italia Ltd. (purchaser); Julius A. Molinaro, "The Casa d'Italia in Toronto: Historical Background (1873-1983)," *Italian Canadiana*, vol. 12 (1996), p. 39.
52 According to R. B. (taped interview, author's collection), V. F. did not honour his pledge because Mussolini, to whom F. had sent a white horse, did not even return a thank-you card, let alone the knighthood that V. F. expected. For a detailed account of this episode, see Angelo Principe, *The Concept of Italy in Canada and in Italian Canadian Writings from the Eve of Confederation to the Second World War*, unpublished Ph. D. Dissertation, University of Toronto, 1989, p. 309.
53 Consul Tiberi $358.00
    Dr. Fontanella and P. Molinaro $95.00
    Zambri, Visconti and Volpi $55.00
    Ciarfella and Guerra $15.50
    Olivero $2.00
    M. Viola and N. Barreca $11.50
    A. Cancelli and Joe De Luca $0.50
    G. Savoia and A. Andreoli $13.00
    Total $550.50
54 *Il Bollettino*, 12 February 1937.
55 In three years, from 1936 to 1939, the corporation was able to reduce the mortgage from $20,000 to $10,000, see Toronto Land Registry Office. J. Molinaro, *op. cit.*, p. 39 writes, "the local Italian-language newspaper, *Bollettino Italo-Canadese*, regularly published a list of individual contributors to the Casa d'Italia, its new name. Funds were also raised through activities such as the dance organized at the King Edward Hotel 11 February 1935 attended by more than 600 persons." After the opening the Casa d'Italia Corporation did well financially.
56 *Il Bollettino*, 29 January 1937.
57 Enzo Santarelli, *Storia del fascismo*, Vol. II (Rome: Editori Riuniti, 1973), p. 367.
58 See Giuseppe Antonio Borgese, *Goliath: the March of Fascism* (New York: The Viking Press, 1937), p. 374.
59 Anthony Eden in his autobiography, *Memoirs: Facing the Dictators* (London: Cassel, 1962), pp. 191-92, wrote, "Mussolini was surreptitiously setting the stage for his aggression, but neither we, nor the world,

nor the Italian people knew it;" Gianpiero Carocci, *Storia d'Italia dall'Unità ad oggi* (Milano: Feltrinelli, 1977), p. 286.
60 See Gian Giacomo Migone, *Gli Stati Uniti e il fascismo* (Milano: Feltrinelli Editore, 1980), p. 345.
61 *Il Bollettino*, 8 and 15 May 1936.
62 *The Toronto Daily Star*, 7 May 1936.
63 *Vancouver Daily Province*, 18 May 1936.
64 *Il Bollettino*, May 1936.
65 *Ibid.*, 15 May 1936.
66 *Ibid.*, 8 January 1937.
67 *Ibid.*, 29 May 1936.
68 *Ibid.*, 1 January 1937.
69 See "Il Valore Italiano" in *La Legione dell'Italia del popolo*, (New York) 16 June 1943.
70 *Il Bollettino*, 17 April 1936.
71 *Ibid.*, 23 April 1937.
72 *Ibid.*, 10 January 1936.
73 Danilo Veneruso, *op. cit.*, p. 199.
74 See appendix No. 9.
75 Quoted by Anonino Spada, *op. cit.*, p. 125. Spada adds, however, that "many years after World War II those gold rings were located, intact, in California. The rings were never sent to the Canadian mint to be melted nor were they ever sent to Italy." He gives, however, no reference to substantiate this important point. Further, Spada's statement does not seem to be accurate. In the sum of $20,816.23 mentioned above is included $3,492.23 obtained from selling gold rings, for details see apendix No. 9.
76 *Il Bollettino*, 24 January 1936.
77 *Ibid.*, 1 January 1937.
78 Antonino Spada, *op. cit.*, p. 111, wrote that *Il Bollettino* "published for some time a smaller newspaper in Vancouver." Alhough the author has searched throughout *Il Bollettino* no reference to this publication has been found.

Chapter Four

1 Vincent Moore, *Angelo Branca: Gladiator of the Courts* (Vancouver: Douglas & McIntyre Ltd., 1981). In discussing Branca's antifascism Moore noted that at Italian-Canadian social events "he [Branca] and his wife remained seated while most of the audience stood to attention for the singing of the Fascist anthem 'Giovinezza.'" Angelo's father, Filippo, "a miner," was more openly hostile to fascism. When fascist songs were played or fascist speeches were delivered, Filippo "would clamp his wide-brimmed hat firmly on his head, glare around the room and walk out," p. 71.

2   See Gabriele Scardellato, "Beyond the Frozen Wastes: Italian Sojourners and Settlers in British Columbia," in *Arrangiarsi: The Italian Immigration Experience in Canada*, edited by Roberto Perin and Frank Sturino (Montreal: Guernica, 1989), pp. 135-162; Angelo Principe, "Note sul radicalismo tra gli italiani in Canada (1900-1915)," in *Canada e Stati Uniti*, edited by Valeria Gennaro Lerda (Venezia: Marsilio Editori, 1984), pp. 147-156. For a more comprehensive view of emigrant workers' radicalism, see Donald Avery, *Dangerous Foreigners. European Immigrant Workers and Labour Radicalism in Canada, 1896-1932* (Toronto: McClelland and Stewart, 1979); A. Ross McCormack, *Reformers, Rebels, and Revolutionaries: The Western Canadian Radical Movement 1899-1919* (Toronto: University of Toronto Press, 1977).

3   See "L'Italiano all'estero" by Fred Tenisci, *L'Eco*, 4 November 1939.

4   Enzo Santarelli, *Storia del Fascismo*, vol. 1 (Roma: Editori Riuniti, 1973), p. 227. Santarelli reports this event as follows: "On November 21 — not without some leggerezza (responsibility) on the part of the ultra-radical socialists maximalists — during the process of exchange of administrative responsibility to the new socialist city council, grave incidents occurred. Fascists broke through the police guards and began shooting at the balcony of palace D'Accursio where Mayor Gnudi was standing. Socialists defended themselves from the palace. In the Piazza, some people, who were caught between the two groups shooting at each other, were felled by hand-grenades. In the Council Chamber the minority chancellor, the lawyer Giulio Giordani, a decorated war amputee, was killed. The episode was never fully explained, but the political provocation by Leandro Arpinati and his fascist band was a factor in this episode and in the occupation and burning of the socialist Camera del Lavoro. There was, as well, a significant amount of responsibility on the part of the socialist leaders."

5   Autarchia, or economic self-sufficiency, was Mussolini's answer to the sanctions imposed on Italy by the League of Nations. Through this policy Mussolini attempted to force Italy to produce within her own borders everything that she needed.

6   *L'Eco*, 12 August 1939.

7   *Ibid.*, 2 and 9 December 1939.

8   See Tracy Phillips' report on "Canadians of Italian Descent" (Ottawa, 9 May 1942), p. 2.

9   *L'Eco*, 19 March 1938. Unfortunately, the issue of the newspaper to which the letter refers has not survived.

10 *Ibid.*, 17 December 1938.

11 *Loc. cit.*

12 *Il Bollettino* (30 April 1937) supported Mitchell Hepburn and his Liberal team because they were against the CIO: "Hepburn, the Premier of Ontario, is the only politician who truly shows the character of a fascist and is closer to this great modern political force. He fought against the

13 abuse and privileges of the dominant class; now he stands against the excesses and the power of foreign proletarian organization [the CIO]."
13 L'Eco, 16 March 1940.
14 The pen-name Littorio was no doubt derived from the Latin lictor, an official attending upon a magistrate. He carried a "fasces" with an axe, symbol of authority and power. Fascists adopted the fasces and the axe as their own symbol and here the term Littorio means fascist. The articles produced by this "author" were: "Corpus Juri Civilis," 10 September; "Corporativismo I" and "Corporativismo II," 17 and 24 September; "Laissez-Faire," 8 October; "Fierezza," 22 October; "Scambio e Produzione," 29 October; "I Due Mondi," 5 November; "Civiltà del Lavoro," 12 November; "Italia e Germania," 19 November; "Roma-Cartagine, Roma-Monaco," 10 December; "Fascismo e Democrazia I," 31 December; and "Fascismo e Democrazia II," which appeared in an issue that is missing.
15 Here, the editor refers to the pactum sceleris ratified among Mussolini, Hitler, Chamberlain and Daladier in Munich, on 29 September 1938; that was the treaty by which dismemberment of Czechoslovakia was decided.
16 L'Eco, 30 December 1939.
17 Ibid., 10 December 1938.
18 Ibid., 17 June 1939.
19 Ibid., 25 November 1939. For the entire speech see appendix No. 11.
20 Ibid., 18 May 1940.
21 Ibid., 13 April 1940.
22 Ibid., 3 February 1940.
23 Ibid., 10 February and 8 June 1940.
24 Ibid., 8 June 1940.
25 Vincent Moore, op. cit., p. 72.

CHAPTER 5

1 For a detailed account of the measures taken against Italian Jews approved by the Italian Parliament on 17 November 1938, see the *Gazzetta Ufficiale*, N. 264, 19 November 1938; also in Renzo De Felice, "Provvedimenti per la difesa della razza italiana: R. decreto-legge 17 novembre 1938-XVII," in *Storia degli ebrei sotto il fascismo* (Torino: Einaudi, 1962 and 1972), pp. 562-68.
2 See Meir Michaelis, *Axis Policies Towards the Jews in World War II* (The Fifteenth Annual Rabbi Louis Feinberg Memorial Lecture in Judaic Studies Program, University of Cincinnati, 1992), p. 1.
3 See Louis Palermo, "The Jews in Italy," *The Globe and Mail*, 6 August 1938.
4 Frederick Edwards, "Fascism in Canada," Part One, *Maclean's Magazine*, 1 May 1938, p. 15.

5 *Montreal Gazette*, 7 February 1938, quoted by Martin Robin, *Shades of Right* (Toronto: University of Toronto Pres, 1992), p. 172.
6 *Le Fasciste Canadien*, December 1937, quoted by Martin Robin, *op. cit.*, p. 172.
7 See Esther Delisle, *The Traitor and the Jew* (Montreal-Toronto: Robert Davies Publishing, 1995), p. 66.
8 *Canadian Jewish Chronicle* (Montreal), 29 April 1938.
9 *Toronto Daily Star*, 22 July 1938.
10 *Il Bollettino*, 29 September 1938.
11 In "The Origins and Development of Racial Anti-Semitism in Fascist Italy," Gene Bernardini writes "While racial anti-Semitism was largely unforeseen and probably unwanted by most Italians, it evolved from Fascist principles and policies, which they generally supported," *Journal of Modern History*, vol. 49 (1977) p. 431.
12 According to Michaelis (*op. cit.*, p. 2), "Mussolini's declaration of war on the Jews was due, not to any irresistible foreign pressure, but to his recognition of Italy's changed alignment in Europe and more particularly to his desire to cement the Axis by eliminating any strident contrast in the policy of the two Fascist Powers." See also by the same author, *Mussolini and the Jews* (London and Oxford: The Institute of Jewish Affairs and The Clarendon Press, 1978), pp. 126-7; R. De Felice, *Storia degli ebrei . . . , op. cit.*, pp. 247-50.
13 In the Gran Consiglio Fascista, only Italo Balbo had the courage to stand against the racial legislation, the rest did not muster enough courage even to speak out. They fell easily and cowardly into line with Mussolini's policy. Renzo De Felice expressed a contemptuous view of these fascists. He wrote: "Nearly no one in the entourage attempted to dissuade Mussolini. Balbo remained an exception . . . Compared to these vulgar Machiavellians, vile instruments of Mussolinian policy, profiteers of it, one is almost tempted to look with respect on a Farinacci or a Preziosi . . . " *op. cit.* pp. 240-241. Not even G. Ciano, who denied his support for Preziosi's anti-Semitic campaign, attempted to dissuade Mussolini from his anti-Semitic policy, Galeazzo Ciano, *Diario 1937-1943*, a cura di Renzo De Felice (Milano: Rizzoli, 1980, entry 29 December 1937).
14 *The Globe and Mail*, 6 August 1938.
15 "Roberto Farinacci (1892-1945) was a lifelong intransigent-recalcitrant school boy, rabble-rousing journalist, anticlerical firebrand, Fascist Party Secretary after the Matteotti affair, champion of the Rome-Berlin Axis, and leader of the anti-Semitic faction in the Fascist Party," Meir Michaelis, *Mussolini and the Jews, op. cit.*, p. 418; R. De Felice, *Mussolini il fascista*, vol. 2. pp. 185-6, 512-14; Farinacci was also a profiteer and cheater who enriched himself by using his influence in the Fascist Party and in the judicial system, Sergio Turone, *Politica ladra: Storia della corruzione in Italia*, 1861-1992 (Bari: Laterza, 1992 and 1993), pp. 140-51.

16 Farinacci to Mussolini, August 5, 1938, IC/ Segreteria particolare del Duce/Jpb 122/033909; quoted by R. De Felice, *Storia degli ebrei* . . . , *op. cit.*, p. 242; M. Michaelis, *Mussolini and the Jews, op. cit.*, p. 418.
17 Sergio Turone, *op. cit.*, p. 150; Re. De Felice, *op. cit.*, p. 241; Galeazzo Ciano, *Diario 1937-1943*, cit., 4 June 1938.
18 Alfassio U. Grimaldi and G. Bozzetti, *Farinacci il più fascista* (Milano, 1972), p. 240.
19 See Antonio Gramsci, *Il Risorgimento* (Torino: Einaudi, 1966), pp. 167-68.
20 Benedetto Croce, *Storia d'Italia dal 1871 al 1915* (Bari: Laterza, 1956), p. 101.
21 Maurizio Molinari, *Ebrei in Italia: un problema di identità (1870-1938)* (Firenze: Giunta, 1991), p. 102. Prato's statement is also confirmed and explained by Attilio Milano. In *Storia degli ebrei in Italia* (Torino: Einaudi, 1992), p. 371, Milano writes that from 1870 on, "the enjoyment of rights which were elementary to any individual, but very new for the Jew, the attraction towards Italian culture and history which to the Jew was easier to assimilate than its Jewish counterpart and, last but not the least, his ambition for personal success destroyed in a short time the solid unity of Italian Jewry."
22 Quoted by Dan Vittorio Segre, *Memoirs of a Fortunate Jew, an Italian Story,* translated by Dan Vittorio Segre (New York: The Bantam Doubleday Dell Publishing group, Inc., 1988), p. 21. "Many observant Italian and foreign Jews strongly protest against such a psychological state of mind. It seems that even Gentiles were disappointed at this"; see also, N. Goldmann, D. Lattes, U. Nahon, G. Romano, *Nel centenario della nascita di Teodor Herzl* (Venezia-Roma 1961), pp. 77-82; R. De Felice, *Storia degli ebrei* . . . , *cit.*, p. 15 n..
23 See Aldo Garosci, *Storia dei fuorusciti* (Bari: Laterza, 1953), pp. 192-193; Massino Adolfo Vitale, "The Destruction and Resistance of the Jews in Italy," in *They Fought Back: The Story of Jewish Resistance in Nazi Europe,* edited and translated by Yuri Suhl (New York: Schocken Books, 1975), pp. 298-303; De Felice, *Storia degli ebrei* . . . , cit., p. 423-424.
24 The Minister of Finance (1932-35) in Mussolini's government was a Jew, Guido Jung.
25 Members of the committee were important Jewish leaders and fascist personalities: President was Pietro Lanza Prince of Scalea, Vice-President was Alberto de Stefani, Secretary, Dante Lattes, Treasurer Angelo Sacerdoti; members were Roberto Cantalupo, Antonio Cippico, Alfredo Baccelli, Roberto Almagià, Ugo d'Ancona, Giacinto Motta, Gino Livetti, Nicola Vacchelli and Gioacchino Volpe.
26 See Maurizio Molinari, *Ebrei in Italia: un problema di identità* (1870-1938)*, cit.*, p. 104.
27 Renzo De Felice, *op. cit.*, p. 173.

28 Not too long before the publication of the Racial Manifesto, the President of the Union of the Italian Israelite communities, Felice Ravenna, recognized that fascism and Mussolini had never made a "distinction between race or religion in the living unity of the Italian people, among which the Jews have always and fully done, as has the rest of the population, their duty." See Luigi Preti, *Impero fascista, Africa ed ebrei* (Milano: Murzia, 1968), p. 189; In a colloquium with Goldmann, Mussolini said: "You must create a Hebrew State. I myself am Zionist. I already said it to Dr. Weizmann. You shoud have a real State, not the national home which England offers you. I'll help you to create a Jewish State," quoted by R. De Felice, *op. cit.*, p. 140.

29 *Il Corriere d'America,* 4 July 1937, quoted by R. De Felice, *op. cit.*, p. 195.

30 See *I Documenti Diplomatici Italiani,* Settima Serie 1922-1935, Vol. XIII (Roma: Tipografia dello Stato, MCMLXXXIX), p. 668.

31 Letter dated November 28, 1933 (XII), Archivio Storico Ministero degli Affari Esteri, N. 4506/815.

32 Archivio Storico Ministero degli Affari Esteri, gabinetto del ministro, letter dated, November 2, 1933, N. 4222 (il 1-12-1933 XII).

33 *Loc. cit.*

34 R. De Felice, *op. cit.*, p. 147.

35 When this case came before the "Tribunale Speciale", in November 1934, only two men were found guilty: Leone Ginzburg was sentenced to four years in jail and Sion Segre to three years, two of which were conditionally suspended.

36 Because of this episode, the fascist Jews of Turin led by Ettore Ovazza created their own newspaper, *La nostra bandiera:* they were against bolshevism and zionism alike, R. De Felice, *op. cit.*, pp. 150-59.

37 See *Il carroccio,* vol. XXXVI, n. 5 (October 1934), p. 452. The radio message in question was also published by *Il Bollettino,* 30 November 1934.

38 *Ibid.*, p. 453.

39 See "Document n. 9" in De Felice, *op. cit.*, p. 518.

40 Graeme S. Mount, John Abbott and Michal J. Mulloy, *The Border at Sault Ste. Marie* (Toronto: Dundurn Press, 1995), p. 49.

41 For the beginnings of Little Italy in the "Ward", see Angelo Principe, "Italiani in Toronto prima del 1861," *Italian Canadiana,* vol. 7 (1991) pp. 98-120; for the development of the Ward's Little Italy, see John Zucchi, *Italians in Toronto: Development of a National Identity: 1875-1935* (Kingston and Montreal: McGill-Queen's University Press, 1988), pp. 34-67; Robert Harney, "Italians in Toronto, 1885-1915," *Italian Americana,* vol. 1, no. 2, (1975) pp. 143-168; Nick Simone, "Italian Immigrants in Toronto, 1890-1930," Discussion Paper No. 26, Geography Department, York University, 1977. For the Ward as a Jewish town, see Stephen Speisman's *The Jews of Toronto* (Toronto:

McClelland and Stewart, 1979), in particular, Chapter 6, "Residential Patterns in the New Community," pp. 81-95.

42 See Cyril H. Levitt and William Shaffir, *The Riot at Christie Pits* (Toronto: Lester & Orpen Dennys, 1987), p. 187; Robert Harney, "The Italian Community in Toronto", in *Two Nations, Many Cultures*, edited by Jean Elliot (Scarborough, Ont.: Prentice-Hall Canada, 1979), pp. 223-224.

43 One of the people interviewed by Cyril H. Levitt and William Shaffir (*op. cit.*, p. 185) said, "when I went to Christie Pits I went with Italian boys... we went up with a dump truck and I had a pick axe. I went with Italian boys, I went with Steve Rocco and Frankie Genovese, and I was partners with a guy called Gene Volpi that I liked very much . . . My father-in law was Italian and we were digging the cellar, and I wasn't about to get my nose broken so I took a handle from a pick axe . . . I remember the kid's name that drove the truck, Andy Bartole."

44 Interview with R.B., author's collection; Luigi Pautasso, "La donna italiana durante il periodo fascista in Toronto (1930-1940)," *Quaderni Canadesi*, vol. 1, no. 1 (1977) p. 10.

45 In a taped interview, R. B., one of the leading fascists in the Fascio Principe Umberto, said that the Consul received a letter from Rome which asked: "Didn't you have anyone else to send to Italy? Only a Jewess!" The letter ordered the Consul to replace her. The reasons, according to R. B., were that "Mrs. Elisa (Rebecca) Palange defended two of the young Toronto women who, it seems, had taken something from the hotel to bring home as souvenirs. In defence of the two youths, Palange was reported to have said, 'Why are you so hard with them? After all, they are Italians like you.'" According to R. B., fascists in Rome took these words as an offense.

46 Etelvina Frediani was replaced in 1937 by Egilda Maria Fontanella, sister of the leading fascist Dr. Pasquale Fontanella. Two years later, Mrs. Filomena Riccio was called to lead the Female Section of the Toronto Fascio, *Il Bollettino*, 1 December 1938.

47 *Il Bollettino*, 18 May and 15 June 1934.

48 *Ibid.*, 18 May 1934.

49 See the chapter "Mosleyites in Canada," in Lita-Rose Betcherman, *The Swastika and the Maple Leaf: Fascist Movements in Canada in the Thirties* (Toronto: Fitzhenry & Whiteside, 1975), pp. 76-84.

50 "Work! Wealth! Wages!" by Brandel Charles in *Il Bollettino*, 12 May 1938. Brandel Charles (alias C. B. Crate) was editor of the *Thunderbolt*, printed in Toronto. "Charles Brandel (Crate) represented the CUF at the Youth Congress held in May 1935, eventually he replaced Simpkin in the leadership of the CUF," Lita-Rose Betcherman, *op. cit.*, p. 79. In the late 1920s and early 1930s *The Thunderer* was published in Toronto where Italian fascists were in contact with the paper and its editor. The great similarity in the names of the two papers leads one to believe that one was the offshoot of the other.

51 "Fascism and the Christian Ideal," *Il Bollettino*, 24 February 1938.
52 *Il Bollettino* (5 January 1934) reviewed positively Jones' book, *Is Fascism The Answer?* (Hamilton, Ontario: Davis-Lisson Ltd., 1933); this review was translated into English and published in the paper's 26 January 1934 issue. Further, in 1938, having just returned from Italy, Jones painted a rosy picture of Italy and its government, in an interview with *Il Bolletino*.
53 *Canadian Jewish Archives*, Montreal: Canadian Jewish Congress, 1978, pp. 62-64.
54 *Il Bollettino*, 17 April 1936.
55 The pamphlet *The Jews in Italy*, appeared in *Il Bollettino*, in three instalments: 24 April, 1 and 8 May 1936.
56 *Il Bollettino*, 5 March 1937.
57 *The Catholic Register*, 3 February 1938; *Il Bollettino*, 10 February 1938.
58 Galeazzo Ciano, *Diario 1937-1943*, cit., entry 15 February 1938, p. 99.
59 *L'Italia nuova*, 26 March 1938.
60 *Loc. cit.*
61 *Le Canada Latin*, a section of *L'Italia nuova*, 5 March 1938: for the complete text see appendix N. 13.
62 The complete text of the "Informazione diplomatica n. 14," is found in Renzo De Felice, *op. cit.*, p. 272.
63 In his *Diario 1937-43*, cit., entry for 15 February 1938, p. 99, Ciano noted: "On my part, I only suggested that the Jewish State he foresaw should not be in Palestine. This would safeguard our relation with the Arabs."
64 *The Canadian Jewish Chronicle* (Montreal), 11 March 1938; see also the issues of 18 and 25 February and 4 March 1938. In its 11 March essue, the Jewish paper reprinted the article which had appeared in *Le Canada Latin*, and it prefaced the reprint with the following note: "The following article appeared in *Le Canada Latin*, a periodical devoted to Canadian-Italian residents. At their own request we are publishing it in order to give the Italian viewpoint on the subject under consideration. Our own comments however are made in the editorial columns."
65 *Ontario Jewish Archives*, Joint Community Relations Committee Collection (OJA JCRCC), file PR142.
66 *Loc. cit.*
67 In this issue there were two more items related to the Jewish question; 1) "The Finnish Government has decided to expel all Jews" who entered the country during the current year 1938 and; 2) "Brazil, Uraguay and Argentina closed their doors to Jews."
68 *L'Eco*, 12 November 1938. The reader will note that there is a difference of 20 in the figures as given by the paper.
69 Vincent Moore, *op. cit.*, p. 2.
70 *L'Italia nuova*, 3 September 1938.
71 *Ibid.*, 1 October 1938.

72 Taking a stand against Mussolini's anti-Semitic policy in July 28, Pope Pius XI said, "we should ask ourselves why Italy has an unfortunate need to imitate Germany... We should say that human beings are first of all one grand and sole race, one large and sole generated and generating, living family. In this sense, humanity is one sole, universal, Catholic race," quoted by Giorgio Angelozzi Gariboldi, *Pio XII, Hitler e Mussolini: il Vaticano fra le dittature* (Milano: Mursia, 1988), p. 81.

73 An infuriated Mussolini threatened to create a wave of anti-clericalism in the country if the Pope insisted on censuring his anti-Semitic measures. See Ciano, *Diario 1937-43*, cit., 22 August 1938, p. 167, who wrote, "contrary to what people believe, I [Mussolini] am a very patient man. But no one should make me lose my patience, otherwise I react furiously (facendo il deserto). If the Pope keeps on speaking up, I will incite the Italians and soon they will return to be anticlerical;" Giorgio Angelozzi Gariboldi, *op. cit.*, p. 81; De Felice, *op. cit.*, pp. 288-289.

74 *L'Italia nuova*, 3 September 1938.

75 *Ibid.*, 3 September 1938.

76 *Loc. cit.*

77 *L'Italia nuova*, 29 October 1938.

78 *Ibid.*, 20 May 1939.

79 Before the infamous "Manifesto", the word "race" was used to mean nation or country or a people who had a common historical experience, language and tradition. In the Manifesto in question the word "race" was used with the meaning of biological distinction.

80 *Il Bollettino*, 11 August 1938.

81 Frank Molinaro, "Italy and the Jews," *The Globe and Mail*, 27 July 1938.

82 On 4 August a decree barred Jewish children, who had neither an Italian (Aryan) mother nor an Italian (Aryan) father, from attending Italian schools and, on 1 September, all Jews who had entered Italy after 1 January 1919 were ordered to leave the country within six months.

83 According to Gemma Volli, "La vera storia dei 'Protocolli dei savi anziani di Sion,'" (*Il Ponte*, fascicolo XI, November 1957, pp. 1649-1662), "The Protocols... was a French satirical novel against Napoleon III. Peter Ivanovic Ratschkovskj, an anti-Semitic Russian agent in France, translated it into Russian and made the Jews, the Elders of Zion, the protagonists rather than Machiavelli [who was the protagonist in the French work]. The book was translated from Russian into French, English, German, Italian and so on. Anti-Semites all over the world naively or dishonestly accepted this fiction as an historical document." There was even a court case about the dubious origin of this book in Switzerland in 1935. Giuseppe Prezzolini defined the Protocols "an anti-Semitic historical novel," in *Il Resto del Carlino*, 8 May 1921.

84 *The Catholic Register*, 26 January 1939.

85 De Felice, *op. cit.*, p. 192.

86 In a long interview with Mari's wife, Giuseppina Gatto Mari, the author learned that once Mari repatriated with the diplomatic corps in the fall of 1940, discovered in Italy the truth about fascism and according to his wife, who had returned to her native land Canada after his death, he went through a new metamorphosis and became anti-fascist. He helped the partisans fighting in the countryside by bringing them food and intelligence. Giuseppina said that he had written a book which she brought to Canada but since no one of the several people who saw it were interested, she burned it.

87 *Il Messaggero italo-canadese*, 4 February 1933.

88 *Il Bollettino*, 8 September 1938, carried five articles on racism ("Gli Ebrei Nel Mondo" by Aschenasi and Sefardim, "Testimonianze Ebraiche," "La Razza e L'Impero," "'Noi Tireremo Dritto' anche per la questione della razza," "Una Domanda al Rabino Edward L. Israel"); on 15 September there were again five pieces related to the Jews ("The Jews in Italy", "La lotta degli ebrei contro i prodotti italiani nel mondo?," "Variazioni sul Problema Integrale della Razza," "L'Austria non vuole medici ebraici," "La Svizzera Caccia Gli Ebrei"); on 22 September three pieces ("'Gli avvenimenti odierni [regarding Jews] Furono Previsti', il Duce," "Democrazia e Razza nei Provvedimenti del Consiglio dei Ministri," and the first of over 25 weekly instalments of the "Protocols . . ." appeared.

89 "The Truth About Spain," *Il Bollettino*, 8 September 1938.

90 *Ibid.*, 2 March 1939.

91 *Ibid.*, 22 September 1938.

92 *Ibid.*, 9 February 1939.

93 OJA JCRCC, file Pr 131.5.35.

94 Letter from the Canadian Jewish Congress to I. Davis of Sault Ste. Marie, Ontario, dated 29 March 1939, OJA CJRCC, file PR 142.

95 *Il Bollettino*, 18 August 1938.

96 *Ibid.*, 1 September 1938.

97 *Ibid.*, 9 February 1939.

98 *Ibid.*, 29 February 1939.

99 See "Berlin Hails Anti-Semite Move in Italy: Fascist Manifesto Regarded as Victory for Hitler's Race Ideology," *The Globe and Mail*, 15 July 1938.

100 *Il Bollettino*, 1 December 1938.

101 See note 72 above.

102 *Il Bollettino*, 1 September 1938.

103 *Ibid.*, 25 August 1938.

104 *Ibid.*, 29 June 1939.

105 *Discorsi di Pio XI*, vol. III, *cit.*, 780, quoted by Sandro Rogari, "Azione Cattolica e fascismo: la crisi del 1938 e il distacco dal regime," in *Nuova Antologia*, vol. 113, no. 534 — fascicolo 2127 (1978), p. 354.

106 See the editorial, "Nazism Creates More Peril than Communism," *The Catholic Register*, 13 April 1939; also 2, 16, 23 February, 27 April

1939, and 20 June 1940. In this issue the paper noted that "Fascism is an evil system. All that could ever be said in excuse for it was that it was meant to save Italy from Bolshevism, but a country is in a bad way when it must call in Satan to cast away Satan"; Sandro Rogari, "Azione cattolica e fascismo . . . ," *op. cit.,* p. 353.

107 *Il Bollettino,* 2 March 1939.
108 *The Catholic Register,* 29 February 1939.
109 *Loc. cit..*
110 *Il Bollettino,* 2 March 1929.
111 See "Bishop Carrell Speaks of Dictatorship in Countries Recently Visited," *The Catholic Register,* 27 April 1939.
112 *L'Eco,* 8 June 1940.
113 *Il Bollettino,* 29 June 1939.
114 *Il Corriere della sera* (Milano), 11 January 1939; Renzo De Felice, *Storia degli ebrei . . . , cit.,* pp. 317-318. Further, Renzo De Felice wrote that Gemelli saw "Guglielmo da Salicento as a champion of the medieval synthesis uniting individual and society, Church and State, religion and politics, science and faith, Church and school. In the centuries following, the disintegration of this unity came about through the activities of the Jewish-Masonic faction and (according to Gemelli) the dissension between Church and State in the nineteenth sentury." Mari may have had this passage in mind when he wrote the article quoted above, note 113, since *Il Bollettino* was receiving *Il Corriere della sera* regularly.
115 OJA JCRCC, file PR142.
116 *Il Bollettino,* 15 September 1938.
117 A similar letter was sent to the following: Alderman Geo. P. Granel, Alderman Wm. Croft, Controller J. D. McNish, Mr. George A. Wilson, Alderman E. C. Bogat, K.C., Mr. Wm. V. Muir, and Mr. Poat V. Roach. OJA JCRCC, File PR 142.
118 *Loc. cit.*
119 Cohen to Purkis, 27 January 1939, OJA JCRCC, file PR 142.
120 Report dated 19 October 1942, by Vittorio V. Restaldi, honorary Italian Vice-Consul in Montreal: "Sul Trattamento degli Italiani al Canada dopo la Dichiarazione di Guerra," *Affari Transoceanici/Ministero Affari Esteri,* Canada, b. 12, f. 2, p. 9.
121 *La voce degli italo-canadesi* (Toronto), 31 December 1938.
122 Angelo Principe, "The Italo-Canadian Anti-Fascist Press in Toronto: 1922-1940," *North East Modern Language Association,* vol. 4 (1980); reprinted in *Polyphony: The Bulletin of the Multicultural History Society of Ontario,* vol. 7, no. 2 (1985).
123 *Il Bollettino,* 9 June 1938.
124 Giuseppe Ricci, *L'orfano di padre: le memorie di Giuseppe Ricci,* Toronto: (n.p., n.d.), p. 221.
125 *Il Bollettino,* 2 March 1939.

126 Taped interview with R. B., author's collection; Mario Duliani, *La ville sans femmes* (Montreal: Société des éditions Pascale, 1945); an Italian version *Città senza donne* (Montreal Gustavo D'Errico, 1946); now in English, *The City Without Women,* translated and with an introduction by Antonino Mazza (Oakville-New York-London: Mosaico, 1994), pp. 127-128.
127 Interview with R. B., author's collection.

Epilogue

1 See "Commenti al discorso del Console Generale: Dopo cinque anni ritorniamo al dilemma: O con Noi — O contro di noi," *Il Messaggero italo-canadese,* 18 November 1933.
2 *Ibid.*
3 Joseph Anthony Ciccocelli (*op. cit.*, p. 25 and n.) writes that Dr. Sansone and "many of his friends disdained the Dictator's involvement in Africa." This, of course, is not the fact: either Ciccocelli misunderstood Sansone or Sansone, who spoke more than three decades after the events, did not recall the facts properly. During the Ethiopian war he, Sansone, was chairman of a Committee whose task was to present to the Canadian public Italy's point of view. He had an exchange of letters with the Mayor of Toronto, Simpson, who had been critical of Italy. Sansone argued the right of fascist Italy to invade Ethiopia. (See *Il Bollettino,* 16 December 1938). Sansone was probably correct when he referred to Mussolini's pro-German policy: "I had fought in the First World War for the Italian forces and sincerely believed that I was fighting for a just cause. But when Italy sided with Germany in 1940, Mussolini had destroyed the years of work which had gone into unifying our homeland," Ciccocelli, *cit.*, p. 35. See also Vittorio V. Restaldi, "Memoriale sul trattamento degli italiani al Canada dopo la dichiarazione di guerra," 19 Ott. 1942, ASEA (Archivio Storico del Ministero degli Affari Esteri, serie affari politici 1931-1945: Canada), 34.R/10411.
4 Interview with Ruggero B., author's collection.
5 See *L'Italia nuova,* 20 May 1939.
6 Letter from F. F. to his wife, private collection, author's possession.
7 Omer Hérouz, "Les étonnements de M. Class, député et organisateur du boycott juif contre la marchandise allemande," *Le Devoir* (editorial), 26 October 1938, quoted by Esther Delisle, *op. cit.*, p. 149.
8 Paolo Orano, *Gli ebrei in Italia* (Roma: Casa Editrice Pinciana, XV), p. 163. Esther Delisle described a similar situation in *The Traitor and the Jew,* referring to Quebec right-wing nationalists.
9 See Indro Montanelli, "Il fascismo della livrea," in *Corriere della sera,* 25 April 1996.
10 See the *Corriere italiano,* 23 March 1929.

11 Joseph A. Ciccocelli, *op. cit.*, pp. 36-38.
12 See *La Favilla* (monthly), October 1940.
13 See Mario Duliani, *op. cit.*, p. 136.

SELECTED BIBLIOGRAPHY

NEWSPAPERS AND PERIODICALS

L'Araldo del Canada, weekly (Montreal).
Bollettino del Circolo Colombo, monthly (Toronto).
Il Bollettino italo-ocanadese, weekly (Toronto).
Canadian Jewish Chronicle, weekly (Montreal).
Il Carroccio, monthly (New York).
Catholic Register, weekly (Kingston, Ontario).
Il Cittadino italo-canadese, weekly (Montreal).
Corriere italiano, one issue only, (Toronto).
Le Devoir, daily (Montreal).
L'Eco italo-canadese, weekly (Vancouver).
L'Emigrato, bi-weekly: five issues only (Toronto).
La Favilla, monthly (Toronto).
Le Fiamme d'Italia, only the masthead (Montreal).
Gerarchia, monthly (Rome).
Il Grido della stirpe, weekly (New York).
L'Italia, weekly (Montreal).
L'Italia nuova, weekly (Montreal).
Il Lavoratore, bi-weekly (Toronto).
Il Martello, weekly (New York).
Il Messaggero italo-canadese, weekly (Toronto).
Il Progresso italo-canadese, weekly (Toronto).
Quaderni canadesi, bi-monthly (Toronto).
La Tribuna canadese, only three issues (Toronto).
La Voce degli italo-canadesi, bi-weekly (Toronto).
La Voce operaia, bi-weekly (Toronto).

TAPED INTERVIEWS

Bacci, Ruggero (Toronto)
Bortolotti, Attilio (Toronto)
Bortolotti, Anselmo (Ottawa)
Di Giulio, Donald (Toronto)
Fera, Carlo (Sault St. Marie, Ontario)
Frediani, Frank (Toronto)
Lamberti, Carlo (Toronto)
Lattoni, Mario (Montreal)
Martino, Quinto (Hamilton)

Zaffiro, Francesco (Hamilton)

PRIVATE CORRESPONDENCE AND PAPERS

Bacci, Ruggero Papers. Private Collection (PC).
Bersani, Rev. Augusto Papers. United Church Archives (Toronto).
Di Giulio, Donald Papers. PC.
Frediani, Etelvina Papers. PC.
Goggio, Emilio Papers. Public Archives of Canada (PAC).
Lamberti, Carlo Papers. PC.
Mari, Giuseppina Gatto. PC.
Missori, Marco. PAC.
Pautasso, Luigi. PC.

UNPUBLISHED RECORDS AND MATERIAL

Archivio centrale dello stato (Euro) Roma: Ministero dell'Interno, Direzione generale affari generali e riservati, Casellario Politico Centrale: b. 772 (Attilio Bortolotti), b. 798 (Beniamino Bottos), b. 905 (Terzo Busca), b. 1168 (Nanni Leone Castelli), b. 5332 (Nicola Giancotti), b. 4885 (Antonino Spada), b. 5408 (Maurizio Vietti).
Archivio Storico del Ministero degli affari esteri (Rome, Italy), Serie affari politici 1931-1945, sezione Canada: Pacco 489; 490; 359; 360; 1168.
Multicultural History Society of Ontario: Italian Section. Archives of Ontario.
Ontario Jewish Archives, Joint Community Relations Committee Collection. File PR 142.
Public Archives of Canada (Ottawa): Ethnic Newspapers Section; Tracy Philipps Papers, Mg 30E 350.
United Church Archives. File on the Italian Mission (Toronto).

THESES

Bayley, M. Charles. *The Social Structure of the Italian and Ukrainina Immigrants Communities: Montreal, 1935-1937.* Master's Thesis, McGill University, 1939.

Brandino, Diana. *The Italians in Hamilton, 1921-1945.* Master's Thesis, The Univeristy of Western Ontario, 1977.

Ciccocelli, J. Anthony. *The Innocuous Enemy Alien: Italians in Canada During World War Two.* University of Western Ontario, 1977.

Principe, Angelo. *The Concept of Italy in Canada and in Italian-Canadian Writings from the Eve of Confederation to the Second World War*, Ph. D. Dissertation. University of Toronto, 1989.

Sidlofsky, Samuel. *Post-War Immigrants in the Changing Metropolis with Special Reference to Toronto's Italian Population*, Ph. D. Dissertation. University of Toronto, 1969.

BOOKS AND ARTICLES

Abella, Irving & Troper, Harold. *None is too many*. Toronto: Lester and Orpen Dennys, 1983.

Anctil, Pierre. *Le Devoir, les Juifs et l'immigration. De Bourassa à Laurendeau*. Québec: Institut québécois de recherche sur la culture, 1988.

Anstey, E. Margaret. "Italy Renascent." In *Social Welfare*, March 1929.

Arendt, Hannah. *The Origin of Totalitarianism*. New York: The World Publishing Company, 1966.

_____. *The Jews as Pariah*. New York: Grave Press, inc., 1978.

Associazioni ed Enti Italiani in Canada, Edizione 1934, a cura dell'Italian Bureau e *Il Bollettino italo-canadese*.

Avery, Donald. *Dangerous Foreigners*. Toronto: McClelland and Stewart Ltd., 1979.

Bagnell, Kenneth. *Canadese. A Portrait of the Italian Canadians*. Toronto: Macmillan of Canada, 1989.

Barrett, R. Stanley. *Is God a Racist? The Right Wing in Canada*. Toronto: University of Toronto Press, 1987.

Bastianini, Giuseppe. "I Fasci italiani all'estero: il valore di un congresso." In *Gerarchia*, October 1925.

Bernardini, Gene. "The Origins and Development of Racial Anti-Semitism in Fascist Italy." In *Journal of Modern History* (49), September 1977.

Betcherman, Lita-Rose. *The Swastika and the Mapple Leaf. Fascist Movements in Canada in the Thirties*. Toronto, Montreal, Winnipeg, Vancouver: Fitzhenry & Whiteside, 1975.

Blake, E. H.. "Awaking Italy." In *The Canadian Forum*, July 1923.

Boissevain, Jeremy. *The Italians of Montreal: Social Adjustment in a Plural Society*. Ottawa: Queen's Printer for Canada, 1972.

Boni, Enrico. "Giovanni Caboto." In *Rivista d'Italia e d'America*, July 1926.

Borgese, G. A. *Goliath. The March of Fascism*. New York: The Viking Press, 1937.

Bottai, Giuseppe. *Diario 1935-1944* (a cura di Giordano Bruno Guerri). Milano: Rizzoli, 1982.

Briani, Vittorio. *La Stampa Italiana all'estero dalle orogini ai nostri giorni*. Roma: Istituto poligrafico dello stato, 1977.

Broadfoot, B. *Years of Sorrow, Years of Shame. The Story of the Japanese-Canadians in World War II*. Don Mills, Ontario: 1977.

Buranello, Robert, ed. *I Giuliani-Dalmati in Canada: considerazioni ed immagini*. Toronto: Legas, 1995.

Cameron, Nish, ed. *Quebec in the Duplessis Era, 1935-1959: Dictatorship or Democracy?*. Toronto: Copp Clark Publishing Company, 1970.

Canadian Jewish Archives (N. 5-8: The Jewish Congress Archival Record of 1936). Montreal: Canadian Jewish Congress, 1978.

Cannistraro, V. Philip. "Fascism and italian americans." In *Cenni storici sulla emigrazione italiana nelle americhe e in Australia* a cura di Renzo De Felice. Milano: Franco Angeli Editore, 1978.

———. "Per una storia dei fasci negli Stati Uniti (1921-1929)." In *Storia contemporanea*, a. XXVI, n, 6, dicembre 1995, pp. 1061-1144.

Cantalupo, Roberto. *Racconti politici dell'altra pace*. Milano: Istituto per gli studi di politica internazionale, 1940.

Carocci, Giampiero. *Storia d'Italia dall'Unità ad oggi*. Milano: Feltrinelli, 1977.

Carbone, Stanislao. *The Streets Were Not Paved With Gold*. Winnipeg, Manitoba: Italian Heritage Committee, 1993.

Caroli, Betty Boyd, Robert F. Harney, Lydio F. Tomasi, eds. *The Italian Immigrant Woman in North America*. Toronto: The Multicultural History Society of Ontario, 1978.

Carter, M. Gwendollen. "Canada and Sanctions in the Italo-Ethiopian Conflict." In *The Canadian Historical Association*. Toronto, University of Toronto Press, 1940.

Ciano, Galeazzo. *Diario 1937-1943* (a cura di Renzo De Felice). Milano: Rizzoli, 1980.

Clark-Grayson-Grayson, ed. *Prophet and Protest: Social Movements in Twentieth-Century Canada*. Toronto: Gage Education Publishing Ltd., 1975.

Clark, Gregory. "London to Paris to Rome." In Addresses to *The Empire Club of Canada*. Toronto: The Printers Guild, 1939.

Colilli, Iuele Diana. *I Friulani di Sudbury*. Toronto: Legas, 1994.

Colonna, Mario. "Italy and World Affairs." In Addresses to *The Empire Club of Canada*. Toronto: The Printers Guild Ltd., 1934.

Careless, J. M. S. and Brown R. Graig, eds. *The Canadians: 1867-1967*. Toronto: McMillan of Canada, 1968.

Cresciani, Gianfranco. *Fascism, Anti-Fascism and Italians in Australia, 1922-1945*. Canberra, ACT, London, England and Trubull, Conn. USA: Australian National University Press, 1980.

———. "Italian Fascism in Australia (1922-1945)." In *Studi Emigrazione/Études Migrations* (anno XXV, N. 90), June 1988.

———. "Italian anti-fascism in Australia (1920-1945)." In *Cenni storici sulla emigrazione italiana nelle americhe e in Australia*, a cura di Renzo De Felice. Milano: Franco Agneli Editore, 1979.

Croce, Benedetto. *Storia d'Italia dal 1871 al 1915*. Bari: Laterza, 1956.

Culos, Marino. *Suvenir* (pamphlet). Vancouver, 1935.

Curcio, Carlo. "Giovanni Caboto." In *Rivista d'Italia e d'America* (anno III), June-July 1925.

———. "I nuovi compiti dei fasci all'estero." In *Rivista d'Italia e d'America* (anno III), October-November 1925.

De Conde, Alexander. *Half Bitter, Half Sweet*. New York: Scribner's Sons, 1971.

De Felice, Renzo. *Intervista sul fascismo*. Bari: Laterza, 1976.

———. *Mussolini il Duce. Gli anni del concenso: 1929-1936*. Torino: Einaudi, 1974.

_____. *Interpretations of Fascism* (trans. by Brenda Huff Evertt). Cambridge Mass.: Harvard Univeristy Press, 1977.

_____. *Rosso e Nero*. Milano: Baldini & Castoldi, 1995.

_____. *Storia degli ebrei sotto il fascismo*. Torino: Einaudi, 1962.

_____ (a cura di). *Cenni storici sull emigrazione italiana nelle americhe e in Australia*. Milano: Franco Angeli Editore, 1979.

De Grand, J. Alexander. *Fascist Italy and Nazi Germany. The 'Fascist' Style of Rule*. London and New York, 1996.

De Grazia, Vittoria. *The Culture of Consent: Mass Organization of Leisure in Fascist Italy*. Cambridge-London-New York: Cambridge University Press, 1981.

_____. *How Fascism Ruled Women. Italy, 1922-1945*. Berkeley-Los Angeles-Oxford: University of California Press, 1992.

Delisle, Esther. *The Traitor and the Jew*. Montreal — Toronto: Robert Davies Publishing, 1993.

De Michelis, Giuseppe. "La politica nazionale della emigrazione." In *Gerarchia* (anno III, N. 10), October 1925.

Diggins, John P. *Mussolini and Fascism. The View from America*. Princeton: Princeton University Press, 1972.

_____. "The Italo-American Anti-Fascist Opposition." In *The Journal of American History*, December 1967.

Di Marzio, Cornelio. "Fascismo all'estero." In *Gerarchia*, 1927.

Documenti diplomatici italiani, settima serie: 1922-1935. Roma: Ministero Degli Affari Esteri, MCMLIII.

Dubro, James and Rowland, F. Robin. *Undercover: Case of the RCMP's Most Secret Operative*. Markham Ontario: Octopus Publishing Group, 1991.

_____. *King of the Mob. Rocco Perri and the Women Who Ran His Rackets*. Markham, Ontario: Penguin Books, 1987.

Duliani, Mario. *La ville sans femmes*. Montreal: Société des editions Pascal, 1945, an Italian version, 1946; now translated into English by Antonino Mazza: *The City Without Women*. Oakville, Ont., Mosaic Press, 1994.

Eden, Anthony (Earl of Avon). *The Eden Memoirs. Facing the Dictators*. London: Cassell, 1962.

Edwards, Fredrick. "Fascism in Canada." In *Maclean's Magazine*, April 15 & May 1, 1938.

Eliot, J. *Two Nations, Many Cultures*. Scarbour, Ont.: Prentice-Hall Canada, 1979.

Fainella, John. "The Development of Italian Organizations in Calgary." In *Alberta History*, Winter 1984.

Foerster, F. Robert. *The Italian Emigration of Our Times*. New York: Arno Press, 1969.

Forbes, Rosita. "Dictators and Democrats." In *Addresses to the Empire Club of Canada*. Toronto: The Hunter-Rose Co. Ltd, 1940.

Forgacs, David, ed. *Rethinking Italian Fascism*. London: Lawrence and Wishart, 1986.

Fox, Sherwood William. "Mussolini and the New Italy." In *Addresses to the Empire Club of Canada*. Toronto: The Printers Guild, 1932.
Franzina, E.. "L'emigrazione schedata." In B. Bezza, ed., *Gli italiani fuori d'Italia*. Milano: F. Angeli, 1983.
Frasca, Isidori Rosella. . . . *e il duce le volli sportive*. Bologna: Pàtron Editore, 1983.
Gaglia, Luigi. "La propaganda italiana a sostegno della guerra contro l'Etiopia svolta in Gran Bregagna nel 1935-36." In *Storia Contemporanea* (anno XV, n. 5), ottobre 1984, pp. 845-908.
Gariboldi, Angelo. *Pio XII, Hitler e Mussolini: il Vaticano fra le dittature*. Milano: Mursia, 1988.
Garosci, Aldo. *Storia dei fuorusciti*. Bari: Laterza, 1953.
Gentile, Emilio. *Il culto del littorio: la sacralizzazione della politica nell'Italia fascista*. Bari: Laterza, 1993.

_____. *La via italiana al totalitarismo*. Firenze: La Nuova Italia Scientifica, 1995.

_____. "Fascism as Political Religion." In *Journal of Contemporary History*, Vol. 25, 1990.

_____. "La politica estera del partito fascista. Ideologia e organizzazione dei Fasci italiani all'estero (1920-1930)." In *Storia contemporanea*, a. XXVI, n. 6, dicembre 1995, pp. 897-956.

_____. *La Grande Italia. Ascesa e declino del mito della nazione nel ventesimo secolo*. Milano: Mondadori, 1997.

Gini, Corrado. "The Demographic Policy of the Italian Government." In *Addresses to The Empire Club of Canada*. Toronto: The Hunter-Rose Co., Ltd., 1931.
Gli antifascisti italiani in America (1942-1944) con prefazione di Renzo De Felice. Firenze: Felice Le Monnier, 1990.
Goggio, Emilio. "Italian Influence on the Cultural Life of Old Montreal." In *Canadian Modern Language Review*, Fall Number, 1952.
Gougeon, Gilles, ed. *A History of Quebec Nationalism* (Translated by Louisa Blair, Robert Chodos and Hane Ubertino. Toronto: James Lorimer & Company, Puglishers, 1994.
Gramsci, Antonio. *Il Risorgimento*. Torino: Einaudi, 1966.
Granatstein, L. Jack. *A Man of Influence: Norman A. Robertson and Canadian Statecraft, 1929-68*. Ottawa: Deneau, 1981.

_____. *Canada's War: The Politics of the Mackenzie King Government 1939-1945*. Toronto: Oxford University Press, 1975.

Grimaldi, U. Alfasio e Bozzetti Gherardo. *Farinacci, il più fascista*. Milano: Bompiani, 1972.
Gualtieri, Francesco M. *We Italians: a Study in Italian Immigration in Canada*. Toronto: Italian World War Veterans' Association, 1929.
Handlin, Oscar. *The Uprooted*. Boston: Little Brown, 1973.
Hannant, Larry. "Fifth-Column Crisis. War jitters on the home front, 1940." In *The Beaver* (Exploring Canadain's History), December 1993-January 1994.

Harney, Robert F. *If One Were to Write a History:Selected Writings by Robert F. Harney* (edited by Pierre Anctil and Bruno Ramirez). Toronto: Multicultural History Society of Ontario, 1991.
    _____. *Italians in Canada*. Toronto: The Multicultural History Society of Ontario, 1978.
    _____. *Dalla frontiera alle Little Italies. Gli italiani in Canada 1800-1945* (trans. by Luigi Bruti Liberati). Roma: Bonacci, 1984.
    _____. *From the Shores of Hardship: Italians in Canada* (edited by Nicolas De Maria Harney). Welland Ontario: Soleil, 1993.
    _____. *Gathering Place: Peoples and Neighbourhoods of Toronto, 1834-1945*. Toronto: Multicultural History Society of Ontario, 1985.
Harney, Robert F. and Vincenza, J. Scarpaci. *Little Italies in North America*. Toronto: The Multicultural History Society of Ontario, 1981.
Heaton, H.. "Fascism Takes Shape." In *The Canadian Forum*, February 1926.
Hillmer, Norman, Kordan Bohdan, Luciuk Lubomyr. *On Guard for Thee: War, Ethnicity, and the Canadian State, 1939-1945*. Ottawa: Canadian Committee for the History of the Second World War, 1988.
Hoar, Victor. *The Mackenzie-Papineau Battalion*. The Copp Clark Publishing Company, 1969.
Hodgins, Bruce and Robert Page, ed. *Canadian History Since Confederation*. Georgetown, Ontario: Irwin-Dorsey Ltd, 1972.
Hoyt, P. Edwin. *Mussolini's Empire*. New York: John Wiley & Sons In., 1994.
Iacovetta, Franca. *Such Hardworking People*. Montreal & Kingston: McGill-Queen's University Press, 1992.
Iorizzo, Luciano J. & Salvatore Mondello. *The Italian Americans* (Chapter 13, "Italian-American Fascism"). Boston: Twayne Publishers, 1980.
Isnenghi, Mario. *Intellettuali militanti e intellettuali funzionari*. Torino: Einaudi, 1979.
Jansen, C. J. *Italians in a Multicultural Canada*. Lewiston, 1987.
Jones, Alfred. *Is Fascism an Aswer?*. Hamilton, Ont.: Davis Lisson Ltd., 1933.
    _____. "Fascism." In *Addresses to The Empire Club of Canada*. Toronto: The Printers Guild Ltd, 1934.
Kealey, Gregory, Warrian Peter, ed. *Essays in Canadian Working-Class History*. Toronto: McClelland and Stewart Ltd., 1976.
King, W. Mackenzie. *Diary* (September 25, 26 & 26, 1928), Transcript 63, Film F., K54.
Kirkconnell, Watson. "The Fifth Column in Canada." In his *Twilight of Liberty*. London-Toronto: Oxford University Press, 1941.
    _____. "European Canadians and Their Press." In *Canadian Historical Society*. Toronto: University of Toronto Press, 1940.
Ledeen, Michael Arthur. *L'internazionale fascista*. Bari: Laterza, 1973.
Levitt, H. Cyril and Shaffir, William. *The Riot at Christie Pits*. Toronto: Lester & Orpen Dennys, 1987.
Liberati, Luigi Bruti. *Il Canada, l'Italia e il fascismo: 1919-1945*. Roma: Bonacci Editore, 1984.
    _____,ed. *Il Canada e la guerra dei trent'anni* Milano: Guerini, 1989.

Logan, A. H. *Trade Unions in Canada*. Toronto: Mcmillan, 1948.
Lozina, Costantino. "Gli italiani nella provincia dell'Ontario (Canada)." In *Il Bollettino della Reggia Società Geografica italiana* (Serie VI, Vol. IV), January-February 1927.
MacCallum, H. Reid. "Fascism and Italian Welfare." In *The Canadian Forum*, October 1923.
MacCormack, A. Ross. *Reformers, Rebels, and Revolutionaries: The Western Canadian Radical Movement 1899-1919*. Toronto-Buffalo-London: University of Toronto Press, 1977.
MacInnis, Grace. *J. S. Woodsworth. A Man to Remember*. Toronto: The MacMillan Company of Canada Litd., 1953.
Mackintosh, W. A.. "Italy Under Mussolini." In *Addresses to The Canadian Club*, November 1935.
Maclaren, Duncan. *Ontario Ethno-Cultural Newspapers, 1835-1927*. Toronto: Toronto Unversity Press, 1973.
Manfredi, Vincenzo. "Riccardo Cordiferro." In *Calabria letteraria* (anno XXXVII, N. 1-2-3), January-February-March 1989.
Martin, Robin. *Shades of Right*. Toronto: University of toronto Press, 1992.
McKenty, Niel. *Mitch Hepburn*. Toronto: McClelland and Stewart, 1967.
McNaught, Kenneth. *A Prophet in Politics*. Toronto: University of Toronto Press, 1963.
Michaelis, Meir. *Axis Policies Towards the Jews in World War II*, (The Fifteenth Annual Rabbi Louis Feinberg Memorial Lecture in Judaic Studies Program). University of Cincinnati, 1992.
_____. *Mussolini and the Jews* (Published for the Institute of Jewish Affairs). London: The Clarendon Press Oxford, 1978.
Migone, Gian Giacomo. *Gli Stati Uniti e il fascismo*, Milano: Feltrinelli, 1980.
Molinari, Maurizio. *Ebrei in Italia: un problema di identità (1870-1938)*. Firenze: Giunta, 1991.
Molinaro, Julius A. "The Casa d'Italia in Toronto: Historical Background (1873-1983)." In *Italian Canadiana*, N. 12, 1996.
Momigliano, Arnaldo. "The Jews of Italy." In his *Pagans, Jew, and Christians*. Middleton, Conn.: Wesleyan University Press, 1987.
Morgan, Philip. *Italian Fascism 1919-1945*. London: The MacMillan Press Ltd, 1995.
Mount, S. Graeme, John Abbot and Michal, J. Mully. *The Border at Sault St. Marie*. Toronto: Dundurn Press, 1995.
Mussolini, Benito. *Opera Omnia di Benito Mussolini* (36 Vol.s) a cura di Edoardo e Duilio Susmel. Firenze: La Fenice, 1951-63.
Muzi. "Viaggio in Canada cinquant'anni fa." In *Mosaico*, Toronto, September 1975.
Napolitano, G. G. *Troppo grano sotto la neve*. Milano: Casa Editrice Ceschina, 1936.
Nelson, Jean Elizabeth. "'Nothing Ever Goes Well Enough': Mussolini and the Rhetoric of Perpetual Struggle." In *Communication Studies* (Vol. 42, N. 1), Spring 1991.

Nolte, Ernest. *Three Faces of Fascism. Action Francaise, Italian Fascism, National Socialism.* New York: Holt, Rinehart Winston, 1966.

Orano Paolo. *Gli ebrei italiani.* Roma: Casa Editrice Pinciana, anno XV.

Painchaud, C. and Poulin, R. *Les Italiens au Québec.* Ottawa: 1988.

Parini, Piero. *Gli italiani nel Mondo.* Milano: Mondadori, MCMXXXV- Anno XII.

Pautasso, Luigi. "La donna italiana durante il periodo fascista in Toronto (1930-1940)." In *Quaderni canadesi* (anno 1, numero 1), 1977.

_____. "Il consolato e la colonia italiana di Toronto alla vigilia della guerra d'Etiopia (1934-1935)." In *Quaderni canadesi*, (anno 1, numero 1), 1976.

_____. "La Propaganda Fascista in Canada alla Vigilia della Guerra d'Etiopia." In *Quaderni canadesi* (numero 3), marzo-aprile 1978.

_____. "1 ottobre 1935: nasce in Montreal l'Agenzia segreta del fascio." In *Quaderni canadesi* (numero 4-5), maggio-agosto 1978

Pellizzi, Camillo. "I fasci all'estero." In *Gerarchia*, April 1929.

Pennacchio, Luigi. "The Torrid Trinity: Italian Priests and Archbishops During the Fascist Era, 1929-1940." In *Catholics at the 'Gathering Place': Historical Essays On the Archdiocese of Toronto, 1841-1991* (Mark George McGowan and Brian P. Clark, eds.). Toronto: Canadian Catholic Historical Association, 1993.

Perin, Roberto. "Making Good Fascists: Consular Propaganda and the Italian Community in Montreal in the 1930s." In G. Gold ed., *Minorities and Mother Country Imagery.* St. John, 1984.

Perin, Roberto and Sturino, Frank, eds. *Arrangiarsi.* Montreal and Toronto: Guernica, 1989.

Poggiani, Euno. "Con gli italiani di Vancouver." In *Viaggio nel Far West* (con prefazione di Roberto Farinacci). Cremona: Nuova Cremona, 1936

Poliakov, Léon. *The Aryan Myth. A History of Racist and Nationalist ideas in Europe*, tran. by Edmund Howard. New York: New American Library, 1974.

Il Ponte. Emigrazione: Cento Anni 26 Milioni, nov.-dic. 1974. Firenze: La Nuova Italia Editrice, 1974

Potestio John, ed. *The Memoirs of Giovanni Veltri.* Toronto: The Multicultural History Society of Ontario, 1987.

Pozzetta, E. Geroge, ed. *Pane e lavoro: The Italian American Working Class.* Toronto: The Multicultural History Society of Ontario, 1980.

Pozzetta, E. George and Ramirez, Bruno, eds. *The Italian Diaspora.* Toronto: The Multicultural History Society of Ontario, 1992.

Prezzolini, Giuseppe. *Fascism*, trans. by Kathleen McMillan. London: Metheuen & Co. Ltd., 1926.

Preti, Luigi. *Impero fascista, Africa ed ebrei.* Milano: Murzia, 1968.

Principe, Angelo and Pugliese, Olga Zorzi. *Rekindling Faded Memories The History of the 'Famee Furlane' of Toronto:1932-1942.* Toronto:'Famee Furlane', 1996.

Principe, Angelo. "The Italo-Canadian Anti-Fascist Press in Toronto (1922-1940)." In *NEMLA Italian Studies* (Vol. Four, 1980) Toronto, 1980, edited by R. Capozzi, J. E. Germano, E. Licastro, A. Principe, & A. Verna; re-printed in *Polyphony*, Bulletin of the Multicultural History Society of Ontario, Fall/Winter 1985.

_____. "Note sul radicalismo tra gli italiani in Canada (1900-1915)." In *Canada e Stati Uniti* a cura di Valeria Gennaro Lerda. Venezia: Marsilio Editori, 1984.

_____. "Note sul radicalismo tra gli italiani in Canada dalla Prima Guerra Mondiale alla Conciliazione." In *Rivista di studi italiani* (Anno VIII, N. 1-2), June-December 1990.

_____. "The Difficult Years of the Order of the Sons of Italy (1920-1926)." In *Italian Canadiana*, Vol. 5, 1989. Toronto, (Centre for Italian Canadian Studies, Department of Italian Studies, University of Toronto).

_____. "Italiani a Toronto prima del 1861. *Italian Canadiana*, Vol. 7, 1991, Centre for italian Canadian Studies, Deparment of Italian Studies, University of Toronto.

_____. "Upper Canadian Protestant Perception of the Italian 'Risorgimento': 1846-1860." In *Papers of the Canadian Society of Church History 1976*. Department of History, Laurentian University, 1976.

_____. "Il Risorgimento visto dai protestanti del Canada alto." In *Rivista Storica del Risorgimento* (Roma), June 1978.

Quarza, Guido, ed. *Fascismo e società italiana*. Torino: Einaudi, 1973.

Rainero, H. Romain. "Politica di potenza e fasci italiani all'estero." In *L'Italia e la politica di potenza in Europa (1938-1940)* (a cura di Ennio di Nolfo, Romain H. Rainero, Brunello Vigezzi). Milano, Marzorati Editore, 1986.

Ramirez, Bruno. *On the Move*. Toronto: McClelland & Stewart Inc., 1991.

_____. *The Italians of Montreal From Sojourning to Settlement: 1900-1921*. Montreal: Associazione di Cultura Popolare Italo-Quebecchese, 1980.

_____. "Ethnic Studies and Working Class History." In *Labour/Le Travail*, 19, 1987, 45-48.

Ratcliffe, S. K. "Mussolini and the Broader Aspects of Fascism." In *Addresses to The Canadian Club*, March 1926.

Razzolini, Esperanza Maria. *All Our Fathers: The North Italian Colony in Industrial Cape Breton*. Halifax, N. S.: Ethnic Heritage Series, 1983.

Ricci, Giuseppe. *L'orfano di padre*, Toronto: n.p., 1981.

Rogers, L. J. "Duplessis and Labor." In *Canadian Forum*, October 1947.

Rose, F. *Fascism Over Canada*. Toronto: New Era Publishing, 1938.

Rogari, Sandro. "Azione cattolica e fascismo. Come la Chiesa si difese da Mussolini." In *Nuova antologia* (anno 113), Vol.s 533 and 534), January-June and July-September 1978.

Rosengarten, Frank. *The Italian Anti-Fascist Press 1919-1945*. Cleveland Ohio: The Press of Case Western Reserve University, 1968.

Rosoli, Gianfausto (a cura di). *Un secolo di emigrazione italiana 1876-1976*. Roma: Centro Studi Emigrazione, 1978.

Salvatorelli, Luigi. *The Risorgimento: Thought & Action* (Trans. by Mario Domandi, Introduction by Charles F. Delzell). New York: Harper & Row, Publishers, 1970.

Salvemini, Gaetano. *Italian Fascist Activities in the United States* edited with an introdution by Philp V. Cannistranto. New York: Center For Migration Studies, 1977.

———. *Under the Axe of Fascism*. New York: The Citadel Press, (first edition 1937) 1971.

———. *Memorie di un fuoruscito*. Torino: Feltrinelli, 1960.

———. *How The Fascist Dictatorship Works* (Pamphlet). New York City: International committee for Poltical Prisoners, 1926.

Salvatore, Filippo. *Le Fascisme et les Italians à Montréal*. Toronto: Guernica, 1995.

———. *Fascism and the Italians of Montreal*. Toronto: Guernica, 1998.

Salvatorelli, Luigi e Mirra Giovanni. *Storia d'Italia nel periodo fascista*. Milano: Mondadori, 1969.

Sanfilippo, Matteo. "Monsignor Pisani e il Canada (1908-1913)." *Annali Accademici Canadesi*, Ottawa, VI, 1990, pp. 61-75.

Santarelli, Enzo. *Storia del fascismo* 3 vol.s. Roma: Editori Riuniti, 1973.

———. *Ricerche sul fascismo*. Urbino: Argalia Editore, 1971.

Santinon, Renzo. *Fasci italiani all'estero*. Roma: Edizione Settimo Sigillo, 1991.

Sarti, Roland, ed. *The Axe Within*. New York: New Viewpoints, 1974.

Scardellato, Gabriele. *Within Our Temple: A History of the Order Sons of Italy of Ontario*. Toronto: Order Sons of Italy of Canada, 1995.

———. "Beyond the Frozen Wastes: Italian Sojourners and Settlers in British Columbia." In *Arrangiarsi* (edited by R. Perin and F. Sturino). Toronto: Guernica, 1989.

Schmitz, F. David. *The United States and Fascist Italy 1922-1940*. Chapel Hill & London: The University of North Carolina Press, 1988.

Segrè, C. G. *Italo Balbo. A Fascist Life*. Berkeley, Calif.: University of California Press, 1987.

Segre, Dan Vittorio. *Memoirs of a Fortunate Jew. An Italian Story*. New York: Laurel, 1987.

Simone, Nick. *Italian Immigrants in Toronto, 1890-1930*. Toronto: York University, Discussion Paper No. 26, n.d..

Simons, Hans. "The Rome Berlin Axis." In *Addresses to The Canadian Club*, October 1937.

Slobodskoi, S. M.. *Storia del fascismo*. Roma: Editori Riuniti, 1962.

Smith, Denis Mack. *Storia d'Italia 1861-1969* (Two Vol.). Bari: Laterza, 1972.

Spada, V. Antonino. *The Italians in Canada*. Montreal-Ottawa, 1969.

Speisman, Stephen. *The Jews of Toronto*. Toronto: McClelland and Stewart, 1979.

———. "St. John's Shtetl: the Ward in 1911." In *Gathering Places: Peoples and Neighbourhoods of Toronto,1834-1945*, Robert Harney, ed. Toronto: The Multicultural History Society of Ontario, 1985.

Spinosa, Antonio. "Le persecuzioni razziali in Italia" (Part I, 'Origini' and Part II 'L'atteggiamento della chiesa.'" In *Il Ponte* (fascicolo VIII), July and August 1952.

Sturino, Frank. *Forging the Chain. Italian Migration to North America, 1880-1930*. Toronto: The Multicultural History Society of Ontario, 1990.

Sturzo, Luigi. *Italy and Fascism*. New York: Harcourt, Brace and Company, 1926.

Tabagi, Walter. *Gli anni del manganello*. Milano: Fratelli Fabbri Editori, 1973.

Tasca, Angelo. *The Rise of Italian Fascism*. New York: Howard Fertin, 1966 (first edition 1938).

Thompson, Doug. "The collapse of 'consensus.'" In his *State Control in Fascist Italy*. Manchester and New York: Manchester University Press, 1991.

Tomasi, S. M. *Perspectives in Italian Immigration and Ethnicity*. New York: Center for Migration Studies, 1977.

_____. "Fede e patria: the 'Italica Gens' in the United States and Canada, 1908-1936. Notes for the history of an emigration association." In *Studi Emigrazione/Études Migrations* (N. 103, anno XXVII), September 1991.

Valli, Suzzi Roberta. "Il fascio italiano a Londra. L'attività politica di Camillo Pellizzi." In *Storia contemporanea*, a. XXVI, n. 6, dicembre 1995, pp. 957-1002.

Vangelisti, Guglielmo. *Gli Italiani in Canada*. Montreal: Chiesa Italiana di N. S. Della difesa, MCMLVIII.

Veneruso, Danielo. *Il seme della pace: la cultura cattolica e il nazionalismo fra le due guerre*. Roma: edizioni Studium, 1987.

Villari, Luigi. "Italy's Foreign Policy," *Addresses to the Canadian Club*, 1934.

Vitale, Massimo Aldo. "The Destruction and Resistance of the Jews in Italy." In *They Fought Back. The Story of Jewish Resistance in Nazi Europe* (Edited & Translated by Yuri Suhl). New York: Schocken Books, 1975.

Volli, Gemma. "La vera storia dei 'Protocolli dei savi anziani di Sion.'" In *Il Ponte* (fascicolo XI), November 1957.

Woodcock, George. *A Social History of Canada*. New York: Penguin Books, 1989.

Woodsworth, S. James. *Strangers Within Our Gates*. Toronto: Federick Clark Stevenson, 1909.

Zucchi, John. *Italians in Toronto: Development of a National Identity, 1875-1935*. Kingston and Montreal: McGill-Queen's University Press, 1988.

Zuccotti, Susan. *The Italians and the Holocaust: Persecution, Rescue, Survival*. New York: Basic Books, Inc., Publishers, 1987.

INDEX

Aloisi, Antonio, 205
Abbott, John, 245
Almagià, Roberto, 244
Alvarado, Maria Ana, 45
Amalgamated Clothing Workers of America: Local 235, 39
Amalgamated Clothing Workers of America: Local 274, 39, 148
Ambrosi, Gian-Battista (Vice-Consul), 54, 55, 59, 87, 88, 102, 231, 236
Amendola, Giovanni, 29, 225
Amendola, Salvatore, 205
Amodeo, Agostino, 207
Amodeo, Atonio, 207
Amodio, Sam, 207
Andreoli, A., 239
Angelony, Tony, 207
Anti-Semitic legislation, 81, 84
Anti-Semitism, 16, 28, 111
Arcand, Adrien, 148
Araldo del Canada, 14, 37, 63, 65
Arpinati, Leandro, 30, 241
Autarchia, 127, 241
Avery, Donald, 241
Avery, F.H., 237
Baccelli, Alfredo, 244
Bacci, Giuseppe, 205
Bacci, Ruggero, 8, 189, 204
Badali, Giovanni, 204
Badali, Leo, 207
Badali, Salvatore, 204, 207
Badalis, S., 204
Bagnell, Kenneth, 11, 19, 20, 224
Balbo, Italo, 23, 29, 243
Balò, Father Settimio, 55, 143, 177, 238
Bancheri, Salvatore, 7
Barbed Wire and Mondulins, 11, 12, 19
Barboglio, Francesco (Vice-Consul), 172
Barreca, N., 239
Barrett, Stanley R., 231
Bartole, Andy, 246
Barzini, Luigi, 44
Basilio, Nino, 206

Basso, Belvino, 143
Bastianini, Giuseppe, 27, 225, 227
Battaglia, Joe, 207
Bayley, Charles M., 36, 69, 227, 234, 235
Belcastro, Father, 55
Bell, Tom, 237
Bellissario, Donato, 205
Benett, Richard B., 51, 56, 57, 59
Bernardi, Amy, 232
Bernardini, Gene, 242
Bernardo, Michele, 204
Betcherman, Lita-Rose, 231, 232, 246
Biagi, S. E., 95
Bianchi, Antonio, 205
Bifolchi, Domenico, 204
Binder, Carol, 226
Binelli, M., 206
Bissolati, Leonida, 43, 229
Blaylock, Selwyn Gwillym, 143
Boccini, Alberto, 123, 135, 144, 168
Bogart, Ernest C., 237, 251
Bolognini, Giulio (Consul), 42
Boni, Enrico, 227
Borgese, Giuseppe Antonio, 23, 225, 239
Bortignon, Father Gioacchino, 141
Bortolotti, Anselmo, 8, 228
Bortolotti, Attilio, 8, 229
Bottos, Benny, 8
Bozzetti, G., 244
Branca, Angelo, 123, 124, 131, 133, 143, 144, 168, 189
Branca, Filippo, 240
Brancucci, Dr. G. (Vice Consul), 25, 125, 139-140
Brandel, Charles (alias Charles Crate), 95, 96, 160, 246
Breglia, Achille, 204
Brigidi, Giuseppe (Consul), 61, 69, 70, 81
Brown, Graig R., 231
Brunetti, Mariano, 204
Buchan, Sir John, 110
Busca, Terzo, 60

Caboto, Giovanni, 15, 35, 65, 66-69, 234
Caboto Lodge N.8,
Calci, Bernardino, 206
Calderone, S., 207
Calderone, F., 207
Camasta, Francesco, 108, 204
Campagna, G., 207
Campana, John, 7
Campanella, Tommaso, 127
Canadian Commonwealth Federation (CCF), 56, 57, 73, 97, 110, 131, 133, 148, 196, 236
Canadian Foresters Association, 104
Canadian Union of Fascists (CUF), 95, 111, 112, 160
Cancelli, A, 239
Canella, Piera Bertoia, 7
Cantalupo, Roberto, 226, 244
Canzano, Carmela, 204
Cappuccietti, Agostino, 205
Capuano, Luigi, 65, 76
Carboni, Angelo Domenico, 105, 237
Careless, J.M.S., 231
Carollo, Pietro, 108, 205
Carrell, Bishop of Calgary, 178, 250
Il Carroccio, New York, 64, 156
Cartier, Jaques, 35, 66
Caruso, Guglielmo, 204
Caruso, Umberto, 204
Casa d'Italia or Fascist Centre, 16, 105, 106, 108, 109, 110, 112, 122, 225
Castelli, Nanni Leone, 42-46, 64, 65, 229
Castelli, Vincenzo, 44
Castronovo, Valerio, 225
Catalano, Carmine, 131
Catelli, Pietro, 227
Catholic Action, 137, 151, 176, 187
Catholic Register, 177
Cavalluzzo, G., 206
Chamberlain, Neville, 130, 242
Chandeler, Bernard S., 7
Charlemagne, 136
Cheli, Father Stefano, 55
Christie Pits Park Riot, 159
Chudleigh mansion, 108
Churchill, Winston, 31, 226
Cialo, Luigi, 205
Ciambini, G., 207
Ciampolillo, Luigi, 204
Ciano, Galeazzo, 71, 163, 243, 244, 247, 248
Ciano, Luigi, 46, 47

Ciarfella, Raffaele, 204, 206, 239
Ciccocelli, Joseph Anthony, 251, 252
Cippico, Antonio, 244
Cira, Joe, 204
Circolo Colombo, 39, 48, 86, 103,
Circolo Matteotti, 39
Clark, Brian P., 231
Club or Fascio Giulio Giordani, 125, 126, 128, 141
Club Roma, 141
Club Ouvrier (Montreal), 80
Cody, Dr. J. Henry, 96, 232, 236
Cohen, Oscar, 180, 181, 182, 251
Colacci, Angelo, 207
Colamartin, S., 207
Colautti, Domenico, 207
Colbertaldo, Pietro (Vice-Consul), 123, 124
Coldwell, M. J., 148
Colombo, Cristofaro, 128
Colonna, count Mario, 232
Colussi, Dante Corti, 172
Comella, Giacomo, 204, 207
Comella, S., 207
Comitato Economico, 102
Comitato Scolastico, 102,
Concilia, Agostino, 207
Conciliation Pact, 28, 52
Conforzi, Pietro, 207
Contini, Fioravanti, 206
Contini, Tommaso, 206
Conzanesi, Joe, 206
Co-operative Garibaldi, 40
Co-operative and Hall Mazzini, 40
Co-operative Meucci, 39
Corfù island, 70
Il Corriere italiano, 38, 40, 43, 48-51, 252
Cortesi, Arnaldo, 150
Corti (Corticelli), Henry (Enrico), 47, 187.188,
Cosentino, Dr. M.C., 237
Cosentino, Dr. V., 237,
Costarella, Napoleone, 207
Coyette (Councillor, Montreal), 79
Crate, Charles see Brandel Charles
Cresciani, Gianfranco, 227
Crispi, Francesco, 37
Croce, Benedetto, 152, 244
Croft, William, 251
Culos, Marino, 143, 228
Culos, Raymond, 7
Culotta, Leonardo, 206

Curletta, Angelo, 207
Cuscania, Emanuele, 205
Cusinamo, Antonio, 207
Cusimano, Giuseppe, 207
Cusinamo, S., 207
Cuthrie, Hugh, 59
Daladier, Edouard, 130, 242
Dalrymble, Dr., 237
D'Amato, Giovanni, 205
D'Amico, Alfonzo, 205
D'Ancona, Ugo, 244
Danesi, Primo, 108, 205
D'Annunzio, Gabriele, 44, 46, 227, 229
Dante, Alighieri, 77
Dante Alighieri Society, 33
Darrigo, Stefano, 205
Darwin, Charles, 175
Davis, I., 174, 250
Davis, L., 160
Day, Mayor of Totonto, 183,
Dell'Angelo, 228
De Biasio, Angelo, 205
De Blasio, Angelo, 205
De Conde, Alexander, 226
De Felice, Renzo, 30, 58, 172, 179, 225, 226, 232, 242, 243, 244, 244, 245, 247, 249, 250
Defence of Canada Regulations, 10
Dejulis, Celestino, 7, 225
Dell'Angelo, Vittorio, 295
Delisle, Esther, 243, 252
De Luca, Joe, 239
De Nino, P., 207
Denton, Frank, 48,
De Rubbertis, Mario, 205
De Stefani, Alberto, 244
Devoir Le (Montreal), 70
Di Cresce, Domenico, 204
Diefenbaker, John, 168
Di Falco, Domenico, 207
Diggins, John P., 168, 228
Di Giulio, Donald, 8
Dilillo, Nicolantonio, 204
Dini, Arduino, 205
Di Pietro, Joe, 207
D'Onofrio, F., 206
Dopolavoro Society, 183
Dubro, James, 231
Duliani, Mario, 11, 76, 224, 151, 252
Dumini, Americo, 225
Dupplessis, Maurice, 57, 58, 81

Eaton Auditorium, 10
Eaton, Lady, 58
Eaton Company, 108
Elliot, Jean, 246
Elsey, W. F., 112, 160
Empire Club of Toronto, 58
Eden, Anthony, 239
Edwards, Frederick, 242
Everett, Brenda Huff, 232
Fabbri, Enedina, 143
Fabbri, Ennio, 125,
Factor, Samuel, 40
Fafaretto, R., 207
Fainella, John, 228
Fantechi-Tavanti Mrs., 238
Farese, Biagio, 80
Farinacci, Roberto, 23, 29, 137, 151, 152, 155, 165, 171, 243, 244
Farr, Joseph, 148
Farthing, Anglican Bishop of Montreal, 119, 149,
Fascio Luparini, Montreal, 64, 233
Fascio Principe Umberto, Toronto, 49, 57, 86, 105, 159, 189
Fascist League of North America, 47, 50, 59,
Father Auad, 231
Father Rutolo, 231
Fattori, Ettore, 86, 91, 237
Fava, Guido, 205
Fava, Ulderino, 205
Favilla La, 47
Federici, Giuseppe, 86, 231
Fera, Carlo, 8
Ferrari, G., 206
Ferrari, Mrs. Fontana, 238
Fiamme d'Italia, 38, 40, 43-45
Fioravanti, Eugenio, 205
Fisher, George, 139
Flandrin, 192
Foà, Jole, 152
Fontana, Edoardo, 237
Fontanella, Maria Egilda, 246
Fontanella, Dr. Pasquale, 189, 228, 231, 237, 239, 246
Formenti, Abramo, 207
Fox, William Sherwood, 234
Franceschini, (James) Vincenzo, 103, 108, 237
Franco, Gen. Francisco, 81
Franklin, Benjamin, 174

Fratellanza Italo-Canadese, 39
Fredericton Camp, N.B., 11
Frediani, Etelvina Sartini, 8, 160, 246
Frediani, Francesco, 8, 205
Fronte Unico Morale, 68, 69, 78
Fuoco, Gregorio, 140
Gariboldi, Angelozzi Giorgio, 248
Garosci, Aldo, 244
Gatto, Antonio, 205, 231, 237
Gattuso, Francesco, 228
Gayda, Virgilio, 165
Gemelli, Father, 250
Genovesi, Frankie, 246
Gente nostra, 38, 43, 46-48
Gentile, Dieni, 71, 234
Gentile, Emilio, 227, 236, 238
Georgi, Mark, 7
Georgi, Angonietta Principe, 7
Giannelli, Chav. V. E., 231
Gianvecchio, Rocco, 207
Ginzburg, Leone, 245
Giofrè, Joe, 207
Gioia, Italo, 21
Giolitti, Giovanni, 37
Giordani, Giulio, 241
Gioventù Italiana del Littorio Estero (GILE), 102
Girardi, Bruno, 123, 169
Gismondi, B., 206
Giurato, Totò, 47
Glionnna, Dr. George A., 189, 231, 231
Gnudi, Ennio (Mayor of Bologna), 241
Godbout, Adélard, 148
Goggio, Emilio, 206, 232, 237
Goldmann, Nahoum, 153, 244, 245
Gramsci, Antonio, 152, 238, 244
Grandi, Dino, 23, 29
Granel, Jeo P., 251
Gregorio, Oreste, 171
Il Grido della Stirpe (New York), 44, 86
Grieco, Francesco, 207
Grieco, F. fu Pietro, 207
Grimaldi, Alfassio U., 244
Grimaldi, Santo, 207
Grittani, Giambattista, 205
Grittani, Joseph, 48, 205, 231, 237
Grittani, Nicola, 205
Guadagno, Dominic, 207
Gualtieri, Rev. Domenico, 47, 183, 193
Gualtieri, M. Francesco, 46, 48, 230
Guerra, Angelo, 207, 239

Guerra, Domenico, 205
Guglielmo, Biagio, 206
Guglielmo da Salicento, 179, 250
Guglielmotti, General, 39
Harny, Robert F., 12, 245, 246
Havas, French Press Agency
Henry, Hon. Premier of Ontario, 93
Hepburn, Mitchel (Premier of Ontario), 58, 93, 241
Herouz, Homer, 252
Herridge, W. D., 110
Hinsley, Cardinal, 177
Hitler, Adolf, 57, 76, 89, 113, 114, 120, 130, 136, 139, 142, 151, 154, 155, 157, 159, 162, 163, 175, 184, 189, 242, 248
Houde, Camillein (Mayor of Montreal), 58,
Hoyt, Edwin P., 225
Iacovino, P., 207
Iagallo, Giacinto, 207
Iannuzzi, D. A., 75, 80
Iannizziello, Antonio, 205
Iannuzziello, Miss A., 238
Indipendent Order Sons of Italy, 39
Informazione Diplomatica No 14, 146
Ingrassia, Ferdinanda Maria, 44, 229
Innocenti, R., 207
Interlandi, Telesio, 155
International Press Service, 70
Inter-social Committee, 48, 49
Invidiata, Dr. Rosario, 189, 205, 231, 237
Iona, Giuseppe, 207
Italian Chamber of Commerce, 65, 73
Italian Red Cross, 70, 120, 121
Italian Veterans' Association, 47, 49, 61, 65, 102, 125, 128
Italo-Canadese Society, 39
Italo-canadian United Political Club, 83
Jabotinsky, Wladmir, 154
Jones, Magistrate Alfred S., 58, 161, 232, 247
Jung, Guido, 162, 244
Kinanaskis Camp, Alb., 144
Kats, Giuliana Sanguinetti, 7
King, William Mackenzie, 9, 31, 51, 53, 73, 131, 132, 133, 196, 230
Kirkconnell, Watson, 62, 232
Ku Klux Klan, 159
Laiola, Teresa, 207
Lamberti, Carlo, 8
Lanza, Pietro Prince of Scalea, 244

INDEX

La Press, Montreal, 70
Lapointe, Ernest, 73, 112,
Lateran Treaty, 32,
Lattes, Dante, 153, 244
Lattoni, Liborio, 8, 67
Laudadio, Romolo, 204
Lavoratore il, Toronto, 8, 125
Lavoria, Giovanni, 205
League of Nations, 70, 74, 114, 115, 196, 241
Lenin, Nikolaj, 157
Lerda, Valeria Gennaro, 241
Lettieri, Michele, 8
Levi, Mario, 156
Levitt, H. Cyril, 229, 246
Liberati, Luigi Bruti, 7, 36, 224, 227, 231, 232, 234, 235
Ligue Latine Canadienne or Canadian Latin League, 81, 82, 83
Lima, Pietro, 205, 207
Liotta, Vincenzo, 207
Livetti, Gino, 244
Livorio, Giovanni, 205
Lo Franco, M., 207
Logan, H. A., 232
Longo, Rev. Joseph, 205, 229
Lozima, Costantino, 41, 228, 229
Lucciola, G., 206
Lupo, Gioacchino, 206
Maccari, Cesare, 50
MaInnis, Grace, 235
Macioce, Aldo, 7
Magi, Massimo Jacopo, 57, 189, 204, 237
Maltempi, Father, 55
Mancuso, Salvatore, 60
Mandalfino, Antonio, 204
Mandalfino, Rocco, 207
Manduca, Teresa, 7
Manfriani, Father Zanobri, 55, 75
Mannoni, Sam, 207
Marconi, Guglielmo, 15, 75, 77-79, 83
Margotti, Pio (Consul), 47, 48,
Mari, Giuseppina Gatto, 7, 172, 249
Mari, Tommaso, 16, 54, 86, 87, 88, 89, 90, 94, 96, 97, 98, 99, 100, 109, 118, 119, 147, 157, 158, 172, 173, 178, 184, 207, 236, 237, 250
Marino, Consular Agente, 161
Il Martello (New York), 44
Marx, Karl, 150, 157,
Masi, Flavio, 231

Masi, Nicola (Consular Agent), 48, 231
Matteotti, Giacomo, 29, 147, 225
Mazza, Antonino, 11, 224, 251
Mazzini, Giuseppe, 195
Mazzotta, Guido, 7
McCormack, Ross A., 241
McGowan, Mark George, 231
McGuigan, Archbishop James, 52, 229
McLaren, Duncan, 228
McLean, Robinson, 116, 117
McMillan, Cathleen, 32, 226
McNaught, Kenneth, 57, 231
McNeil, Archbishop Neil, 55, 92,
McNally, Bishop, 52, 119
McNish, J. D., 251
Meconi, Luigi, 59
Medora, G., 206
Messaggero italo-canadese (Toronto), 66
Messineo, Father Antonio, 120
Michaelis, Meir, 242, 243, 244
Mivhelin, Walter, 207
Miclet, Arnaldo, 204
Migone, Gian Giacomo, 240
Milano, Attilio, 244
Minculpop (Ministry of Popular Culture), 27, 71, 115, 130, 135, 171
Missori, Alessandro, 205
Missori, Marco, 48, 204, 237
Mitchel, Hunphrey, 235
Mizzoni, Giovanni, 205
Modona, Guido Neppi, 225
Molinari, Maurizio, 244
Molinaro, Frank, 114, 115, 162, 163, 171, 232, 249
Molinaro, Julius, 239
Molinaro, Pasquale, 206, 231, 239
Mollo, T. O., 64
Montanelli, Indro, 192, 252
Moore, Vincent, 240, 242, 247
Mora, Frank, 206
Morandi, Luigi, 204
Moretti, Vito, 7
Morgan, Philip, 234
Morgan, prof., 99, 100
Morra, L., 207
Mosley, Sir Osvald, 158
Motta, Giacinto, 244
Mount, Graeme S., 245
Muir, William V., 251
Mulloy, Michael J., 245
Muraca, Antonio, 205

INDEX

Murphy, Edward J., 237
Mussolini, Benito, 13, 14, 19, 20, 21, 22, 23, 29, 30, 31, 32, 33, 35, 36, 37, 42, 43, 47, 51, 52, 53, 55, 57, 58, 59, 60, 65, 70, 71, 76, 81, 88, 89, 90, 95, 96, 97, 98, 102, 103, 111, 113, 114, 115, 116, 117, 118, 119, 120, 129, 130, 133, 137, 141, 142, 144, 147, 149, 150, 151, 152, 153, 154, 155, 156, 157, 158, 160, 162, 168, 171, 175, 176, 177, 178, 179, 182, 184, 185, 186, 188, 189, 190, 191, 182, 193, 194, 195, 218, 220, 224, 225, 228, 232, 239, 241, 242, 243, 244, 245, 247, 248
Muzi, Dr., 41
Nahon, U., 244
National Congress of Italians, 11, 224
National Christian Party, 148
National Film Board, 11
Nationalist Party, 148
Neri, Damiano, 119
Ney, Major J. Fred, 102,
Nicoletti, Marino, 206
Nietzsche, Friedrich, 115
Nitti, Francesco Saverio, 37
Nordau, Max, 153
Notari, Giuseppe, 205
O'Brien, Mila, 8
O'Brien, Bishop, 224
October (or Bolshevik) Revolution, 23, 29,
Oliver, Michael, 232, 239
Ontario Lodge, O.F.d'I., 207
Orange Order, 159
Orano, Paolo, 146, 171, 192, 252
Order Sons of Italy, 35, 39, 40, 44, 61, 64, 65, 102, 118, 121, 124, 188, 207
Order of the Flower of Italy, 40
Orlando, Eliseo, 204
Orlando, Maria, 204, 207
Orlando, Vittorio Emanuele, 37
Ovazza, Ettore, 245
OVRA (Opera Volontari Repressione Antifascista), 30
Paassen, Van, 116
Padlock Law, 58
Palange, Elisa (Rebecca), 159, 160, 246
Palange, Pasquale, 159, 204
Palermo, Louis, 148, 151, 242
Pancaro, Luigi, 19-22, 25, 224
Pantaleo, Felice, 204

Paolucci, Dominic, 204
Papini, Giovanni, 47
Parini, Pietro, 103, 104, 105, 106, 109, 238, 239
Parisi, P., 207
Parisi, Giuseppina, 204, 206
Partito Nazionale Fascista (PNF), 30, 107, 124
Partito Popolare Italiano, 88
Pasquale, Enrico, 65, 76
Pautasso, Luigi, 7, 233, 237, 246
Pelletier, G., 53
Pellizzi, Camillo, 34, 227
Pennacchio, Luigi, 7, 231
Penne, Captain, 140,
Perfetti, L., 207
Perilli, Attilio, 85, 167, 184, 185
Perin, Roberto, 7, 59, 227, 232, 234, 235, 241
Perley, Sir George, 235
Petawawa Camp, Ontario, 11, 20, 144, 172, 184, 188
Petrucci, Luigi (General Consul of Italy), 21, 50, 53, 54, 73, 74, 84, 109, 154, 155, 187, 188, 118, 235, 238
Petrucciani, Gino, 204
Phillips, Tracy, 241
Pilo, Isabella, 121
Pinto, Bernardino, 205
Pisani, Monsignor, 226
Pizzigalli, P., 69
Polenta, Romano, 204
Pope Leo IX, 236
Pope Pius XI, 55, 137, 139, 169, 176, 177, 187, 236, 248, 250
Pope Pius XII, 137, 238
Pope, Generoso, 154
Portoghese, Giuseppe, 204
Poveromo, Amleto, 225
Prato, David, 152, 153
Preti, Luigi, 245
Preziosi, Giovanni, 151, 155, 243
Prezzolini, Giuseppe, 226, 249
Price, M., 59
Principe, Concetta, 7
Principe, Sandra Gourlay, 7
Progresso italo-americano (New York),
Progresso italo-canadese (Toronto), 37, 85, 86,
Puccetti, Rosa, 141
Pugliese, Guido, 8

INDEX

Pugliese, Olga Zorsi, 7
Purkis, Thornton, 182, 251
Quaranta, Pasquale, 204
Quarza, Guido, 225
Quattrocchi, luigi, 205
Quinn, Councillor F., 77
Quinn, Hebert F., 235
Quinto, Martino, 8
Rader, Italo, 141
Ravenna, Felice, 153, 245
Raynault, Ademan (Major of Montreal), 77, 78, 79
Re, Frank, 204
Reconstruction Party, 57, 111,
Regina, G., 207
Renzoni, 121
Restaldi, V. Vittorio, 121, 233, 251, 252
Revedin, count of, 21
Rezza, G., 204
Ricci, Giuseppe, 183, 251
Ricci, Vilma, 7
Riccio, Filomena, 246
Riddell, W. A., 114
Risimini, O., 207
Roach, Poat V., 251
Robin, Martin, 36, 227, 228, 231, 243
Rocco, Steve, 246
Rochat, Giorgio, 225
Roche, David, 79
Roebuck, Arthur W., 40, 237
Rogari, Sandro, 250
Rogers, H.A., 232
Roland, Robin, 231
Romano, A., 207
Romano, Giovanni, 244
Romano, Giulio, 64, 75, 76, 77, 78, 79, 80, 81, 169, 222
Romeo, Francesco, 204
Roosevelt, Franklin D., 196
Rosano, Giuseppe, 205
Rose, Fred, 82, 235
Rosen, Samuel, 169
Rotstein, Meyer, 237
Rubin, Rabbi Eli (Sozius), 161
Ruffo, Raffaele, 204
Ruocco, W., 123
Sabetta, Antonio, 107, 238
Sabetta, Dr. Vittorio, 118, 224
Sacerdoti, Angelo, 153, 244
Salandra, Giovanni, 37
Salvatore, Filippo, 227, 232, 233

Salvemini, Gaetano, 43, 60, 230, 232
Somerville, H., 177
Sanci, Sam, 207
Sanfilippo, Matteo, 226
Sansone, G. F. C., 48, 237?
Sansone, Dr. Donato, 47, 189, 205, 231, 237, 251-252
Santarelli, Enzo, 226, 239, 241
Santinon, Renzo, 225
Saporita, Joe, 227
Sarfatti, Margherita, 153
Sarti, Rolando, 225
Sauro, Ersilia, 223
Sauro, Rev. Libero, 207
Savoia, Egle, 205
Savoia, Giovanni, 204, 239
Scandiffio, Lawyer, 189, 237
Scandiffio, Raffaele, 205, 206, 207
Scanga, Francesco, 205
Scardellato, Gabriele, 7, 228, 241
Schiralli, V., 206
Schmmitz, David F., 31, 226
Schwartz, Rabbi J. Jesse, 161
Scinocca, 160
Scoccia, Mariano, 204
Scolaro, Giacomo, 207
Scorsone, Vincenzo, 206
Sebastiani, A. D., 77
Segre, Dan Vittorio, 244
Selvaggio, Nicola, 228
Serio, Nicoletta, 234
Sguigna, Dante, 207
Shaffir, William, 229, 246
Shannon, Alderman J. L., K.C., 181
Silone, Ignazio, 150
Simone, Kick, 245
Simpson, James (Mayor of Toronto), 56,
Singer, E.F., 237
Smith, Mrs Joshua, 237
Snoidero, Carlo, 207
Società Colombo, 134
Società Figli d'Italia Inc., 40, 123, 128, 134
Società Veneta, 40
Soddu, General, 142
Sokolov, Nahum, 153
Somerville, H.
Spada, Antonino, 60, 65, 228, 233, 240
Speisman, Sthephen A., 7, 245
Sperapane, Ruggero, 205
St. Stephen, King of Hungary, 170
Stevens, H. H., 57, 110, 111

Stitt, Dr. M. L., 161
Stoangi, Augusto, 206
Sturino, Frank, 7, 241
Sturzo, Don Luigi, 88, 89, 236
Swastika Club, 159
Tambosso, A., 207
Tammaro, S., 207
Tardieu, Andre, 76
Tasca, Angelo, 23, 225
Taschereaw, L. A., 52, 53, 69
Tedesco, Giuseppe, 205
Telford, Lyle (Major of Vacouver), 131
Tempora, Angelo, 45
Tenisci, Fred, 141, 241
Teolis, Angelo, 205, 231
The Daily Star, 99, 102, 103, 116, 118,
The Globe and *The Globe and Mail*, 10, 99, 116
Tiberi, Giorgio (Vice-Consul), 105, 107, 109, 239
Toboni, Giulio, 207
Tomasi, Silvano M., 226
Tomasicchio, Giuseppe, 86, 205, 231
Tomasoni, Antonio, 205
Tommaso, S., 207
Tosti, Gustavo, 226
Traube, Ludwig, 149
Tribuna canadese, 14, 37, 46, 63, 85, 86
Trombetta, Domenico, 86, 231
Trombetta, Michele, 205
Truffa, father Peter E., 55, 231, 237
Turano, Salvatore, 206
Turone, Sergio, 243, 244
Union National, 57
Ururi, Campobasso, 107
Vacchelli, Nicola, 244
Vagnini, Colombo, 129
Valoppi, Augusto, 205, 206
Valloppi, Mr., 207
Veneruso, Daniele, 120, 240
Vangelisti, Guglielmo, 235
Vattoli, Corrado, 205
Velocci, Isidoro, 207
Veneruso, Danilo, 236
Verdon, A, 206
Vetere, Camillo, 42, 45, 46, 57, 64, 75, 76, 77, 228, 233
Villari, Luigi, 99, 232
Villeneuve, Cardinal, Primate of Canada, 155
Vince, Rocco, 205
Viola, Giuseppe, 225, 239
Visconti, (n.f.n.), 239
Vistorino, Vincenzo, 206
Vitale, Adolfo Massimo, 244
Vittorio Emanuele III, King of Italy, 29, 46, 74, 138, 230
Vizzaccaro, Orazio, 205
Voce degli italo-canadesi la, 8, 125,
La Voce operaia, 8
Volli, Gemma, 249
Volpe, Francesco, 206
Volpe, Gioacchino, 244
Volpi, Gene, 246
Volpi, (n.f.n.), 239
Weizmann, Chaim, 153, 245
Whittaker, William, 160
Wilson, George A., 251
Wilson, President Woodrow, 227
Winstandley, R., 139
Withcombe, Brenda, 7
Woodsworth, James S., 56, 73, 74
Zaffiro, Francesco, 7
Zambri, Teodoro, 207, 239
Zanussi, Giuseppe, 205
Zavaglia, Nicola, 11, 19, 224
Zeppieri, R., 206
Zucchero, Giuseppe, 207
Zucchi, John, 36, 227, 228, 229, 245
Zullino, Captain, 140

Printed in April 1999 by
VEILLEUX
ON DEMAND PRINTING INC.

in Longueuil, Quebec